I0759507

BULLIES

CATCHING UP WITH THE HOUND, THE HAMMER, AND THE STANLEY CUP CHAMPION PHILADELPHIA FLYERS

SAM CARCHIDI
AND JEFF HARE

Library of Congress Cataloging-in-Publication Data available upon request.

This book is available in quantity at special discounts for your group or organization. For further information, contact:

Triumph Books LLC
814 North Franklin Street
Chicago, Illinois 60610
(312) 337-0747
www.triumphbooks.com

Printed in U.S.A.
ISBN: 978-1-63727-628-0
Design by Nord Compo

To James and Marlowe: You'll never know how much joy you
bring Poppy and how you bless my life every day!
I am so proud of both of you and love you
to the moon and back!

Also, to the late, great Tony Ciabattoni, a sports-loving man
whose passion and vision helped jump-start
this wonderful project. Rest easy, my friend.
—Sam Carchidi

To the Bullies.... Your LOVE changed Philly and the fate
of a nine-year-old boy forever; may you always walk together!
To my friends and family, but especially my mom and dad,
who taught me the love of all Philly sports pretty much at birth.
And finally, to the three people I'll always drop the gloves for—
my beautiful, amazing children, Thompson and Charlotte,
and the love of my life, Margie Campolongo Hare.
See you back at da' park, Margie!
—Jeff Hare

CONTENTS

FOREWORD

IF I HADN'T BEEN A PROFESSIONAL HOCKEY PLAYER, I probably would have become an engineer because math was always my strong suit. Or maybe I would have become a farmer because I enjoyed that kind of work and lifestyle.

But, as you may know, I not only became an NHL player, but I gained fame—unfortunately—because of my fists. I became the Philadelphia Flyers' enforcer and was known as "The Hammer."

What was I thinking to always be fighting on the ice? I must have lost my mind. Fighting, quite honestly, is something I hated to do. I'd look at the schedule and mentally prepare for whom I would probably fight next. I would rather have spent my time concentrating on moves I could make against a specific player to help our team score goals.

Numerous Jobs

I've done a lot of things in my life after hockey. I've dabbled as a standup comedian, author, motivational speaker, and (ahem) singer. I've been a minor-league hockey coach and general manager—I even drove the team bus. I've been a rink manager. I've owned a limousine company, and I've sold electricity for a company I run.

Hockey, however, was my love. I spent four years with the Philadelphia Flyers, and during that span, we won two Stanley Cups and got to the Finals three times.

Some of my hockey memories are filled with joy. We had a great group in Philly, and we all got along, which was a big part of our success. Our line, which included Orest Kindrachuk and Don Saleski, had its own identity. We were tough to play against, and we chipped in with some goals. And when we'd have a good shift—even if we didn't score—we'd give our team some momentum.

I loved playing in Philly and gave my heart and soul to the organization, so it was a sad day when general manager Keith Allen traded me to the Los Angeles Kings in September of 1976. To be honest, that bitter feeling of being sent away has stayed with me all these years later.

But we had some magical times during my years in Philadelphia.

Fifty-plus years ago, I was part of a Flyers team that shocked the NHL and won the franchise's first Stanley Cup. That was in the glorious 1973–74 season. We were tough, we were talented, and we shared our journey with a remarkable and passionate fan base.

Thank you, fans.

Philly fans are the best. They were always in our corner, and they helped lift us to great heights—and that's an important part of this book.

Something Missing

As for me personally, winning two Stanley Cups didn't give me a lifetime of happiness and financial security.

I'm not looking for sympathy. I'm just telling my story. *(Editor's note: See Chapter 9 for more of Schultz's compelling story.)* Maybe there are some lessons that will help some people along the way. That's my hope.

Being a Stanley Cup champion in 1974 and again in 1975 with the Broad Street Bullies was very satisfying. Especially the first one—winning the Cup in '74 was the highlight of my career. The '75 title wasn't as rewarding for me because I had been hearing rumors all season that I might get traded.

Indeed, I was traded after the 1975–76 season. I began to drink way too much, and I have always struggled financially.

Hopefully, my life is on the right path now.

I have been going through Alcoholics Anonymous and feeling more comfortable in my own skin. I have a book coming out—it's tentatively called *Hammered by Life*—and better days are ahead.

Some of you probably remember me as the NHL's most penalized player, a guy who frequently dropped his gloves and helped the Flyers win two Stanley Cups. What you may not know is the mental strain I experienced to prepare for each game. I visualized going to war with an opponent—whether it was Terry O'Reilly, Keith Magnuson, or whomever—in the hours that led to our game.

As I mentioned, I despised fighting. It was totally different than who I am as a human being. To this day, I have never had a fistfight away from hockey.

Growing up, I was a pretty small kid. When someone threatened me, my big brother, Ray, handled it. I was totally intimidated, but that all changed when I got into a fight while playing for the Salem Rebels in the Eastern Hockey League. After numerous fights, I discovered I was pretty good at it.

But being a good fighter doesn't make you immune to life's problems.

And my life was filled with them. I was molested as a youngster by a neighbor, and I turned into an alcoholic after my hockey career ended. I later got divorced and it is still one of my biggest regrets. My brother, Ray, died at 46, and my precious nine-year-old granddaughter, Annalise, died of brain cancer in 2020.

I'm now trying to focus on the good things in my life, like the time I spend with my sons, Chad and Brett. They are among the best parts of my life.

This book isn't just a 50-year reflection about the happy times of the Flyers and the championships. It's also about some of the obstacles many of us have faced along the way. It's about real life, and it's about the people who made the Flyers feel like a true family. The players' wives were a big part of that.

I'm happy I was part of that Flyers family, and grateful we have such a great alumni association. We are still actively involved in the community, and we still get to see one another.

I'm not so sure that many other pro teams still feel that type of bond, especially 50-some years after the fans fell in love with us…and we fell in love with them.

Bullies forever!

—Dave Schultz
Two-time Stanley Cup winner
with the Philadelphia Flyers

CHAPTER 1

DID ED SNIDER'S JEW-HATING ENEMIES INDIRECTLY CREATE THE BROAD STREET BULLIES?

As the decades have passed since the Philadelphia Flyers last won the Stanley Cup, the appreciation of their 1974 and 1975 championships has grown even greater—if that is possible.

Back when the Flyers were captivating the city with their Cups, Philadelphia was in disarray and badly in need of some positive news.

Crime and inflation were high in Philly. Spirits were low. The sports teams were so bad that Philadelphia was known as the City of Losers before the Flyers shocked the NHL and won the franchise's first Stanley Cup in 1974. They beat the favored Boston Bruins in the Finals, giving them the championship in just the franchise's seventh year of existence.

With that as a backdrop, how did the Flyers—then known as the Broad Street Bullies because of their arena's location and the aggressive way they played—accomplish such an unimaginable feat so quickly? How did they come to be loved by so many people? How did they go from having 20 people at their introductory parade in 1967 to what was called "the mother of all parades" in 1974, when two million fans saluted them?

Well, the genesis of the story may be in the 1940s, when Ed Snider, who years later would become the Flyers' owner, was a youngster in Washington, DC, and was victimized by anti-Semitic kids in his neighborhood.

After a while, Snider could not take any more. He turned into a tough kid of sorts. Snider decided he would never be pushed around again as he fought someone from the neighborhood.

About three decades later, he had that same attitude as he watched his Flyers get pushed around by the St. Louis Blues in back-to-back Stanley Cup playoff series losses.

Never, he said, will that happen again, either.

Bottom line: The Broad Street Bullies' birth has Snider's fingerprints all over it.

Their rise captivated a city back then, and 50-some years later the players from those teams are still deeply appreciated, still treated with reverence. They still don't have to buy a drink if they walk into a bar. They are still recognized and respected when they bump into hockey fans in Philadelphia, Florida, and many places around North America.

And beyond.

The Broad Street Bullies were known for their fists, but they were more than fighters. Much more. They received brilliant goaltending and had several high-quality players. They were also relentless. No NHL team outworked them. No team had players who understood their roles better than the Flyers.

Around the NHL, fans loathed them. That fueled the Bullies as they won consecutive Stanley Cups in 1974 and 1975.

The road to their championships, however, was filled with potholes—and heartbreak—during their early years.

In the Flyers' second season, the Blues embarrassed them by sweeping four straight games in Round 1 of the 1969 playoffs.

St. Louis outscored Philadelphia by a combined 17–3. Physically, the Blues had their way as Barclay Plager and his brother, Bob, and Noel Picard got under the Flyers' skin.

It was one thing to lose a seven-game playoff series like the Flyers had against St. Louis the previous season. It was another thing to be overmatched in every game and brutalized in most board battles.

After that series, Snider made up his mind to "get big, tough players."

Snider went to general manager Keith Allen, telling him to find the meanest, biggest players around, telling him he was sick of watching the Flyers get bullied.

Lou Scheinfeld, the Flyers' vice president when the franchise was formed, was sitting with Snider in a Spectrum super box during home games in that 1969 playoff series. The Blues' owners were sitting at the other end of the box.

"We lose, and the Blues guys are cheering, and Snider is steaming," Scheinfeld, who named the Spectrum, recalled in 2023. "You don't fuck with Ed Snider on his turf. He looked over at those guys and you could see steam coming out of his head, and those guys are cheering and clapping and running down to the locker room to celebrate."

Snider went to the Flyers' locker room. He told Scheinfeld he was going to have a discussion with Allen, the coach at the time, who would become the general manager the next season.

"If we're going to have a choice between two guys in the draft, we're going to pick the bigger one," Snider told Allen. "If we can't beat them on the ice, we're going to beat them in the parking lot."

The street fighter was coming out in Snider.

Highly Successful Draft

In the summer of '69, the Flyers would later be hailed for drafting center Bobby Clarke, who slipped to the second round because he was diabetic, and teams considered him a health risk.

Two other players from that draft—left winger Dave Schultz in the fifth round, and right winger Don Saleski in the sixth—didn't get much publicity at the time.

But they would become major players in the Broad Street Bullies' identity.

Clarke was the Flyers' meal ticket, a tenacious player who would win three MVP awards.

Schultz and Saleski were blue-collar players who contributed some important goals, but their value was in their hard-nosed style of play.

When you think of the Broad Street Bullies, those two players and left winger Bob Kelly, who was drafted in the third round in 1970, and defenseman André "Moose" Dupont come to mind as the physical ringleaders. Dupont was acquired from St. Louis.

It should also be noted that all four players had some skill that frequently gets overlooked because of their aggressive, brawling, and fearless play.

They also had colorful nicknames that added to their mystique.

Saleski was "Big Bird" because his wild hair reminded people of the *Sesame Street* character. It started when Clarke overheard a young fan tell his mom that Saleski "looks like Big Bird" during a pregame warmup. Clarke excitedly shared the story with his teammates. "And that was it," Saleski said with a laugh. The nickname would never leave him.

Schultz was "The Hammer" because of his punching prowess and the way he nailed opponents with his fists.

Kelly had many nicknames, but "Hound" was the most popular; he earned the nickname because of his dogged style on the ice. If you look at a small metal ball bouncing around crazily in a pinball machine, that was Kelly as he ricocheted off opposing players and the boards.

Dupont was "Moose" because of his huge size—he was listed as 6'0", 200 pounds, but his teammates say he weighed much more—and his hard-hitting style. He was dealt to the Flyers in 1972 at the request of coach Fred Shero, who had coached him in Omaha in the Central Hockey League.

They were the main fighters on Flyers teams that no longer got pushed around. They did the pushing.

"They brought in Schultz, they brought in Saleski, traded for Dupont. We had Kelly," Clarke, the team's heart and soul, said five decades after the Flyers won their first Cup. "All of a sudden, we had a personality. It was built around guys fighting a lot. But that also hid the talent that [Rick] MacLeish had, and some of the other guys' talent. [Bill] Barber was a Hall of Famer. We got Reggie Leach.... Keith made some good trades.

"We had a really good team, but we also had a personality," Clarke added. "We had a personality to live up to. The team had to play hard, had to play tough. And because of our talent, we won a lot of games."

Clarke said fighting "didn't win games, but it gave you a notoriety, a personality of what you are. And, of course, everybody hating us helped us. It made us closer."

Going Too Far?

Still, even some who worked in the Flyers' front office wondered if the team was going too far.

Fitz Eugene Dixon was one of those people.

Dixon was a minority owner of the Flyers, and he was a man of sophistication. "He was a tweed jacket, Main Line kind of guy," Scheinfeld said.

Dixon was not a fan of the Flyers' fighting antics, and he sent Snider a letter about it.

Snider called Scheinfeld into his office and asked him to read the letter. He wanted Scheinfeld's advice.

According to Scheinfeld, Dixon said, "I abhor all this fighting," and asked Snider, "What are you going to do about this debacle?"

"How do I answer this?" Snider asked Scheinfeld.

"Just tell him if this keeps up, we're going to have to put in more seats," Scheinfeld cracked.

Snider loved the suggestion, called in his secretary, and dictated a letter to Dixon.

"Fitz never confronted him after that," Scheinfeld said.

Snider's Roots and the Bullies

Interestingly, those associated with Snider wonder if the true genesis of the Broad Street Bullies is connected to his childhood in Washington, DC, where he had his share of Jew-hating enemies who tried to intimidate him.

Some of the neighborhood kids called him "Jew-boy," and it infuriated him.

Snider grew up during World War II and heard the stories about Jews being slaughtered in Europe. His parents owned a grocery store called Snider Market, and Eddie (as he was known at the time) worked there as a youngster, mopping the floors, setting up displays and the meat counter, unloading trucks, cutting meats, and cleaning the vegetable drawers. He took pride in everything he did.

Walking to and from school, he would get harassed by anti-Semitic kids. They were neighborhood bullies who would throw his glasses to the ground and smash them.

"Jew-boy, Jew-boy, don't you cry, you'll be a rabbi, by-and-by."

That was a chant he heard, according to Alan Bass in *Ed Snider: The Last Sports Mogul.*

Jay Snider, one of Ed's sons, said his father had lengthy talks with him about that time period.

"He was getting bullied," Jay Snider, who served as the Flyers' president from 1983 to 1994, said five decades after the team won its last Cup. "And he said one day he just made up his mind" to fight back.

Eddie "waited in some bushes" for the ringleader, Jay Snider said. "And when the kid walked by, he basically ambushed him and beat the crap out of him."

Snider became a tough guy. He became respected for standing up for himself. He developed a swagger and joined a group of friends who looked out for each other.

His family said he was also enamored by tales of his uncle Sam, who told Eddie that when he was younger, he would deliberately walk through anti-Semitic neighborhoods and display a huge Star of David, goading the people to fight him.

Eddie applauded his uncle's chutzpah.

So, when Snider years later proclaimed, "We will never be pushed around again" after the Blues physically manhandled the Flyers in the 1969 Stanley Cup playoffs, he was speaking from personal experience.

"Ed was a street fighter," said Scheinfeld, a onetime Flyers executive and Snider's drinking buddy for many years. "Ed would fight you. I mean, I pulled him back from getting into fights in restaurants when somebody said something to him or bumped into him. I stopped him from going over the glass after a referee."

Keith Allen, the Flyers Hall of Fame general manager, had to intervene between Snider and a heckler during a 1973 playoff game in Minnesota. In *Keith the Thief*, a book written by his son, Blake Allen, Snider recalled the incident.

Snider and Allen were sitting in the stands with their wives, Myrna and Joyce, respectively. They were cheering loudly whenever the Flyers scored or did something positive, and it caught the ire of a North Stars fan who was sitting a handful of rows in front of them.

"Snider, you're a bum! You stink, Snider," said the fan, who added some profanity-laced statements.

This went on for a while, until Snider couldn't take it any longer.

"Let's go outside!" Snider screamed.

The man stood up. He towered over Snider, and he had arms like Dwayne "The Rock" Johnson.

Allen, a former NHL defenseman who was an imposing figure, went with him. They went outside. Cooler heads prevailed.

Thanks to Allen's presence, Snider went back inside and was still in one piece.

Scheinfeld recalled the time Snider made an unsuccessful attempt to go into the referees' locker room, planning to fight one of the officials.

There were many other Snider eruptions, including one when he worked for Philadelphia's NFL team.

"He got into a fight in Hershey at an Eagles preseason game because fans were giving him some shit," Scheinfeld said. "He got into a fight at Madison Square Garden at a Flyers game."

It was a continuation of his youth.

"He was a tough kid," Scheinfeld said. "He was in a lot of fights as a kid."

One night after work, Scheinfeld and Snider planned to go to dinner. They walked out of the Spectrum when Ed decided to use one of the arena's public restrooms, which was jammed because a concert was being held that night.

"He pushes right through, gets right to the front, and some guy yells, 'What in the hell? What's the matter with you?'" Scheinfeld said. "And Ed gets up in the guy's face."

Scheinfeld was stern with his boss.

"Ed," he said, "let's get the hell out of here."

As they walked toward the exit, Scheinfeld shook his head.

"Why the hell did you do that?" he asked. "That was unnecessary."

"Because you were right behind me," Snider cracked, figuring Scheinfeld would jump in if it came to blows.

As Snider aged, his fighting urges reduced, or at least they were more under control. But his desire to win became magnified.

"He was so intense," said Jay Snider, one of his sons. "You really couldn't talk to him during a game."

That's why he once kicked Donald Trump out of his owner's suite because Trump wasn't paying attention to the game and was talking too much, distracting Snider from watching his beloved Flyers.

"Even between periods, you tried to talk about the weather or something else, and his mind was someplace else," Jay Snider said about his father. "He was so focused and emotional. The only thing he was passionate about was the Flyers. Ever. And he lived and died with it—every win, every bad call, and everybody was against us [in his mind]. And he was infamous for running down to the referees' room."

That intensity wore off on some of his children.

His daughter Lindy Snider remembers being in school and being upset about a game the Flyers had lost the previous night.

She couldn't stop talking about the painful loss to one of her friends.

Another classmate interrupted her.

"It's just a game, Lindy."

"What do you mean it's just a game?!" Lindy replied. "This is not just a game. It's never just a game. This is our life!"

Bullies Are Born

The Broad Street Bullies were hated by the NHL establishment because they were tarnishing the league's image with their fighting and aggressive play, leading to fines, suspensions, court dates, and even a few battles with fans.

In a December 29 game in Vancouver in 1972, Bob Kelly got into a fight with the Canucks' Jim Hargreaves in the third period. As that was unfolding, Don Saleski and Vancouver's Barry Wilcox got into a scuffle near the boards at the Pacific Coliseum. Saleski had the upper edge, and a fan reached over the boards and pulled the right winger's hair. More chaos ensued as Flyers backup goalie Bobby Taylor went after the fan, who, as it turned out, was a dentist. Barry Ashbee then punched the dentist several times, according to Jay Greenberg in *Full Spectrum.*

"I left my stick on the ice, but I got the guy with a couple of good shots," Ashbee said at the time.

Some believe this was the advent of the Broad Street Bullies.

The Flyers' Ed Van Impe and Bill "Cowboy" Flett jumped into the stands swinging their sticks, as if to say, *"Do NOT mess with our players!"* Fans ducked for cover, but the players swung their sticks at the vacated wooden seats as they tried to scare the paying customers but not harm them, according to the *Bulletin*'s Jack Chevalier.

"We had to protect Bobby Taylor," Van Impe said.

Flett rescued Taylor, who was known as "Chief." Afterward, Taylor said: "That's the first time a Cowboy ever saved an Indian."

Flyers players Joe Watson and Ross Lonsberry were also involved with the fans. In addition, Taylor knocked down a Vancouver policeman who had entered the scene.

Coach Fred Shero was incensed. He said fans were hollering and throwing things at his players earlier in the game and that because he "expected trouble," he'd requested some security in the building, but nothing was done.

After the game, the Flyers boarded their team bus, which was parked a few feet from their locker room door to prevent another riot. About 100 angry fans shouted insults.

"Animals!" many yelled.

Several Flyers were taken away by police after the game, a 4–4 tie. All told, seven Flyers were charged with creating a disturbance "by using obscene language and by fighting with spectators with fists and by wielding hockey sticks against and in close proximity to spectators in the general seating area," according to the police report. They appeared in court during their next trip to Vancouver in February, but the case was postponed until June.

A Vancouver columnist sarcastically chastised the Flyers' behavior.

"See, kids, this is how you do it in the bigs," Jim Taylor wrote. "Something goes wrong, you climb into the stands and hit people with sticks.... But this is the NHL. You've got autographed pictures and bubble gum cards and pajamas with signatures on them. If they did it, it must be okay."

As for the Flyers and their June court hearing, Lonsberry was cleared of charges, but $500 fines were assessed to Van Impe, Ashbee, Bobby Taylor, Flett, Saleski, and Joe Watson.

In addition, Bobby Taylor received a 30-day jail sentence for punching a police officer; the sentence was appealed and later suspended.

If You Want Pretty Skating...

The Flyers teams that won Cups in 1974 and 1975 were deeply talented, but there's no denying they played with an edge. That opened things up for gifted players like Bobby Clarke, Rick MacLeish, and Bill Barber, among others.

"A lot of us are not considered smooth skaters," Kelly, known as the "Hound," said after the Flyers won their second Cup. "I guess you'd call our style helter-skelter."

"People think of hockey and they think of everything graceful and flowing," center Terry Crisp added. "The Flying Frenchmen stuff.

"And then we come along..."

Shero never apologized for the Flyers' bruising style of play. It wasn't necessary. Like football, toughness was a part of the sport.

"If it's pretty skating they want," he said in 1974, "let 'em watch the Ice Follies."

After winning Cup II in 1975, *Philadelphia Inquirer* columnist Bill Lyon wrote that other teams wore tuxedos and glided to a waltz, while the Flyers wore jeans and T-shirts and stomped to discordant blaring.

"So, you can call this the Cup that sweat built," wrote the always-eloquent Lyon. Other teams "fill Lord Stanley's Cup with champagne. But the Flyers drink beer. That may be the best explanation yet of why the Flyers have won it twice now."

In a way, the old-school, nothing-fancy style unified the team even more.

The Flyers were an amazingly tight-knit group. They seemingly did everything together off the ice—partying, fishing, hanging out with each other's families—and had a special bond when they played.

Their brawling style united them.

"That in itself brought us so close together," right winger Gary Dornhoefer said 50 years after the Broad Street Bullies created havoc. "You go down fighting. You're not going to win every game, but if you're going to lose, leave a reminder for the opposition that you're going to be in for a tough game."

The Flyers' transformation started in 1972–73, when they finished second in the West with a 37–30–11 record and won the first playoff series in franchise history, beating the Minnesota North Stars in six games.

That was one year removed from a loss in Buffalo that was more tragic than a *Dexter* rerun. The Flyers, in Shero's first coaching year with the team, needed just a tie to secure a playoff berth in their final regular season game.

Instead, they lost 3–2 on a long shot by former Flyer Gerry Meehan with four seconds left in regulation.

But the 1972–73 season was all about making amends. Not only did the Flyers do that, but they set the foundation for winning the Stanley Cup the next year.

Bobby Clarke raised his game to another level in 1972–73, scoring 104 points and winning the Hart Trophy as the league's MVP. Rick MacLeish also blossomed into a star, collecting 50 goals and 50 assists—he became the youngest player (23) in NHL history to reach the 50-goal mark. Rookie left winger Bill Barber (30 goals) also burst onto the scene, and Dornhoefer erupted for a career-high 30 goals.

In addition, Keith Allen made shrewd trades that landed left winger Ross Lonsberry (21 goals in his first full year with the Flyers) and right winger Bill Flett (career-high 43 goals) from Los Angeles, and they excelled in their first full season in Philadelphia. Rugged defenseman André "Moose" Dupont, pilfered from St. Louis, was also a key addition.

"If anything happened in front of the net, Moose and Eddie Van Impe cleared the bodies so Bernie [Parent] had a good look at the shots," Joe Watson said.

Herculean Task

After beating the North Stars in Minnesota in Game 6 to advance to the 1973 Stanley Cup semifinals, the Flyers had a gargantuan task against the mighty Montreal Canadiens.

The fact that the heavy-underdog Flyers split the first two games of that series—with each matchup in Montreal's fabled Forum—opened eyes around the league.

The Flyers returned to the Spectrum and received a heroes' welcome from the fans, many of whom had slept outside the arena so they would be in line to buy tickets when they went on sale. The fans were excited about the Flyers' first home game since capturing the playoff series in Minnesota and nearly sweeping the Canadiens on the road.

So, when the Flyers took the ice for pregame warmups, they were given a standing ovation that wouldn't end. It was like everybody in the stands looked at each other and said, "*Do NOT stop applauding.*"

Fifty years after that scene, Dornhoefer said beating Boston to clinch the Cup in 1974 and that pregame salute in the 1973 semifinals were probably the loudest times he ever experienced at the Spectrum.

The '73 pregame adulation against the Canadiens left a lasting impression.

"You couldn't even talk to anybody else on the ice," he said. "You couldn't hear anybody."

The cheering crowd drowned them out.

Although the Flyers were ousted by Montreal, four games to one, in the 1973 playoffs, they were moving in the right direction.

They had played the Canadiens almost evenly. Three of the games were decided by a goal and two went into overtime. In Montreal's series-clinching win, the Flyers had a third-period lead before dropping a 5–3 decision.

Clarke gathered the players in the locker room.

"We have something special going here," he told them.

Some players believed the Flyers would have beaten the Canadiens if they had a more consistent goalie than Doug Favell, who had an .892 save percentage in the series. Montreal's Ken Dryden had a .916 mark.

The Flyers management decided to make a bold move because there was a piece missing.

Allen found that piece in the offseason, reacquiring goaltender Bernie Parent from Toronto.

For Allen, it was an agonizing deal because he had to include Favell in the trade. Favell had played extremely well during the stretch run and in the Stanley Cup quarterfinals (.943 save percentage) against Minnesota. He was popular among teammates and fans.

Allen said even his family was upset with him for trading Favell.

As fate would have it, the Flyers started their historic 1973–74 season against the Maple Leafs at the Spectrum, where Parent outdueled Favell 2–0.

Parent, who improved dramatically after playing next to his idol, Jacques Plante, in Toronto, was on his way to stardom. So were the Philadelphia Flyers.

Interestingly, when the Flyers traded Parent to Toronto in a three-way deal in 1971 that also included Boston, Philly received MacLeish, who turned into a borderline Hall of Famer.

"Ricky," Barber said, "was like poetry in motion on the ice. He was so fluid with his skating style and his wrist shot."

MacLeish was arguably the best player in Flyers history during pressure situations. He was the NHL's top point producer during the Flyers' playoff runs that culminated with Stanley Cups in 1974 and 1975. In the '74 playoffs, he had 13 goals and 22 points in 17 games, including the Cup winner in the 1–0 Game 6 victory over Boston. The next year, he had 11 goals and 20 points in 17 playoff games.

"The trades to get Bernie and Ricky MacLeish, that was the glue," Saleski said. "That's what propelled us to win the Cup."

Numbing Numbers

With Parent having a season for the ages in 1973–74, the Flyers finished tied for No. 1 in the NHL with a 2.10 goals-against average. The previous season, they were 11th out of 16 teams with a 3.28 GAA.

Parent topped the NHL that season in goals-against average (1.89), save percentage (.932), shutouts (12), and appearances (73).

Besides having a terrific goaltender, the Flyers had a stellar defense and a multitude of offensive stars. They also had tough, gritty players who backed down from no one.

This wasn't your father's Flyers who'd gotten pushed around by the Blues.

This was the Flyers of Schultz, Kelly, Saleski, Dupont, Orest Kindrachuk, et al. They were complementary players who knew their roles and weren't a liability whenever they were on the ice.

Fact is, they were assets. Huge assets. During the regular season that led to the 1974 Stanley Cup, Dupont finished at plus-34, Schultz was plus-25, Kindrachuk and Saleski were each plus-20, and Kelly was plus-10.

The defense had Ed Van Impe, Dupont, and Barry Ashbee (he had a team-high plus-53 rating in 1973–74) providing the toughness, and the Watson brothers (Joe and Jimmy) and power-play specialist Tom Bladon playing key roles.

"They've got a great goaltender and the best defense in the league," Rangers coach Emile Francis said during the 1974 playoffs.

And even utility players like Terry Crisp and Bill Clement were important to the team's success.

The Broad Street Bullies weren't just brawlers. Far from it. They were composed of players who thrived in their roles and had much more skill than their critics wanted to admit. Their penalty kill, which got more work than any NHL team, was No. 1 in the league (88.4 percent success rate), and their power play was No. 3 (22.3 percent success).

The Flyers were virtually unbeatable at the Spectrum.

"Our fans," defenseman Jimmy Watson said, "were worth a goal a game at home."

Opposing teams "did not really want to play in Philadelphia," Saleski said. "The persona was a huge intimidation factor and big advantage for us."

But the Bullies weren't exactly pacificists on the road. They were hated by opposing crowds—and that seemed to inspire Philly to maintain its swagger and aggressiveness in road arenas. Some of those arenas struggled to draw fans, but many sold out their venues when the Flyers came to town. In fact, five of those enemy arenas set franchise attendance records when their teams hosted the Flyers in 1973–74.

"Getting fans riled up on the road was a great thing for us," Saleski said, "because that just adds to your fuel and gets you fired up. It helps pump you up. But that persona probably impacted Schultz more than other people on our team because he was the Broad Street Bully. Yeah, Mr. Broad Street Bully."

And, yes, they knew how to get fans riled up. They set an NHL record in the 1973–74 season with 1,750 penalty minutes. That broke the record they had set the previous season, and that was 603 minutes more than the second-place team.

The Flyers had the penalty-killing skill to offset being shorthanded. They were shorthanded 422 times in 1973–74 but allowed just 49 power-play goals. Moreover, they scored an NHL-best 20 shorthanded goals, including five by Clarke and four by MacLeish.

Confrontations with Fans

Fans in other cities didn't come to watch the Flyers, however, because of their skill. They came because of the likelihood of seeing bench-clearing brawls. They came because they wanted to see Schultz, who had become a showman of sorts, get the snot beat out of him by one of their players.

This led to some emotional confrontations between the Flyers and visiting fans. Some of them took place after games.

Five decades after their Stanley Cup glory days, members of the Broad Street Bullies were nearly unanimous when asked about the worst fan behavior in the NHL.

New York. Madison Square Garden. Home of the Rangers.

Fans would "fire bottles off our bus when we pulled out after beating them," defenseman Joe Watson recalled. "Jesus Christ. They turned all the lights out on the bus, and they're firing whiskey bottles off the bloody windows of the bus. We were not well liked."

To get to their bus after games at The Garden, the Flyers had to walk through a winding tunnel and down to a parking area.

When the bus pulled out, fans would chase it for "two or three blocks and throw all kinds of stuff at us," Kelly said. "It was just crazy New Yorkers who were wrapped up in their team."

One crazy New Yorker chased the bus from Madison Square Garden to the Lincoln Tunnel. He "beat the bus with chains" the entire time, backup goalie Bobby Taylor said.

"We thought it was funny for a while," Taylor said, "and then we stopped at a red light and a couple of our guys said, 'Open the door. We'll stop this guy.'" The bus driver opened the door. Out went the Broad Street Bullies.

The fan "took one look and started running. We never saw him again," Taylor said.

On another exit from New York, Clement remembers standing by the bus with Saleski, Dupont, and Kelly. "We were waiting for the other guys, and these fans behind a barricade really got to me. They're yelling, 'You gutless fucking Broad Street Bullies. We fucking beat the shit out of you.'"

Clement hadn't played that night, so he had lots of energy.

"Let's go over there and see how tough they are," he said to his teammates.

They walked on the other side of the barricade. Clement put up his fists.

"I fucking squared off with this guy in army boots, and he started kicking at me," Clement said. "So, I moved in really quick and threw a punch. He had really long hair, and I grabbed it and threw him down to the ground. And all of a sudden, I feel somebody punching the shit out of the back of my head."

No worries. Just like on the ice, the Flyers came to the rescue of a fallen teammate.

"Moose, Saleski, and Hound pulled him off me, and the kid who jumped on me ended up pressing charges," Clement said. "We had to go to court in New York City after the season."

When they arrived in court, the players were greeted by a judge who told them: "So, you are the guys who beat up on my favorite team, the Montreal Canadiens?"

The players rolled their eyes. This wasn't going to go too well, they thought.

But the judge dismissed the case if there were no more New York incidents in the next year. The Flyers, in effect, were cleared.

MSG Misadventures

There were many other misadventures at Madison Square Garden.

Clarke remembers a fan throwing a knife onto the ice during warmups.

There was also the night a Rangers fan waited for some of the Flyers to leave Madison Square Garden. "Where's this Schultz? Where's this Kelly?" the fan asked. "Bring them out. We'll see how tough they are!"

Dupont heard the guy and pulled him into the locker room. The fan looked stunned.

He dragged him to Schultz's locker, where the menacing left winger was getting dressed.

"This guy wants to see you," Dupont announced.

Schultz, unaware of what was transpiring, turned around from his chair.

The man ran out of the locker room.

The Broad Street Bullies preferred playing at the Spectrum, but they didn't mind playing away from home. It gave them a chance to have dinners and drinks together, and they thrived in enemy cities.

"We loved playing on the road," Dornhoefer said.

The road is where the Flyers had an "Us Against the World" attitude.

"I know some people think they're just a bunch of animals and headhunters," Atlanta left winger Keith McCreary said after the visiting Flyers beat the Flames in the 1974 quarterfinals en route to their first Stanley Cup, "but they're a whole lot more than that."

Still, many hockey purists didn't agree. That fueled the Flyers for their Cup run in 1975 because they wanted to show their first championship wasn't an accident.

They knew they would be a target because of their 1974 championship, knew teams would circle meetings with the Flyers on their calendars.

But they didn't want that target to grow. That's why the players met and discussed the Stanley Cup patches that Snider decided they would wear on their jerseys.

Snider was rightfully proud of the Flyers' 1974 accomplishment and wanted to shout it to the rest of the league by showcasing the huge patches of the Stanley Cup.

The players thought they were too ostentatious. They understood Snider's pride, but they wanted the patches removed.

"I remember Ed's disappointment," Scheinfeld said.

The Flyers wore the patches during preseason games but not during the 1974–75 regular season.

Looking back on it 50 years later, Scheinfeld said "the players were right. The patch would have been a garish, in-your-face challenge to opponents."

That said, he also knew the jerseys with a Cup in the front would have been a marketing bonanza, and that the Flyers would have sold "a zillion sweaters" if they had worn them during the season.

The players didn't care about the profits; they cared about successfully defending their Cup.

The Flyers made some additions heading into the 1974–75 season, the most significant being right winger Reggie Leach, Clarke's linemate in juniors. Clarke recommended the Flyers acquire him. GM Keith Allen listened, showing the power the captain carried.

It turned out to be one of the best trades in Flyers history. The Flyers got Reggie the Rifle from the California Golden Seals.

In eight years in Philadelphia, Leach would score 306 goals, including a franchise-record 61 in 1975–76. He was acquired for Al MacAdam, who became a two-time All-Star, Larry Wright (106 NHL games, including two with the Seals), Ron Chipperfield (83 NHL games, but none with the Seals), and George Pesut (92 NHL games). Chipperfield turned out to be the player the Seals drafted with the first-round pick they received in the deal, and Pesut was the player acquired as "future considerations."

After a slow start, Leach scored 45 goals in his first season with the Flyers in 1974–75, playing with Clarke and Bill Barber on what became the iconic LCB Line.

Other newcomers that season included defenseman Ted Harris and backup goalie Wayne Stephenson.

Harris was acquired from St. Louis for future considerations. His steady play and veteran leadership were needed because Ashbee suffered a career-ending eye injury in the 1974 Stanley Cup semifinals.

Harris was a four-time Cup champ in Montreal, but he wasn't expected to play a main role with the Flyers. He was 38 and toward the end of his career. But instead of being a spare part, he became a valuable regular.

He called it "one of the most enjoyable seasons of my life," after winning the '75 Cup with the Flyers before departing to coach the Minnesota North Stars. "I've never seen a team like this…where everybody loves everybody else, where the players can sit down and have a beer with the coach."

Something to Prove

The Flyers' 1975 championship had special meaning.

"There was a lot of noise last year, saying it was a fluke," Dornhoefer said after the Flyers outlasted the Sabres in Buffalo

2–0 to win Game 6 and clinch their second straight Cup. "We had something to prove. I'm glad we won it here so people couldn't say we could only win at home."

In the Cup clincher, the Flyers scored two third-period goals that were symbolic of their work ethic. In a way, the first goal, scored by Bob Kelly, was the brainchild of assistant coach Mike Nykoluk.

After the second period, Nykoluk made a recommendation to head coach Fred Shero while the teams were in a scoreless deadlock.

"We might want to put Hound out there," Nykoluk said. "He hasn't played in a while. He might give you the energy."

On the first shift of the third, Shero sent Kelly onto the ice on the top line. The left winger was usually a bottom-six player who created havoc with his relentless checking and his fearless play.

He now found himself on the top unit, alongside Clarke and Leach.

As the third period started, Leach dumped the puck into the Sabres' zone. Kelly chased it behind the net and took a nasty hit from Jerry Korab, a 6'3", 220-pound defenseman.

Enter the irrepressible Clarke, who cleverly shielded Korab off the play, enabling Kelly to pick up the puck and spin out front. Using a backhander, he beat goalie Roger Crozier 11 seconds into the period.

"Clarke bumped Korab, and Korab forgot about the puck," Kelly said. "I was at the right place at the right time."

Kelly skated right to Shero on the bench.

"Hey Freddy, you owe me five bucks," Kelly told him.

It turned out the Flyers had practiced that behind-the-net play frequently, and Shero had promised $5 to a player who scored that type of goal.

"Hey, five bucks used to fill up my Corvette in those days," Kelly said five decades after scoring the biggest goal of his career, a goal that turned out to be the winning tally in a Stanley Cup clincher.

Fifty years later, he was still the only player in Flyers history to score a Cup-clinching goal in a road game.

The second goal in the Cup-winning game was scored by another hard-working non-star. With 2:47 left, Clement put a shot through Crozier's legs on a breakaway. Kindrachuk did the dirty work on the goal. He was checked hard into the boards by Korab just after threading a pass to Clement.

"I felt like I went through the boards," Kindrachuk said at the time.

"You've got to admire 'O,'" Dornhoefer said. "He knew he would get creamed, but you have to take a check to win."

For Dornhoefer and Kelly, two hard-nosed players who exemplified the Broad Street Bullies, winning the 1975 Cup was extra special. Both were injured and did not play in the historic Cup clincher against Boston the previous year.

"When you're not in there bleeding with the guys and suffering with the guys and what they're going through, it hurts," Kelly said. "It was just so much more fulfilling to go from start to finish for the whole season for the second Cup, and as a team, we proved the first one wasn't a fluke."

Dornhoefer had similar sentiments.

"When you're not there and you won, you kind of feel left out and not a part of it," he said. "You don't get the same feeling as when you're on the ice, like I did in Buffalo. That was very gratifying."

It was also gratifying for Snider, who unknowingly had the Broad Street Bullies' seeds planted in his mind when he was showing he wasn't a pushover in DC in the 1940s.

CHAPTER 2

A NICKNAME FOR THE AGES

OVER THE YEARS, team nicknames have become a part of every sport's lore. They enhance a team's popularity and give it lasting power, or in rare cases (see the "Black" Sox, the White Sox team that threw the 1919 World Series), they bring shame for their misgivings.

The Philadelphia Flyers' "Broad Street Bullies" label, a nickname that started in January of 1973 thanks to reporter Jack Chevalier and copy editor Pete Cafone from the *Philadelphia Bulletin*, helped give those hockey teams a mystique in the 1970s. It fueled hatred from fans in opposing cities, adulation from those in hard-scrabble Philadelphia, a city that prides itself on toughness and a no-nonsense attitude.

It's also a nickname that has withstood the test of time. If you say "Broad Street Bullies" in the 2020s, most casual sports fans know who you are talking about.

Heck, even some who live on a different continent are aware of the nickname, which was embraced by Philly's fans of all walks of life.

The players from those powerhouse teams also liked the nickname.

"You know why? It's intimidating," said Joe Watson, a key defenseman on the Philadelphia Flyers' two Stanley Cup champions of the 1970s.

He recounted a story about the Broad Street Bullies, saying it revolved around a friend of his who traveled to Prague in the Czech Republic around 2020 and waved down a taxi driver.

Cabbie: "So where are you from?"

Tourist: "Philadelphia."

Cabbie: "Ah, the home of the Bullies. The Broad Street Bullies."

"Fuck. That's 45 years ago" when the Bullies were around, Watson said. "And he knew them—in Prague, of all places."

The Broad Street Bullies became a part of pop culture. In 2020, a Saturday Night Live sketch had Jim Carrey, portraying Joe Biden, looking at the audience and thinking he sees Bobby Clarke during a "town hall."

Clarke, of course, was the captain of the Broad Street Bullies.

"I'm just so excited to talk to America with real-life Americans," Biden/Carrey says after addressing Clarke in the sketch.

The Broad Street Bullies have been portrayed in a countless number of national TV spots, even in a 1993 *Simpsons* episode.

After Homer sold his soul to the Devil for a donut, he was summoned before a jury to determine his fate. Satan's "Jury of the Damned" was composed of notorious figures, including Lizzie Borden, Benedict Arnold, Richard Nixon, John Dillinger, John Wilkes Booth, and (drum roll, please) the starting lineup of the 1976 Philadelphia Flyers.

Flyers fans didn't seem insulted that their team was listed with the bad guys. In a way, it was a compliment. The Flyers were despised around North America, loved around Philly.

For their fans, it was a badge of honor.

Preserving Memories

Sports nicknames generate smiles and precious memories from those who followed their beloved teams. They stir thoughts of more innocent times, when younger fans lived and died with their teams' exploits—long before adulthood and enhanced responsibilities changed their priorities, perhaps making their fandom a little less intense.

Brooklyn Dodgers fans had their version of the "Broad Street Bullies." For them, it was "The Boys of Summer," a nickname created by Roger Kahn's book, and it conjures invaluable memories of the 1950s. "The Whiz Kids" moniker does the same for fans of the young Phillies teams of a similar era, or the "Miracle Mets" of 1969, or the "Gashouse Gang" for the 1934 St. Louis Cardinals. Even if people who followed those teams are no longer around, those fans passed along stories to younger generations. That has kept those nicknames at the forefront, and it seems probable that even in 2074—a century after the Flyers won their first Stanley Cup—Philadelphia sports fans will still take pride in the "Broad Street Bullies" nickname.

Legendary teams, and nicknames, are not easily forgotten.

Catchy nicknames, like the Broad Street Bullies, have a way of perpetuating a team's accomplishments. A handful of other examples: the St. Louis Rams' "Greatest Show on Turf" at the turn of the 21st century; the Denver Broncos' "Orange Crush" from the 1970s; the Dallas Cowboys' "Doomsday Defense" in the 1960s and 1970s; the Detroit Pistons' "Bad Boys" of the 1980s, a nickname spurred by their aggressive defensive style; the San Diego Chargers' high-powered offense that was known as "Air Coryell" after their coach, Don, in the 1980s and 1990s; Michigan's men's basketball team got the label "Fab Five" because it started five standout freshmen in 1991; the powerful Cincinnati Reds were known as "The Big Red Machine" in the 1970s; the Chicago Bears were known as "Monsters of the Midway" in the 1940s and again in 1985; and Pittsburgh had its "Steel Curtain" as its defense led the way to championships in the 1970s.

The Broad Street Bullies is as good as any of those nicknames, and its origin came from a Philadelphia sportswriter after he watched the Flyers' penalty-filled 3–1 victory in Atlanta on January 3, 1973. That was a season before the Flyers won their first Stanley Cup.

At the time, Jack Chevalier, who was known as Chevy, covered the Flyers for the now-defunct *Philadelphia Bulletin*.

After the Flyers' aforementioned win in Atlanta, Chevalier filed a story and called the Flyers a nickname that, as it turned out, was never printed.

He later reconsidered and phoned Cafone. This, of course, was long before the Internet put stories online seconds after a game ended. Chevalier wasn't writing for an online site. He was writing for a newspaper that had a late deadline, so he had plenty of time to change what he had written.

Chevalier didn't like his first version, one in which he called the Flyers "the Blue Line Bandidos." A few hours later, he instructed Cafone to change it to the "Bullies of Broad Street."

"He said he liked Bullies of Broad Street better," Cafone said in 2023, "and I agreed with him. Simply put, I didn't think there were Mexican bandits in Philly at the time.... There were some criminals, yes, but not actually Bandidos."

Broad Street is where the Flyers' home arena, the Spectrum, was located in those days.

Chevalier's original nickname, Cafone said, made him think of Mexican bandits, "especially as represented in movies and popular culture. We actually had that discussion on why the Bullies of Broad Street was much better, because I was sure there were bullies on Broad Street somewhere," Cafone said.

Cafone kept the "Bullies of Broad Street" in Chevalier's story. But the nickname was too long for the headline. The copy editor wanted something snappier and shorter. The headline he wrote: *Broad Street Bullies Muscle Atlanta.*

Little did he or anyone else know that he had created poetry of sorts, that the nickname would become famous. Since it was created, the nickname has been used on T-shirts, hoodies, hats, German Army helmets, and probably hundreds of other items. Heck, there's even a Broad Street Bullies Pub next to the Wells Fargo Center, the home of the current Philadelphia Flyers.

After the *Bulletin* folded, Chevalier worked for other newspapers, including the *Philadelphia Inquirer* and *Philadelphia Tribune*, while Cafone moved to California and worked for big newspapers in San Francisco. The two remained close over the years. Cafone would visit with Chevy and his family when he traveled back east. The two newspaper guys would go to the racetrack, the seashore, baseball games.

At some point, they would kid about their missed opportunity of having their famous nickname copyrighted.

"The amazing thing is, we didn't know anything about trademarks," Cafone. "We never even thought about putting a trademark on a name. We never thought it was going to be something that stuck."

Chevalier, an unpretentious sort who had a strong and trusting rapport with the players and coaches he covered, died at 83 in 2019. Fittingly, after he died, a celebration of his life was held at the Broad Street Bullies Pub.

As a writer, "he was fair, and that's all you could ask," said Bill Barber, star left winger of the Broad Street Bullies.

These Nicknames Didn't Stick

The Fred Shero–coached Flyers of that era had other nicknames, including The Mad Squad—which played off a popular TV crime show at the time, *The Mod Squad*—Freddy's Philistines, and City of Brotherly Mug.

But the Broad Street Bullies is what resonated.

Fifty-plus years later, the nickname still draws smiles.

"The Flyers were a little intimidated before they became the Bullies, and they didn't fight as much on the road," said Lou Scheinfeld, the team's first vice president.

The nickname seemed to give them an obligation: live up to it and give opposing fans their money's worth.

Most of the time, Dave "The Hammer" Schultz, Bob "Hound" Kelly, Don "Big Bird" Saleski, and André "Moose" Dupont made them happy they bought tickets.

Schultz was, by far, the player who did the most fighting. But Kelly didn't back down from anyone, either.

While Schultz was someone who never got into a fight off the ice while growing up, Kelly had a much different background. Kelly grew up working on a farm and was in a gang as a youngster in Ontario. Fighting was part of his identity in his teenage years.

He remembers getting into his first scrap back in third grade.

"My mom put me in police pants," he recalled.

It was not a good look to his classmates. They shouted insults and chased him around the school's hallways, got into his face at the water fountain.

"So, I was kind of retaliatory from that point on," Kelly said.

It carried onto the ice, where he became a player known for his hustle and great fighting ability.

Getting the "Tap"

Fred Shero never ordered Kelly to go out and start a fight to change the game's momentum. He did it in a more subtle way.

The studious coach would walk behind Kelly on the bench before his next shift and gently tap him on the shoulder.

Kelly knew what it meant.

"You're going out there next and do what you have to do," Kelly said.

Kelly didn't need a tap on the shoulder when Clarke was hit in the head by the stick of Barry Cummins on December 2, 1973, igniting a bench-clearing brawl in which the California Golden Seals rookie defenseman was pummeled. Kelly, followed by several teammates, left the bench to assist Clarke and bloodied Cummins.

"In those days, you stood up for your teammates," Clarke said. "You were supposed to protect each other."

But sometimes, the Broad Street Bullies went too far, forward Bill Clement said decades later.

He recalled a game early in the 1974–75 season—again against the California Golden Seals. Notice a pattern? Schultz and Saleski were in the penalty box, as was the Seals' Mike Christie, Clement said. What followed was a third-period melee in which 23 penalties were assessed in what turned out to be a 4–1 California win in Oakland.

In that game on October 25, 1974, the teams combined for a then-single-game NHL record of 232 penalty minutes—144 for the Flyers, 88 for California.

The melee started when Christie, a rookie defenseman, and Orest Kindrachuk fought on the ice. A short time later, Clement said, Schultz and Saleski went after Christie in the penalty box, and California's Jimmy Neilson jumped into the box to even up the skirmish. "I jumped in on Neilsen and grabbed him and threw him down," Clement recalled. "I had my knee on his chest and said, 'You're not fucking going anywhere.' And what made me feel bad about that story is that Schultzy had one side of Christie's face and Saleski sucker-punched him and cut him for about 15 [stitches] right near the eye. And I almost wanted to cry because it wasn't honorable."

Saleski later said in *Full Spectrum* it was the "one thing I look back on with regret."

Other accounts say Kelly also took a punch at the outmanned Christie.

Christie had blood running down his face and said, "You guys think you're tough. You've got two of you. Go ahead, hit me again."

Saleski declined, Clement said. Years later, Saleski and Christie became teammates and friends in Colorado. Christie had a big scar near his eye from the fight. "It's hard for me seeing myself having done those things," Saleski said, regretfully.

Clement said, "there were times when our team would just beat the fucking snot out of other teams and players, where I felt really bad for them. I wanted to win and was happy with the win, and I got over it pretty quickly. I wasn't a bleeding-heart liberal. I'm a hunter and a killer like everybody else, and I've been in fights off the ice. I think I was in as many fights off the ice as I was on the ice. But there were times where I felt really bad for our opponents because they came into a fucking gunfight with no knife or anything."

Fighting on the Reservation

Saleski could protect himself, but he wasn't nearly as good with his fists as the other Bullies. Like Kelly, Saleski learned how to fight as a kid. He lived on an Indian reservation, and he and his sister would get picked on because they were "the only white kids in the school," according to the former right winger.

But fighting really wasn't his strength.

Barry Ashbee knew it as well as anyone. The night before the former Flyers defenseman and assistant coach passed away from leukemia in 1977, Saleski visited him.

Ashbee: "Bird, I love you, man. You've got them all bullshitted."

By that, Ashbee meant Saleski had always been dubbed as one of the key figures in the Broad Street Bullies, but that he couldn't come close to Schultz, Kelly, or Dupont when it came to fighting ability.

"I wasn't a tough guy," said Saleski, a deeply devout Catholic who played with a scrappy style and never backed down from a fight. "I've never been a tough guy."

But he has been accident prone.

Take the night Saleski was in a fight against the Kings in Los Angeles and received stitches over one of his eyes. "I probably had a concussion," Saleski said. "I was dizzy and feeling woozy."

After the game, his teammates went partying or to some bars, but Saleski decided to go back to his hotel room. He needed some rest, not some disco music intensifying his pounding head.

"The guys came looking for me around 1:00 AM," Saleski said. "I heard Kelly at my door, so I got up and figured I'd open the door just a crack. And just then, he kicked the door open and split my other eye. They had to take me to the emergency room at a hospital to get it stitched up. The next morning, I had two huge black eyes with stitches over both of them. I walk into the dressing room and Freddy [Shero] says to me, 'What the hell happened to you?' I said, 'Freddy, you don't even want to know. Two concussions in one night.'"

Or, as Chevalier wrote in the *Bulletin* following a game in which the Broad Street Bullies did their thing: "Bullies on the loose. Hammer, Big Bird, Hound, and Moose."

Chevalier's nickname, along with the Flyers' fighting style, gave them an identity.

"It was good because, I can assure you, we instilled fear in a lot of teams," Saleski said. "Teams like Los Angeles didn't want to come to Philadelphia. They'd get the Philadelphia Flu or the Flyers Flu."

"When your team has a personality, it gives you something to live up to and it motivates you—and all those things fall in place," Bobby Clarke said 50-plus years after the Broad Street Bullies were born.

On the road, the Flyers, partly because of their nickname, were Enemy No. 1. Fans in Buffalo hung an effigy of Schultz with a noose around his neck. Fans in Minnesota would wait for Schultz after a game to shout insults and threats at him.

"It wasn't just one of two people, it was 25 or 30," backup goalie Bobby Taylor said.

Clarke said the team would receive death threats "at times" on the road.

"But it was never taken seriously or anything," Clarke said.

The hatred in Boston was palpable. After all, the Broad Street Bullies had unseated the team known as the Big, Bad Bruins in toughness.

"You knew when you were playing in Boston you were in for a battle," Saleski said, "and you were in this small bandbox with people throwing shit at you. They were right on top of you and pouring beer on you…because you had to walk through the crowd to get to the dressing room."

In Pittsburgh, a fan near the glass would always throw a chocolate bar at Clarke, a diabetic. "Here you go, Clarkie, eat this!"

Clarke would smirk but wouldn't acknowledge the fan. He would use it as motivation and, more times than not, steer the Flyers to another win.

The Broad Street Bullies, as Chevalier said, were always on the loose, always supporting one another, always doing whatever it took to make his nickname—arguably the best in Philadelphia sports history—seem oh, so appropriate.

CHAPTER 3

REXY'S: OH, IF THESE WALLS COULD TALK

BACK WHEN THE PHILADELPHIA FLYERS were winning Stanley Cups, they were scoring goals for cases of Tastykakes.

They were also celebrating their good times at Rexy's, a friendly bar in West Collingswood Heights, New Jersey, that was owned by "Pat" Fietto.

Or Pasquale, as Bobby Clarke affectionately called him.

Clarke and his teammates became very close with Fietto.

So close that the restaurateur would cash their paychecks.

So close that Clarke and his wife, Sandy, would vacation with Pasquale and his wife, Virginia ("Ginnie").

According to teammate Joe Watson, it was Forbes Kennedy—an original Flyer in 1967–68 who spent two seasons with the team—who "knew every watering hole in Jersey" and was the player who "discovered" Rexy's.

Then Clarke began showing up at Rexy's in 1969, his first year with the Flyers. Bernie Parent and others followed. Before too long, it became the Flyers' unofficial hangout. It was like their second home.

They would get there after their morning practice, and some of them would stay until dinner time. Or later.

"They'd come after practice in the morning, and some of them, like Ricky MacLeish and Billy Barber, they'd still be there at 11:00 or 12:00 at night," said Patty Fietto, one of the owner's daughters.

Players would sometimes eat three meals a day there.

"It was better than going home and cooking," left winger Bob Kelly, among the players whose checks were cashed from the Rexy's owner's pocket, said with a laugh.

Practices would start around 9:00 AM, Kelly said. He and most of his teammates would then head to Rexy's and "kind of have breakfast and a couple beers, and then lunch rolls around. Around 2:00, you ate lunch. And then next thing you know, you're still there at nighttime. So, it was our home."

"Outside of the hockey rink," said Bobby Taylor, a Flyers backup goalie during their peak seasons, "Rexy's was our headquarters."

The players would sit at the bar and mingle with the patrons. They liked the interaction, liked being respected for their on-ice exploits.

They also liked drinking a "Bob-a-louie"—Joe Watson's nickname for beer.

"We started going there after practice because most of us lived right in that area," Clarke said. "We practiced early, so we always stopped for lunch together. And in those days, lunch was two or three beers and a sandwich, just like the rest of the people in the bar. They're working people. We were all the same."

"Rexy's was just a gathering place for us," recalled Jimmy Watson, a young defenseman on the Flyers' Stanley Cup championship teams. "It was a nice, comfortable place to have a bite to eat and then BS after practice, and then you'd go back to your house. For some guys, maybe they would have a few beers. I really watched myself. But some guys would have a few beers."

And a few more.

"I don't know how the hell they did it," Watson said. "And the next day, they would do the same thing. But they always kind of gathered themselves and were ready to play when the game came. But it was a dangerous situation because if you weren't careful, you'd start drinking too much."

Most of the Flyers in that era lived in South Jersey, so Rexy's was a convenient stop. And the players who lived in Pennsylvania, which banned Sunday alcohol sales at the time, made their way to Rexy's on that day.

Thus, the women in the bar had more players to choose from.

"I was the only single guy on the team for I think my first two years there," Watson said, smiling. "And the guys all said I got the girls by default."

Dad's Mandate

Before she was old enough to drink, Patty Fietto, the owner's daughter, was at the restaurant a lot. "But my father would not let my sister, Kim, and I out in the bar. I mean it," she said. "We were not allowed past the doorway between the center dining room and the bar. Never."

She later became the general manager of the old-school Italian restaurant/bar, which was in the family for three generations. Her grandparents were South Philadelphians who bought the bar in 1943.

Her grandfather, Guido Fietto, was a bricklayer and a hard-nosed boxer, but he wanted to open a bar. The location of Rexy's, then known as The Homestead, was perfect.

"It was a little corner bar with an apartment upstairs," she said. "And my grandparents and their four kids lived there."

When Guido Fietto boxed, his nickname was Rexy. The establishment took the name. Guido died in 1965, and Fietto's dad,

Pat, and her uncle, Tony, took over the business. Pat was the more active one.

Pat had a big heart. He went out of his way to help those in need. He gave a lot of young people opportunities to work at Rexy's and took pride in nurturing them and teaching them the business.

"When my father died, there were a lot of them at his funeral," Patty said. "They were in their sixties and seventies and they were actually crying."

Pat Fietto had that kind of impact on people. He was caring and honest, and loved to laugh. His humorous stories made Clarke and the Flyers feel comfortable, like they were back home in Canada with one of their favorite uncles.

In a way, he was a surrogate father to the young players.

"He was such a good guy," Clarke said. "Treated everybody so good."

Fietto, who sold Rexy's in 2009 and died in 2019 at age 91, also had business smarts.

"For a kid who grew up shining shoes in South Philadelphia and really had no education because he hated school, he was a great businessman," his daughter said. "But he never forgot where he came from and was humble. He never lived over his means."

A devoted husband, Pat Fietto was stern with his two daughters, but they had him wrapped around their fingers. "We didn't want for anything," Patty said, smiling. "He'd give us a hard time before he would allow it. Whatever it was we wanted, we'd end up with it. Of course, we had our mother pulling for us, too."

Some of the original Flyers from the 1967–68 season—guys like Kennedy, Bill Sutherland, and Jimmy Johnson—were the first players from the organization to frequent Rexy's, Patty Fietto said. Players from the Jersey Devils, the Eastern Hockey League team that played at the Cherry Hill Arena, were also regulars.

Why was Rexy's so popular with the early-day Flyers?

"I think a lot of them lived in Barrington Manor, so it was close," said Patty, who babysat for original Flyers like Gary Dornhoefer and Simon Nolet, players whose families lived in those apartments.

The proximity to their homes—and the fact it was the first bar over the Walt Whitman Bridge into South Jersey—was only part of it. Pat Fietto was a bigger part. He made the Flyers feel comfortable and at home.

"He had a personal relationship with all of them," Patty said. "He was good to those guys when they first came over here. He would take them and introduce them to people when they were nothing, when they were looking for mortgages or whatever it was they needed. I guess it was just my father's personality. I mean, I know some of these kids came out of coal mines up in Flin Flon and from Ottawa and they didn't know" many people from the area. "They weren't college grads. They were kids that worked hard and played hockey since they were probably four or five years old. So, what did they know about business?"

The Flyers' Father Figure

The players believed in Pat Fietto. They knew he was honest, and that when he gave you his word on a situation or a person, it was golden. He introduced them to realtors such as Ed Parvin and whatever professionals they needed. Most of them decided to settle in South Jersey.

"They trusted my father with their lives," Patty said.

The players gravitated toward him. Clarke brought his father, Cliff, to meet Pasquale. The Watson brothers, Joe and Jimmy, introduced their dad, Joe Sr., to him.

Pat Fietto had become a father figure to most of the players. He and Sal the bartender/manager—another person with a South

Philadelphia background—would tell them uproarious stories that kept them entertained and longing for more. Pat would talk about his upbringing, about South Philly neighborhoods, about his dad's boxing days.

He was a Philly guy, through and through, and he was educating a group of mostly twentysomethings about their adopted city and what made its people tick.

The players were amused by some of Pat's habits. One of them was reaching into his pocket and pulling out a wad of money—the one-dollar bills were always on top—that was wrapped in a rubber band.

When Pat passed away, Flyers broadcaster Steve Coates, who was a minor-leaguer in Philadelphia's system and a Rexy's regular, whispered to Kim Fietto (Patty's sister) asking if her father's trademark rubber band had been placed in the coffin.

Kim teared up.

"It's a lot of little things that people just remember about him," Patty said. "I think my dad was just such an honest man, and such a man's man that he was just able to [connect with the players]. My father came from nothing, just like these kids came from nothing."

They worked hard to excel in the workforce. Pasquale, "Pat," brought the Flyers together at Rexy's. The Flyers, simple guys who meshed seamlessly with the blue-collar, no-frills locals, brought the city together with their dominance at the Spectrum.

Pat Fietto, a salt-of-the-earth sort with a hard-to-match work ethic, became a confidant of the players. And, sometimes, he found himself in the middle of uncomfortable situations, like the time one of the older players got into an argument with his wife and left her stranded at a nearby hotel. The woman phoned Pat and asked if he could help her.

He drove to the hotel and helped calm the situation.

Becoming Rock Stars

When the Flyers were winning Stanley Cups in 1974 and 1975, they would head to Rexy's after home games. The place became packed with fans, causing Fietto to hire off-duty cops to be at the door so there wouldn't be any problems.

The players were still unassuming, small-town guys.

But they became rock stars to the fans, especially the young women who followed them to Rexy's and threw themselves at them.

Taylor, the goalie, remembers a woman in her forties or fifties, "asking me to sign her panties—while they were on."

He complied as the woman pulled down her pants.

"If she was a 22-year-old model, it would have been great," he said of the experience in the 1970s. "But that, I didn't like it. I closed my eyes a little bit. I'm not sure if I even spelled my name right.

"I don't know what it is with people and so-called celebrities," he said. "They just lose their sense of values."

Or offer to take off their clothes for a one-night tryst.

"I don't know how I'd word it, but they'd go nuts," Taylor said. "They would just do stuff that I know darn well they wouldn't normally do. People were flashing us all the time. I remember one time, with my first wife, this lady comes up to me, or I should say came up to her, and offered her a $4,000 diamond ring if she would allow me to sleep with her."

Taylor said this happened at a team appearance in Northeast Philadelphia, where the players were signing autographs and had a social gathering afterward.

He didn't know an "offer" had been made for his services until he got home and his wife "accused me of screwing around with this lady. I didn't even know who the heck it was that asked her.

And then when she kept explaining what she looked like, I said, 'Oh, I remember that woman coming up to me and just talking.'

"My wife says, 'Yeah, she offered me a $4,000 diamond ring if I let you sleep with her.' I said, 'You should have (accepted).'"

Brazen Women

At Rexy's, the women patrons were brazen. It didn't matter that the players' wives were frequently with them after a home game. The young women—rink rats, the players and their wives called them—would hand the players their phone numbers and beg for them to call.

They made their advances and were oblivious that the players' wives were seated next to their husbands.

The wives were astonished.

"The women thought they owned them," said Carolyn DeSimone, who was married to Rick MacLeish at the time.

Taylor said it was difficult for the married players to avoid temptations.

"Now I know why Adam took the bite from the damn apple," he said. "But I think the guys did a pretty good job of it."

Some did, some didn't. Many players from the 1974 and 1975 championship teams ended up getting divorced.

"It's not always a happy marriage because you're traveling so much," Joe Watson said shortly before the 50th anniversary of the Flyers' 1974 championship. "If you look back on our team now, only four or five guys are still married to the same person."

Rexy's Invaded After Cup Win

When the Flyers won their first Cup on May 19, 1974, it seemed like half of South Jersey drove to Rexy's, hoping the players would arrive and they could celebrate with them.

"The cops had to block off the Black Horse Pike because it was so crowded," Patty said.

Pat Fietto tried bringing the Flyers from the Spectrum, site of their Cup-clinching 1–0 win over Boston, to Rexy's. He phoned his brother, who was at the bar.

"He said there were 8,000 people outside the place," Fietto told the *Philadelphia Inquirer* in 2010. Police on the scene, however, said the number was more like 6,000. "People were standing on the roof singing 'God Bless America.' I told him to close the place. A friend of mine owned a place nearby"—Compton's—"and we went there instead."

At Rexy's, people had packed the bar, the parking lot, and the adjacent streets. (A handful of Flyers had reportedly gotten into the bar, but others were called and told not to come because of all the commotion.)

Several hours after the Flyers' epic Cup-clinching victory, police arrested 22 people—most for disorderly conduct after a 20-minute brawl broke out—and used billy clubs and dogs to disperse a boisterous crowd that had gathered. In front of the bar, traffic was blocked on the Black Horse Pike for more than six hours.

"Eventually, they had to bring in the [police] canines," Patty said. "And like a SWAT team from Camden. They all lined up on the pike because no one would leave. I believe my dad sent them to another place, because they would have gotten mobbed going into Rexy's. They wouldn't have been able to get in. It was packed between the people that were in there and the people who were outside.

"It was bedlam."

At 11:30 PM, 6½ hours after the game ended, a policeman with a bullhorn announced: "The Flyers won't be here tonight. Please clear the road."

Witnesses complained about police brutality. Police officers said they had beer bottles heaved at them.

Tony Fietto surveyed the damage at Rexy's and the debris surrounding his building and was distraught.

"This is some way to show appreciation" to the Flyers, he said.

The scene at Rexy's was boisterous earlier in the series, but there wasn't any violence displayed like after the Cup-clinching victory.

When Bobby Clarke scored to give the Flyers a 3–2 overtime win in Boston in Game 2 of the '74 Finals, Rexy's patrons erupted. The victory tied the series at one win apiece and made the Flyers realize they could beat the favored Bruins. It made the fans believers, too.

It was the Flyers' second win ever in Boston, ending a 19-game winless streak (0–17–2) in Beantown since their first game in the city in 1967, a 4–2 Philadelphia victory.

Fans hugged and kissed and pounded their mugs on Rexy's bar. "Let's Go Flyers!" chants echoed around the jam-packed establishment. About an hour into the celebration, someone had an idea.

"Airport!" someone shouted.

More than half of Rexy's emptied. The patrons hopped in their cars and took the 20-minute ride to Philadelphia International Airport to greet the team upon their return from Boston.

Philadelphia was officially a hockey town.

The next year, the Flyers were again on their way to a Stanley Cup championship when an electrical fire blazed through Rexy's while fans were watching the team's second-round playoff game against the New York Islanders. The Isles would win the matchup 2–1 to force a Game 7.

"The place was packed, and everybody had to get out of there right away, but they didn't want to get out. They didn't want to leave the bar, honest to God," Patty said.

The next day at practice, the Flyers players wore black armbands on their jersey sleeves as a tribute to their beloved bar.

They then whipped the Islanders 4–1 to win the series, four games to three, and advance into the Stanley Cup Finals. Following the clutch victory, Flyers winger Bob Kelly lifted a beer and made a toast.

"To Rexy's," he said as the players clinked beer cans.

Let the Good Times Roll

Rexy's was where the Flyers let down their hair. The players and their wives would party in a private back room. Rick MacLeish was once seen wearing a black Sinatra-style hat as he sang into a beer bottle while atop a table.

There was a time Barry Ashbee sat at the bar next to teammate Bill Flett, who was nearly set aflame. Some say it happened at a Vancouver bar. Some say it was at Rexy's.

Ashbee took out a lighter and nonchalantly lit Flett's bushy beard on fire. Flett quickly put it out by dipping his beard into his mug of beer. He finished his burnt beer in one gigantic gulp.

The people at the bar laughed until their bellies ached.

"A round for everybody!" Ashbee instructed the bartender.

Life around the Broad Street Bullies was never dull—on or off the ice.

One night Pat Fietto was sipping a drink at the bar, and as he got down to the bottom, he thought he came across some odd-looking ice cubes.

They were Bobby Clarke's fake teeth.

"Clarkie did that to a lot of people," Patty Fietto said.

Clarke, a quiet sort, loved Rexy's so much that he and his wife, Sandy, would take two of their young children, Wade and Jody, into the establishment for a little while after a weekend game.

Inside Rexy's, the kids would feast on a bowl of maraschino cherries. The parents would then put the kids back in the car in Rexy's parking lot, tell them to behave, and return to the bar.

"We were obsessed with the cherries. Straight sugar," Jody recalled. "So now we're bouncing off the walls, sitting in the back of the car, beating the crap out of each other while my parents are enjoying Rexy's."

Jody said she and her brother "weren't in any danger," but it's funny to look back on it five decades later.

Almost all the Flyers—or those connected to the team—have numerous stories about Rexy's.

Center Bill Clement vividly remembers the first time he visited Rexy's.

The Flyers had been planning to recall Clement, then 20, from the minors as an insurance policy for the playoffs. But he had suffered ankle and cheek injuries playing for the Quebec Aces in the AHL, and general manager Keith Allen wanted him to see the Flyers' medical staff in Philadelphia.

That gave him a chance to try Rexy's.

"I was shy and I was talking to these people and I had a half-buzz on," Clement said, "and all of a sudden, everything kind of stops and everybody looks at the door."

Entering was "this white guy with a big Afro; he stood about 6'4", and he's with this gorgeous girl with long black hair. And I'm like, 'Who's that?'"

"That's the crazy linebacker who plays for the Eagles," said the man next to him.

It was Tim Rossovich, who professed to eating fire and glass.

"Holy shit," Clement said. "He looks scary."

Clement talked to his new bar buddies for about another hour.

As he stood against the wall, Clement noticed Rossovich's companion, Tara, was suddenly standing next to the future Flyer, while the big linebacker was across the other side of the bar. Clement made small talk with her. Within 10 minutes, "we're exchanging saliva like crazy." Clement said. They finally unlocked their lips, and Clement could feel a glare from across Rexy's bar.

"Oh, fuck. My life is going to end early," he thought to himself.

He looked at Tara.

"I think we have a problem here," he said. "Your boyfriend is staring at us."

"Don't worry," Tara said. "I'll take care of him."

She walked to the other side of the bar. They talked for three or four minutes. The man who ate glass for kicks walked out the door.

Bill Clement would live and become a key player for the Flyers, scoring the goal that iced the team's Cup-clinching win against Buffalo in 1975, and then eventually becoming an elite hockey analyst for ESPN and the Flyers.

He took Tara back to a hotel that night.

"That," he said, "was my introduction to the major leagues."

Not all of Clement's drinking had a happy ending.

In the early '70s, before they had gotten to be a powerhouse team, Clement remembers drinking with Flyers teammate Willie Brossart before a late-afternoon road practice.

"I chugged down a couple of gin and tonics," Clement said. "I went to practice, and I was fucked up, but I made it through."

Clarke noticed Clement wasn't himself.

"Don't ever fucking do that again," Clarke scolded. "You fucking asshole. What the fuck were you thinking?"

"Clarkie, I don't know," Clement replied. "I didn't plan on it turning out like this."

At the time, Clement said, there were no standards. It was a freewheeling time in society. And for the players between games.

"But Clarkie knew the standard," Clement said.

Not only did he know it, but he would set it for years to come. The Flyers would follow his hard-working lead. Five decades after they sat atop the hockey world, the Broad Street Bullies are still the most popular champions of any of Philadelphia's title winners, including the 1980 and 2008 Phillies, the 1967 and 1983 76ers, and the 2018 Eagles. Only the 2025 Eagles are comparable, but they didn't draw as many fans in their victory parade as the Flyers did in 1974 or 1975.

"The reason for that," said Lou Scheinfeld, the Flyers' former vice president, "is that almost all the players from the Broad Stret Bullies remained in the area and stayed visible. They stayed connected to the fans."

After they retired from hockey, many of those Flyers started businesses in the Philadelphia/South Jersey area, and the players from those championship teams were always doing charity work in the community.

"They all stayed around here," Scheinfeld said. "I don't think they wanted to move too far away from Rexy's."

Wives' Perspectives

The wives had a love-hate relationship with Rexy's. They loved that their husbands could relax and be themselves there. They hated that they sometimes parked themselves on a Rexy's barstool for a good part of the day.

"The girls spent a lot of time alone," Patty said. "It was a good thing they had the other girls to keep each other company."

Some of the wives felt they came in second place to Rexy's. When the team was on a homestand, the players would be at the bar almost every day.

"After a while, I became not-too-fond of the place," said Cathy Schultz, who at that time was the wife of Dave. The wives "would complain all the time to each other."

Patty Fietto understood the wives' gripes about her family's establishment.

Said Patty: "If my husband was at practice and I knew he was done at 11:00 AM, and now I'm looking at 5:00 and then 9:00 and he's not home yet..."

MacLeish's wife, Carolyn, said the Flyers always went to Rexy's, and that the place got a little stale for their companions. She said the players and wives met some "very nice people" there and that the owners were lovely people.

"But it was where we'd always go after games, and after a while, it was like, 'Guys, can't we go someplace else?'" she said. "It got a little old."

During game days, the players took afternoon naps. Their wives fed them dinner, and off they went to the Spectrum. After the game, it took them time to get dressed and talk to the media. They and most of the wives would then head over to Rexy's.

Rinse. Repeat. Drink.

"The guys loved it there," Carolyn said.

While the wives weren't especially fond of Rexy's—especially with women eyeing and approaching their husbands unabashed—it turned out they did acknowledge it was a good spot for people to congregate. Years later, they even had reunions at the bar-restaurant, organized by Jenny Barber, the wife of the Flyers star left winger.

Jenny, 48, died in 2001 after a battle with lung cancer, but she was one of the driving forces behind the group of Flyers wives.

"She kept us all together," Carolyn said. "She was an amazing lady."

A Place to Bond

More than anything, Rexy's was a place for the players to bond with each other and the fans.

"People would come in, sit down and buy you a beer," said Bob Kelly, the kinetic left winger who 50 years earlier scored the winning goal as the Flyers captured their second Stanley Cup. "Our guys were just as friendly as anybody. I mean, we're no different than anyone else. Sure, we put on a pair of skates to go to work. The guy next to you maybe puts on a suit to go to work. There's no difference. We're both doing our job, and at the end of the day, you're still who you are, right?

"We didn't have any jackasses on our team. If you were, you didn't last long. They kind of got the boot in a hurry."

In other words, the Flyers were just down-to-earth people who happened to attract more than two million people to consecutive parades.

"It was brotherly love, wherever we went," Kelly said. "It was awesome."

Rexy's sponsored a benefit golf tournament each year. The Stanley Cup they had won was there, and Flyers defensemen Joe Watson and Ed Van Impe decided to have some fun. They distracted the security guard who was watching the famous trophy and hid the Cup.

"The poor guy was running all over the place trying to find it," Watson said. "They were about to call the cops, and we decided to bring the Stanley Cup back."

Some of the players who lived in Pennsylvania had after-game hangouts on the other side of the Delaware River.

Those players would be in a downtown Philadelphia bar, celebrating after a victory.

"This is the kind of stuff that used to go on," right winger Don Saleski recalled. "We're downtown, partying after a game. One night, it had to be 1:00 AM because we were leaving to go to an after-hours place. We'd leave the bar and the cops—they would wait for us everywhere we went—and they'd say, 'Uh, you don't want to drive over there. Get in.'"

So, the players jumped into the police car and were escorted to their next bar. They later would drive the players—supposedly sober by then—back to their cars.

"You can't make this shit up," said Saleski, who had a successful business career after retiring from hockey following the 1979–80 season.

You also can't make up what happened to Rick MacLeish in a Los Angeles bar in 1978.

The Flyers had played the Kings earlier on that April 1 night, and as MacLeish dove to break up a pass, his throat was accidentally slashed by the skate of Los Angeles star Marcel Dionne. One of the Flyers' doctors on the trip, oral surgeon Everett Borghesani, rushed onto the ice. Several towels were needed to sop up the blood as MacLeish was taken to the locker room.

Reportedly, 88 stitches were needed to close the two gashes, though one estimate said 180 were used.

"He started stitching me in the first period and didn't finish until the end of the game," MacLeish told Zack Hill, then the Flyers' public relations director, in 2005.

Now for the funny part and the bar in Los Angeles…

After the game, some of the players went out to drink beers and smoke some cigarettes. "Joe Watson said there was some smoke and beer coming out of my neck," MacLeish told Hill. "I'm not sure what it was, but it was definitely something. Around 4:00 that morning, I woke up and I was bleeding all over the place because the stitches had broken. We called the team trainer, and he took me to get new stitches."

MacLeish recovered and starred in the playoffs that spring. But not before one of his teammates had some fun with the locker-room blackboard, writing: "What's the difference between Rick MacLeish and Frankenstein's monster? Two stitches!"

Road Bars

On the road, Los Angeles (where one Flyer had a fling with a famous actress), Atlanta, Vancouver, and Chicago were among the team's favorite stops.

"You'd go into some towns and there'd be chicks all over guys," Saleski said. "Some guys were more excited about the opportunity than others."

Atlanta was the best city, bar none, because it was the headquarters for Eastern Airlines and Delta Airlines, another player said. "With all the clerical workers, secretaries, and stewardesses, the ratio of women to men was probably five to one," he said.

The player added that as soon as their road game ended, "we couldn't wait to get out. And then we would close the bars. Depending on what happened first—you either picked somebody up and went back to the hotel, or the bar closed—one of those two events would signal the end of your evening."

There were no rules, no moral boundaries on the road, said the player, who wasn't proud of it.

"We all thought we were bulletproof with a big 'S' on our chest," he said.

This was an era when platform shoes and checkered suits were in style.

"We were the semi-cleaned-up version of the *Slap Shot* guys," said one of the Flyers' regulars from their Cup-winning years.

In Chicago, the Flyers stayed at the Drake Hotel, which was across the street from the Playboy Club.

A woman named Rhonda was the housemother at the Playboy Club, but she still looked like a centerfold, according to one ex-Flyer.

Several Flyers went to the club, which liked them there because they attracted more people. One night, Rhonda and two centerfolds went out for drinks with three Flyers players.

Supposedly, nothing much happened that night, but word got around that the Flyers had a sweet contact in Chicago.

In the coming months, whenever the Flyers were en route to the Windy City and the pilot would announce "we're in our final descent to landing," the commercial flight would get noisy with a Beach Boys song.

"Help me, Rhonda. Help, help me, Rhonda," blurted the 40 or so members of the Flyers' traveling party. "Help me, Rhonda. Help, help me, Rhonda.... She was gonna be my wife, and I was gonna be her man."

The rest of the people on the plane would look at the Flyers like they had gone insane.

Vancouver was also a popular bar scene for the Flyers, especially at the Ritz Hotel. The players frequently drank there for free, thanks to teammate Reggie Leach.

"There'd be six or seven of us there, and Reggie would arm-wrestle those loggers and miners who would come in from work," Joe Watson, a colorful Flyers defenseman of that era, recalled 50 years later. "He'd arm-wrestle for a whole table of beer, and each table would have 20 or 30 beers on it. We'd be there for maybe five, six hours, and by the time we'd leave, we had five full tables of beer. That's how good he was at arm-wrestling, so it was nice to go to a bar with Reggie because he'd put those guys down."

The beers went down, too.

Beer the Beverage of Choice

The players were simple folks with simple tastes. Beer was their drink of choice.

After the Flyers won their second Cup, the team's physical therapist, Matt DiPaolo, decided to put a workout room in the Spectrum for the players. Bikes, weights, and weight benches were among the numerous exercise items.

"We had all this equipment, and it never got used," Saleski said.

Shero had the equipment removed. Vending machines were installed with milk and healthy food choices. Shero had a better idea. He had a pool table put in the room, and he added beer to the vending machines.

Suddenly, the room started to fill up.

"I want you guys to be around here and hang out," Shero told the players.

Whatever you say, Coach.

CHAPTER 4

FLYERS WIVES CLUB

THE PHILADELPHIA FLYERS' WIVES were the unsung heroes of the team's success. Besides taking care of the kids, and doing most of the duties around the house, they made sure their husbands could concentrate on one thing: hockey.

Like the players, the wives had an unbreakable bond with each other, one that still exists 50 years later.

"We're like sisters," Carolyn MacLeish DeSimone said. She was married to star center Rick MacLeish during the Flyers' golden years. They later divorced, and Rick MacLeish died in 2016.

The Flyers' leaders, designated by a "C" or an "A" on their jerseys, were captain Bobby Clarke and alternates Gary Dornhoefer, Joe Watson, and Terry Crisp.

The wives' unofficial leaders were Myrna (wife of owner Ed) Snider, Jenny (wife of Bill) Barber, Carolyn (wife of Rick) MacLeish, and Cathy (wife of Dave) Schultz, among others.

The women arranged get-togethers for the wives, sat next to each other at home games, gathered at each other's houses to watch road games, and went on vacations together while their husbands were traveling with the team.

They were confidantes of each other, and they assisted one another during pregnancies.

In short, they were always there for one another, which was important because most came from small Canadian towns, and it was easy to be overwhelmed by big-city life and not having family around.

So, they leaned on each other. Happily.

"We clung together," Carolyn MacLeish DeSimone said of the wives. "If it wasn't for those girls, I don't know what I would have done."

Most of the wives felt the same way.

"When the guys were on the road, we'd get together and do things," said Isabel Leach Stevens, who was married to star right winger Reggie Leach when the Flyers won the Cup in 1975. "We were just each other's family. You have to understand, these were all young women, most of them Canadian. And we were at a place with no family near us. But we had each other."

Myrna Snider was the person who helped the wives and their families bond. Her husband, Ed, built the organization. Myrna built relationships.

It was Myrna who was concerned about the culture of the players and their families, about the Flyers being active in the community, about the Spectrum workers being happy at their jobs.

"I don't care if they were running a hot dog stand or sweeping the stands. Mom knew them. They knew her. We looked at everybody in that building as a member of our family," daughter Lindy Snider said.

Myrna was a social butterfly. She was outgoing and friendly. She was a good listener and wanted to know about other people's lives and interests.

"In her later years, she traveled the world, and we used to say that everywhere she went, she was practically the mayor," Lindy said.

In a way, she was mayor of the Spectrum.

"She made everyone feel important," Lindy said. "It didn't matter what position they held. And if somebody had a sick kid, or someone's daughter was getting married, she acknowledged them or did something for them. She brought to this organization the culture of family."

At Christmas, for instance, the players and their families had a skating party at the Spectrum. Santa was there for the kids.

Myrna was there with presents for everyone—players, wives, their children.

"She was the best. She loved to have fun. She loved to keep everyone together, and she loved us girls," Carolyn MacLeish DeSimone said, referring to the players' wives.

Myrna had a room designated for the wives at the Spectrum. It was a place to grab something to eat and relax, a place to mingle and share common experiences.

It was even a place to look at naked men. Sort of.

"I don't know if it was Valentine's Day or what holiday," Carolyn said, "She had a little party for us down there. Oh my God, she was crazy. She had things like *Playgirl* magazines and fake penises around.... Using the magazines, getting our husbands' and Mr. Snider's faces and taping them on [the bodies]. We put them all around the room."

The wives were having a great time, and then a man came into the room with a food delivery. "And we're like, 'Oh my God!' We weren't expecting him," Carolyn said. "Myrna came in and she was dying laughing."

Myrna was so well-loved that even after she and Ed divorced, many of the Flyers wives rented a limo and made a surprise visit to her apartment.

"We just thought the world of her," Carolyn said. "She treated us like her daughters."

She made the Flyers feel like a true family, Cathy Schultz said. She added that when Dave later played in Los Angeles, Pittsburgh, and Buffalo, none of those teams had the same close-knit atmosphere Myrna had created in Philadelphia.

Jay Snider, one of Myrna's sons, said when he became the Flyers' president and went to league meetings, he would get asked about his mom.

"I hate to say it, but the first person they asked about [wasn't his dad]; it was my mom," Jay said. With the other owners, "it wasn't, 'How's your dad?' It was, 'How's Myrna doing? I haven't seen her in a long time. I love her.' Everybody asked about her."

A Lasting Bond

Carolyn MacLeish and Cathy Schultz were extremely close and, 50 years later, they still are.

The players were on the road a lot, so when Carolyn and Cathy were in the latter stages of their pregnancies, they slept at each other's houses in case one went into labor. "Rick wasn't home for either of my births," Carolyn said. "It wasn't like today where they [the husbands] come home for the birth. You were just by yourself. You're on your own. Cathy was spending nights with me in case I had to go, which I did with Danielle. So Cathy was Danielle's 'dad'" at the hospital.

Before Carolyn went into labor, she and Cathy were with the other Flyers wives and watching an away game. Carolyn thinks they were at Diane (wife of Ed) Van Impe's house in the Philadelphia suburbs. Carolyn and Cathy didn't return to the MacLeishes' Cherry Hill, New Jersey, home until after midnight.

A few hours later, Carolyn went into labor.

"Thank God that Cathy was there," she said. "She drove me to the hospital."

The players were an incredibly tight-knit group, on and off the ice, and the fact their wives got along just as well with each other made for one big Flyers family.

Even the players' children became close. They would hang out together, and on game days and nights, they would play and get in trouble—they liked to go into the Flyers' locker room and erase Fred Shero's blackboard messages and leave their own creative words—on the bottom floor of the Spectrum. "GIRLS RULE!" was not written by Shero.

Players' Afternoon Ritual

If the Flyers were playing at night, afternoon naps were part of the players' ritual.

Jody Clarke, one of Bobby's daughters, remembers her mom scolding her and her siblings if they were making too much noise.

"Keep it down! Keep it down!! Your dad is sleeping," she recalls her mom, Sandy, telling her children.

Most of the Flyers' children from that time have similar stories.

Jody said she was lucky because they had a big house, and their parents' bedroom was on one side, and the playroom was on the other side. "I imagine that was intentional when they built that house," she said.

Sandy was always looking out for her husband, who has battled diabetes since he was a youngster.

Around the house, "she did everything," Jody said. "She took care of him behind the scenes and asked for nothing—absolutely nothing—in return for it. He never looked after the kids; he never changed a diaper. He wasn't even there when I was born. He was at an optional practice."

Jody wasn't complaining. Her dad, she said, was loving in his own way, and his focus was on hockey.

Her mom's focus was on the kids and her husband.

"She's Saint Sandy," Jody said. "She is literally the rock. And I would say for a majority of the players, that was probably the case with their wives."

Most of the Flyers and their wives got married at young ages.

"I mean, we were kids," said Cathy Schultz, who was married to Flyers enforcer Dave Schultz at the time of the team's heyday. "So, the wives really bonded. We would get together at each other's houses and watch the away games. We did things together. I have lifelong friendships with them."

She became especially close with Carolyn MacLeish.

"When we came here, when the players went to training camp, they put all the married guys at the International Motel. Everyone else was in the city," Cathy Schultz said. "So that's how I met Carolyn. And Kelly's and Clement's wives and others. Anyway, I had not brought my hair dryer, so Dave said, 'Well, try MacLeish's wife.' I knocked on their door and we just kind of Vulcan-eye locked. And I said, 'Help!'"

Those early days, while their husbands were trying to prove themselves and earn Flyers roster spots, weren't just tough on the players. They were also a strain for the wives.

"You're stuck in this motel that was not very pleasant," Cathy Schultz said. "No car because the car would be at practice and might not show up until eight [beer] rounds later. So, that was my introduction, and I was like, 'Holy Smokes, folks!'"

They later rented apartments for a while. Nothing luxurious. The furniture was rented, and they stayed at places with month-to-month leases in case they were sent down to the minors.

The players eventually became heroes. Women swarmed around them. Never mind if a player was sitting with his wife at a bar or restaurant. That didn't matter to the women who threw their phone numbers at the players, sometimes running into the wives as they did so.

People even went to the players' houses, including the Schultzes' in Cherry Hill.

"There was a lot of stuff that happened," Cathy Schultz said. "I opened the door one night and there were three drunk people there who wanted to party. Two of them were girls."

The Flyers were playing on the road that night. "So, your first thought is, *Wow, people know I'm here alone*," Cathy Schultz said. "And I had an infant in the house. I heard later they actually went to Clarke's house, too. They wanted to party with me. It was creepy. I slammed the door and called Dominic, my neighbor, and he came over with a bat. I mean, he didn't hurt anybody, but he scared them off.

"So, there was always that. There were always people sitting outside our house or in cars, or girls—groupies—hanging out around our house."

She said it was "very unnerving. And in broad daylight, too."

The players and their wives "couldn't really go anywhere because we would get mobbed," Cathy said. "One time we were on the Atlantic City Boardwalk—the Taylors, Kindrachuks, and us—and we got mobbed."

Some of the people had attitudes that Cathy Schultz couldn't understand.

"The guys started signing autographs, and this older woman came up to me and said, 'Get him to sign this for me,'" she said. "And I said, 'I'm sorry. He's signing as people come up to him.' And I just kind of turned away, and she called me a name and kicked me in the butt."

These types of experiences made the wives' bond even stronger. They shared stories about the groupies—the players, and later the wives, called them "rink rats"—and commiserated with each other.

Their husbands, they concluded, seemed connected to each other's hips. Even after returning from a long road trip, "they had to be together and have a guys' day or night," Carolyn MacLeish said. "I'd be like, 'Really?' Sometimes us girls would drop them off…to a golf course or wherever they were going, and we'd go to Rexy's."

Shero's Letters to Wives

At Rexy's, or wherever they gathered, the wives liked talking about coach Fred Shero's "code of conduct" that he created for them.

"It was like something out of *Good Housekeeping*, 1949," one of the wives said.

At the top of one letter, which was typed on Philadelphia Flyers letterhead, it read:

TO: ALL HOCKEY PLAYER WIVES

RE: ICE RULES FOR HOCKEY WIVES

Shero started the letter by asking: "How can you as Mrs. Hockey Player become a member of the hockey club without ever scoring a goal?"

He then listed eight ways:

1. Talk about other players only as you want [it] heard about your own husband.
2. Don't let the ups and downs of your husband's career or the way he is [playing] on the ice, at any given time, affect your behavior.
3. No error is funny, because your man has eighty games a year in which to duplicate it and maybe a worse one.
4. Fans may upset you, but as long as he is on the ice, he belongs to the team and the game, NOT TO YOU.
5. Trades are made by the front office. Though good friends are leaving, the merits of a trade belong in the front office. No trade is ever approved by *GOOD HOUSEKEEPING*.

6. Since your husband is in the NHL, he is a star. The life of the wives of the stars is a happy one. The paydays have been healthy and regular for a long time. Your husband plays every game, and every night seems like Academy Award Night. The biggest question may be deciding what products to endorse. The wives of the stars must become the natural leaders of the hockey wives society. You must be careful not to form a tight clique, or the hockey club could find itself in a struggle between the high-rent district and the middle class instead of one for the title.
7. Tell your husband, "You don't play hockey, you WORK at hockey." The true hockey wife knows that hockey is not a game when your paycheck depends on his ability to perform.
8. Your husband is something special to us and to you. Help us care for him.

SINCERELY,
FRED SHERO,
HEAD COACH

In another letter Shero sent to the wives on Philadelphia Flyers stationery, the coach implored them to dote on their husbands.

Here's what he wrote:

"A MESSAGE TO THE WIVES

How to keep a husband?

Be to your husband all these:

A Chinese cook in the kitchen,

A Japanese wife in the bath,

A French mistress in the bedroom,

An English hostess in the living room.

Do that and your husband will be true to you all your life! Maybe he'll look at another woman now and then, but only with his left eye. He'll keep the right one on you all the time.

Compliments of, Fred Shero."

One of the wives mentioned Shero's statement that the players "'belong to the fans. Once they go on the ice, they don't belong to you.' The girls really had to stick together, so we were just there for everything. Going through our children together. Going through difficult times together."

Today, the wives laugh at Shero's letters to them. They understand it was a different time and that he meant no harm. But they laugh at the sexist time period and are glad times have changed.

One of the wives said the tone of one letter was a "dress like a lady, be a whore in the bedroom kind of thing."

The message to the wives was for them to show up to all home games, look good, take care of the children, and don't talk about stuff surrounding the team. Bobby Clarke, like a lot of the players of that era, said he grew up at a time when the "traditional family" had a dad who worked and a mom who cooked, and took care of the kids and the house.

"It was what I knew," he said 50 years after the Flyers won their first Cup. "I didn't really pay attention to it until after I stopped playing and [realized] how important your wife is to your ability to play hockey. She looked after the kids and raised the kids and fed you. She'd come to the games, get the babysitters, and do all the things that you never had to worry about. I just had to play hockey."

Added Clarke: "I was just like a teenager, you know. Go to the rink, practice, come home, get something to eat, get ready to play hockey. She did everything else. So those wives in those days were the stability of the hockey players' lives."

The wives also arranged for trips together, including one to Florida for some sun, and one to Colorado for some skiing.

"We were like, *If the guys are going on a trip, why can't we go on a trip?*" Carolyn MacLeish DeSimone said.

Carolyn, Jenny Barber, and Cathy Schultz got in the car and drove to Daytona Beach, renting an efficiency near where Jenny's aunt and uncle lived.

"We weren't even old enough to drink," Carolyn said. "Our last morning there, they had this freak freeze. It was like 30 degrees so we said we might as well go home. We start driving home and we got caught in the [worst] 50-year storm and got stuck in the snow in Savannah, Georgia."

The road crews weren't prepared for it.

"They didn't know how to get rid of the snow," she said. "They were out there sweeping it. There was snow all over the palm trees. We got the last room in a hotel, and we got stuck there for two or three nights."

The women had a bad traveling experience, but at least it gave them plenty of good stories to tell.

"All the girls had just a great chemistry together," Carolyn said of the players' wives. "I think that's another reason why the guys did so well. They were close, but the girls were close, too, and it was really a good mesh."

As the saying goes: happy wife, happy life.

For the Flyers, that was especially the case during the 1973–74 and 1974–75 seasons, but as the years progressed, many of the couples drifted apart and got divorces. The players' drinking habits and infidelities were major factors, say those close to the teams.

The players remain close, however. So do the wives and former wives.

Different Era

The players in the 1970s didn't make the kind of money that most earn in the 2020s. Today's players are making inflated salaries that are mostly in the millions.

"They weren't making life-changing money back then," said Jody Clarke, Bobby's daughter. "We were probably the wealthiest of the group. But [most] were raising kids on what was essentially just a normal income. The husbands weren't home. The trips were long because they were commercial flights back then. Practice came first. When they weren't doing that, half the time they were out partying. They were rock stars."

Clarke made $19,000 in his first year, including a $5,000 signing bonus. Gradually, his salary climbed to that of a superstar, but he and his wife weren't materialistic, weren't interested in fancy things.

"My parents said all the stuff they have and have been blessed with, they don't care about that stuff," Jody said. "My mom still doesn't care. I have to convince her to buy jeans from somewhere other than Target. I'm like, 'Come on, Mom. You can afford normal pants now.' My dad grew up okay [financially]. When my mom was growing up, her dad died when she was 13 and my grandma was pregnant with their seventh kid, so they were poverty, poverty, poverty."

Many of the Flyers wives came from backgrounds that stressed family, not money. Perhaps that helped them keep their husbands grounded when their salaries started to increase.

The players and their wives were mostly in their early twenties, or younger, when the Flyers were winning their Stanley Cups. Some were in their teens when they became part of the NHL club.

"They were kids themselves," said Mark Stevens, a onetime singer with the Philadelphia doo-wop duo The Dovells. Stevens became close with the Flyers players and their families and later married Reggie Leach's ex-wife, Isabel. He and Isabel now live next door to Reggie and his wife, by Lake Winnipeg in Manitoba. "These were very young people. They were not worldly traveled. They all came from small towns. And the wives were women who, for all intents and purposes, never left Canada" before coming to Philadelphia. "That's not what they did. They weren't like American women, where six of them will go to Cabo together and raise the roof. Not these women. These women had a lot of fun, but they were a different breed."

They were close-knit, friendly people who were comfortable being in the background and made it easy for their husbands to flourish.

CHAPTER 5

BOBBY CLARKE: THE ULTIMATE CAPTAIN AND HOOKY HOCKEY

JODY CLARKE, WHOSE FATHER, BOBBY, became the most iconic player in Philadelphia Flyers history, sat in the team's practice facility in Voorhees, New Jersey, as the calendar approached 2024, and the discussion turned to something she learned about her dad when he was a youngster.

There were many times he would cut school, walk down a hill, and head to a little outdoor rink near his house in the closely knit mining town of Flin Flon, Manitoba. There, he would join other kids in a game of hooky hockey.

If his parents found out, "he wasn't worried about my grandpa catching him," Jody said, more than 60 years after her dad's early love affair with the sport. "He was just worried about my grandma. She would try to hit him with a [hockey] stick."

That's a snapshot of Clarke as a kid. Hockey over school. Always hockey over school. It didn't matter that he was a diabetic. As he got older and starred for the Flin Flon Bombers of the Western Canada Amateur Hockey League, he started to think he might have a future in the NHL, not in the zinc and copper mines, where his father, Cliff, worked. (His mom, Yvonne, was the disciplinarian in the house. She was also a terrific long-distance runner who had Olympic aspirations until she became pregnant with Bobby.)

About 50 years after he led the Flyers to their first Stanley Cup, Clarke, unlike the scouts, said he was oblivious to the thought that diabetes would prevent him from playing professional hockey.

"That never crossed my mind," he said in the unassuming way that had become his long-ago trademark. "I was stubborn and dumb, I suppose. I just played hockey, and no one ever tried to stop me from playing."

Perfect Match

Philadelphia and Bobby Clarke were made for each other.

The city's residents and the Flyers captain were gritty and devilish (Clarke would deliberately pee on unsuspecting teammates in the shower), and had a passion for things they liked.

Never was that more evident than in the Flyers' heyday, when Clarke and his spirited teammates lifted a downtrodden city that was ridiculed around the nation for its sports teams.

That is, until the Flyers changed the narrative.

Clarke inspired the change.

He looked like a choirboy but played the game with an unparalleled mean streak.

Opponents called him a dirty player because of the sneaky way he wielded his hockey stick at them to take the puck away or shield them from getting to it.

"He was the meanest player I ever saw—and I mean that as a compliment," said Lou Nolan, the Flyers' iconic public address announcer. "He would almost kill you to win. Losing wasn't an option."

During the Flyers' run to their second Stanley Cup championship in 1975, Clarke speared his friend and former Team Canada roommate, Toronto's Rod Seiling, during an NHL game that was nationally televised in Canada.

"I like Bobby as a man," Seiling told *Sports Illustrated* at the time, "but he carries the aggressiveness a bit far on the ice. I don't think he has to use the stick on people's bodies as much as he does to be effective."

The incident was replayed ad nauseam. Clarke said, "things like that happen in the heat of the moment," that he didn't mean to cut Seiling near his eye, and that he phoned him the next morning and apologized.

The NHL, meanwhile, was besieged with angry, anti-Clarke mail.

Scotty Bowman, who directed teams to nine Stanley Cups and became the winningest coach in NHL history, understood their ire. He once called Clarke the "dirtiest player in hockey."

Clarke's teammates, mindful that No. 16 was their meal ticket, shook their collective heads. Clarkie was being Clarkie. Going full-bore to make a play.

The Flyers called him the game's most intense player, someone who played (mostly) within the rules and had a hockey IQ that was beyond genius.

"He could get you going with a great pass or a goal, or he could send a message to his team by going out of his way to agitate an opponent with a well-placed stick or glove," Nolan said. "Talk about tough guys. Clarkie would be bleeding all over the place and he didn't even care. It was just part of his shift, part of who he was."

"I don't think I'd call Clarke dirty," former Toronto coach Leonard "Red" Kelly once said. "Mean is a better word."

Hail, Flin Flon

Clarke had a fortitude that was unmatched, and some of it came from his small-town upbringing in Flin Flon. Now in his seventies,

Clarke, who was usually called "Clarkie" by his teammates but was also known as "Whitey," smiled fondly when talking about his roots.

"It was always us against the rest of the world," he said.

The little guys against the guys from the big city.

"It was us against them, and we were going to beat them," he said. "So, you learn that the way you're going to do it is by working your ass off."

Almost every kid who came through tiny Flin Flon "learned to work because it's your town against everybody else," Clarke said. "Everybody's against us. It was a great philosophy to have and a great teaching tool for the coaches. It was like, *We're small towners; we're tougher than that. We'll show those rich kids from the city*. It was, *Look at all those kids with their fancy jackets and their fancy bags to carry and stuff. Us poor kids from Flin Flon. We'll show them*."

Though it seems impossible to fathom, "Clarkie worked harder off the ice than he did on it," said Steve Coates, the onetime Flyers broadcaster and a longtime close friend of Clarke's. Coates was a Flyers minor-leaguer during the mid-'70s.

"He was ahead of his time," Coates said. "He worked out all the time. If he wasn't working out in the gym, he was running. And there were a couple of times I ran with him on the beach, and I fell into a hole—and I could have died out there and he never would have known because he just kept going. He didn't give a shit. He was just going to work out, and that's why he had such an outstanding ability to work 100 percent of the time."

The relentless work ethic Clarke displayed on the ice, Coates said, was something "he did all the time. Twelve months of the year. I'll tell you what, there weren't many players that had that kind of dedication in those days."

Back in the 1970s and 1980s, most players used training camp to get into shape because their summers were filled with too much eating and drinking. Clarke, however, was already in shape when camp started.

During the season, Coates said, a normal day for most players went like this: Go to the rink for practice in the morning. Go to the bar and get out of there at 2:30 or 3:00 in the afternoon. Go home and have another beer and get a bite to eat. Get up in the morning and "feel shitty." Go to practice and feel good again and go back to the bar.

More Motivation

"I think one of the things that really pushed him back then was that he was our second draft pick," Bobby Taylor, a backup goalie during the Flyers' glory days, said more than 50 years after Clarke was the 17th overall selection in the second round of the 1969 draft. "He wasn't even our first draft pick."

The Flyers took center Bob Currier in the first round (sixth overall) in 1969, the NHL's first universal draft. He never played in the NHL.

In the second round, they nabbed Clarke, a junior-level sensation who only dropped because teams were concerned his diabetes made him risky. The consensus among scouts: Clarke couldn't withstand the rigors of an NHL season. (Footnote: Clarke and Phillies third baseman Mike Schmidt were both second-round picks who became the greatest players in their franchises' histories.)

If NHL teams had a redo, Clarke would have been the top overall pick in 1969. Of the 84 players in that draft class, Clarke finished with 1,210 career points—by far the highest total of those draftees. Butch Goring was second with 888 career points. Clarke was also No. 1 with 852 assists (Goring was No. 2 with 513), and he had the highest plus-minus rating (plus-502) in the class. André "Moose" Dupont (plus-302), drafted by the Rangers with the eighth overall pick and later Clarke's teammate with the Flyers, was second (plus-302), and Réjean Houle was third (plus-179).

Interestingly, Broad Street Bullies wingers Don Saleski (plus-72) and Dave Schultz (plus-41) were fourth and fifth, respectively, in that draft class. In addition, Saleski was seventh in goals (128) and Schultz was 12th (79) from that less-than-scintillating class.

Drafting Saleski and Schultz helped form the Broad Street Bullies, and it gave the Flyers two important pieces.

Selecting Clarke, however, was monumental.

Fast-forward to the 2023 draft. The Flyers took a different type of risk when they drafted gifted Russian right winger Matvei Michkov in the first round. There were no guarantees Michkov would ever leave Russia because of the political climate, but he did join the Flyers for the 2024–25 season.

Clarke was a risky choice because of his health. The only reason the Flyers selected him was because scout Gerry Melnyk pressed the issue with the brass and would not take "no" for an answer.

"If you don't draft him, you're making a big mistake," he said at the time, with conviction.

Years later, Flyers chairman Ed Snider said general manager Bud Poile didn't want to take Clarke in the second round because he had drafted a center in the first round and didn't want another one.

An argument ensued at the Flyers' draft table.

Melnyk was furious. He wanted the Flyers to take Clarke in Round 1. As the draft progressed in Montreal's Queen Elizabeth Hotel, Melynk spoke his mind.

"I don't care if Clarke's got only one arm," Melnyk told Poile, according to Jack Chevalier in *The Broad Street Bullies*. "If he can play hockey that way, take him."

Snider asked coach Keith Allen, who would later become the team's general manager, to check his scouting sources on Clarke.

At the time, Snider didn't know anything about Clarke. But he soon learned Melnyk believed Clarke would step right into the NHL and probably be the Flyers' best player.

He instructed Poile to pick Clarke if he was still available.

More than a half century later, it is still the best draft selection the Flyers ever made.

Clarke said the 1969 draft didn't have the fanfare it has today. The fact is, it had no fanfare.

When Clarke was chosen, he didn't even find out until "a couple days after the draft, when a part-time scout from Winnipeg who worked for the Flyers called and told me I went. I said, 'Great.' I was excited."

But Taylor was right. Clarke did use the fact he lasted until the second round as motivation.

The more he thought about being bypassed until No. 17 overall, the more he developed a chip on his shoulder. "Ordinary men were making decisions that I wasn't going to be good enough to play in the NHL, [that] I was not going to be strong enough because I have diabetes," he said years later. "You know, your natural reaction to that is, 'Fuck you. I'll show you.'"

Just before the start of his rookie season in 1969–70, Clarke, who worked briefly in the mines as a teenager, called his dad after signing his first contract with the Flyers.

"I got $5,000 to sign and $14,000 to play," Clarke said. He impressed the Flyers by leading them with eight points during his first exhibition season. "At the time, my dad had 25 years underground in the mine. He was making $12,000. He said to me, 'Holy shit! Why are they paying you all that money? All you're doing is playing hockey.'"

Intangibles > Diabetes

Clarke didn't have great size (5'10", 182 pounds) and he wasn't among the league's fastest players. But he outworked everyone, and his hockey instincts were off the charts.

Growing up, Clarke learned he had diabetes at age 11 or 12.

"As your blood sugar goes up and gets high, you're going to the bathroom all the time, and you're thirsty all the time," Clarke said. "You're eating enormous amounts of food and losing weight, so when that was happening, my mom took me to the doctor, and I was diagnosed right away."

He was hospitalized for about a week, received insulin, and had his blood checked frequently.

When he returned home, he began giving himself insulin shots.

"I was lucky. I wasn't afraid of it or anything," he said. "Lots of kids, rightfully so, are afraid of taking needles every day and stuff like that. I was a big worry to my parents because I was a little reckless."

His mom was on top of his eating habits. She made sure he had three meals and snacks in between.

"It becomes a routine that probably all of us should have," he said of his diet. "You take the insulin in the morning, and then you take food all day to balance the insulin."

When he first joined the Flyers and went to their training camp in Quebec City, Clarke, who had just turned 20, broke away from his routine. He took his insulin but skipped breakfast because he didn't want to be late to a practice.

"I had never really had an incident where I had low blood sugar to the point where I didn't know what I was doing," Clarke said. "Now I get through practice and get in the car, and I'm sweating [profusely], and the other guys I'm riding with tell me this, and they take me right to the hospital. I wake up and I'm in the hospital."

From that point, he never skipped a meal. "You're better off eating more than less, obviously," Clarke said. "So, it never happened again."

Coke to the Rescue

When he played and felt his blood sugar was getting low, he would drink a Coke between periods.

Right winger Don Saleski remembers being at a hockey camp in which Clarke "started blacking out on me, and I fed him two chocolate bars."

On another occasion, Saleski sat next to Clarke on a plane headed to Vancouver. The previous night "we were partying real hard," Saleski said. "We get to the airplane and we're sitting in first class, and you could see he was starting to go. He says, 'Get me a Coke.' I asked the flight attendant to get my buddy a Coke right away. And she came back with a Coke and brought ice. He says, 'No, no, no. Just give me the Coke,' and I asked her to bring him another one. He downs two warm Cokes and, wow, he came right back."

Taylor, who was Bernie Parent's backup, recalled Clarke once "had a seizure at home, and his son, Wade, didn't know what to do.... Wade was young, and he was crying his eyes out; he was angry and scared at the same time. He later said to him, 'You have to let me know what to do if this happens.' It really hit home to Whitey."

That, Taylor said, is what he believes made Clarke realize he should probably spearhead a drive to make people more aware of diabetics and their needs.

"Before that, he was involved, but not a lot, because he hated public appearances," Taylor said. "He didn't really like that, but that's why he became a spokesman for the Juvenile Diabetes Association in the Philly area."

Jody Clarke said her dad "looks like a drunk person, slurs his words, and sweats a lot" when he is having a diabetic episode.

Back in the day, a Coke seemed to remedy things, "but now we know that artificial sugar is not what he needs," Jody said. "So now it's a teaspoon of sugar in a glass of orange juice. That will bring him back faster, and it's a little safer than straight Coke."

She said her dad also has glucose tablets he puts under his tongue to help, "but if it's gotten too far, you can't put your hand in there because he'll bite you. He won't know [he's doing it], but he'll bite you."

Clarke's career started rather innocently—15 goals and 46 points as a rookie. But as he got more comfortable with the pace of the NHL, he improved dramatically. His career skyrocketed when the Flyers put better players around him and also added guys who protected him.

Clarke's point totals went like this in his first four seasons: 46, 63, 81, and 104. And his goals also climbed in each of his first four seasons: 15 to 27 to 35 to 37.

Teams couldn't contain him. He was on his way to becoming a superstar. And he was unfazed when someone taunted him about his diabetic condition.

"This guy in Pittsburgh used to run down to the glass and throw a chocolate bar at me," Clarke said. "He'd yell, 'Here you go Clarke. Eat this!'"

It was probably a Clark Bar, but the Flyers center just shrugged and continued his dazzling play.

Clarke was the Flyers' indefatigable leader, and his teammates knew it. If an opponent went after No. 16, they could expect retaliation from Schultz, Bob Kelly, or someone else.

His First NHL Mentor

Clarke also benefitted by the presence of veteran Ed Van Impe, a stay-at-home defenseman he called his mentor.

During Clarke's arrival to the NHL, Van Impe was the Flyers captain.

"He kind of looked out for me when I was a kid," Clarke said. "He recognized long before I recognized it that I was going to be a pretty good player. And he helped me out and watched over me for years."

Clarke would confide in Van Impe, who was nine years older than him and was like a big brother.

In the second half of the 1972–73 season, Clarke replaced Van Impe as the Flyers captain. He was 23, making him the youngest captain in NHL history at that point.

Coach Fred Shero wanted him to be the captain not just because of the way he played, but because of the way he led. He said he noticed "right away" that Clarke "wasn't a yes man. If I tried something, he would question me. He would question openly, where others wouldn't open their mouths because they were afraid of me because I was the coach."

Shero liked that quality. A captain, he said, "has to be like the coach. He has to fight for his team and be willing to stick his neck out."

Making Clarke the captain was a stroke of genius. Never did Bill Clement realize that until after he was traded to the woeful Washington Capitals in June 1975 and talked to club president Peter O'Malley.

O'Malley drove Clement around the area and told him about all the appearances the team would make in the offseason, trying to build a fan base.

"We want to fill this roster with guys just like the Flyers—guys that just love to win," O'Malley told Clement.

Clement, a deep thinker, contemplated what O'Malley said. "And for the first time in my life, I realized the difference between loving to win and hating to lose," he said.

He turned toward O'Malley.

"Peter, can I make a suggestion?" he said.

"Sure," O'Malley replied.

"You might want to fill the team with guys who hate to lose, because everybody loves to win, but not everybody hates to lose," Clement told him.

It was at that point that Clement realized the impact Clarke had made on the Flyers.

"I really think Clarkie's hatred of losing was stronger than his love for winning," Clement said. "And that's ultimately what motivated him and what motivated a lot of our team to follow his lead. It was just unacceptable to lose."

Clarke's all-out style made him a perfect captain. It also gave him a platform, and when he spoke, you snapped to attention.

Oh, Captain, My Captain

In the 1974 Stanley Cup Finals, for instance, Clarke was incensed by Rick MacLeish's listless play in Game 5 in rowdy Boston Garden. The Bruins won 5–1 and narrowed the Flyers' lead to 3–2 in the best-of-seven championship series.

MacLeish was ultra-gifted—Clarke always calls him the most talented player of the 1974 and 1975 champions—but he had a habit of loafing at times.

"Ricky was just going through the motions," Clement said about Game 5 in the '74 Finals, "and Clarkie was just chomping and chewing on his gum, saying, 'That cocksucker. Fucking Ricky. That motherfucker.' Ricky finishes his shift, and he sat down on one side of me, and Clarkie was on the [other] side. He waits about 10 seconds for Ricky to catch his breath, and he says, 'I sure as fuck hope you're saving it for Sunday, you cocksucker.'"

Clarke, a quiet sort who was usually more subtle when he called out a player, sat back and never said another word to MacLeish that night.

Before what turned out to be a historic Game 6, Clarke remembers following MacLeish into the team's washroom. He double downed on his comments made during Game 5.

"If we're going to win the Stanley Cup, we need you to be our best player today," Clarke told him. "If you don't play a good game, we're not going to win the Stanley Cup. Our team needs you."

MacLeish was never a man of a lot of words.

"Don't worry," he said. "I'll be good."

He was probably the best player on either team in the Flyers' 1–0 win that gave them their first Cup.

"Ricky was dynamic in Game 6 and scored the only goal," Clement said. "He came to play. I have no doubt that the message delivered by Clarkie was the reason."

Clarke's messages were usually more subdued than the mini tirade on the bench in Game 5. It was rare that he had a one-on-one confrontation with a teammate. If a player struggled or made a glaring mistake in the opening period of a game, for instance, Clarke might give them a "let's get going here" comment at the first intermission. They took the comment to heart. They knew why he had made it.

Right winger Don Saleski, who came from Saskatchewan, said Clarke monitored the dressing room. He remembers having his injured knee taped before a 1976 game and Clarke walking into the room. The Flyers were already missing several injured players.

"Hey, Satch, you going to play tonight?" Clarke asked.

Saleski: "Yeah, I think so."

"Well, your knee is a long way from your fucking heart, ain't it?" Clarke responded in a matter-of-fact tone.

Saleski laughed at the memory from nearly 50 years ago.

"I guess his message was, *You're playing tonight*," Saleski said.

Like in any job, it's difficult for all employees to get along. Hockey wasn't any different. Saleski said there were some players on the team that he wasn't personally friendly with. "It was nothing against them, but they had different interests," he said. "But when we went on the ice, there was no doubt we had each other's backs. It was a team like I've never seen [before]. A lot of that goes to Clarkie and his leadership."

And his hate for losing, and his desire to get an edge in any possible manner.

Clarke also hated players who disrespected the team. When Clement struggled at a practice because he had a hangover, Clarke got in his face.

Clement's respect for the captain grew.

Fifty years after the Flyers won their last Cup, Clarke downplays his role as captain.

"I was always given a lot of credit for being a leader and being vocal and all those kinds of things," he said. "But I was not vocal. I was part of the team.... I wouldn't say, 'You've got to do this.' I mean, I might quietly say to you, 'You've got to pick your game up. We need you,' and stuff like that."

Anything to Gain an Advantage

Jimmy Watson tells the story about a 1973–74 game against the Toronto Maple Leafs. But to put Clarke's intensity into context, you have to go back to the previous year, when hockey superpowers Canada and Russia met in the Summit Series.

Team Canada had gone 1–3–1 in the first five games and needed to win the last three contests in Moscow to capture the series. Canada knotted the series at 3–3–1 heading into the final game in late September of 1972.

Facing a 5–3 deficit heading into the third period of the final game, Canada scored three unanswered goals and won 6–5. Paul Henderson scored the winner with 34 seconds left, and some call it the most iconic goal in Canadian hockey history.

"It was our society against theirs," Phil Esposito, a member of that Canadian team, told Sportsnet. "As far as we were concerned, it was a damn war."

Henderson, a winger, scored the winning goal in each of the last three games. He was on a line with his Toronto Maple Leafs teammate, Ron Ellis, and the Flyers' Clarke.

Here's where Watson picks up the story as the Flyers were about to play a 1973–74 game against Henderson, Ellis, and the rest of the Maple Leafs.

"We're getting ready for a faceoff, and Ed Van Impe was lined up against Paul Henderson," Watson said. "Clarkie's going to take the faceoff, and of course, he played with Paul on Team Canada. Clarkie goes over to Van Impe, and he says, 'Eddie, spear the son of a bitch.' Just like that."

Henderson overheard the conversation. After the faceoff, he skated back about four feet so Van Impe couldn't spear him, Watson said. It opened space for the Flyers.

"Clarkie had just played with the guy [Henderson]. And poor Henderson is like, 'Holy shit!'" Watson said. "And that's just the way Clarkie was. That's how competitive he was. He hated the opposition, man."

In the 1972 Summit Series, Clarke, using a two-handed slash, broke the ankle of Russian star Valeri Kharlamov in Game 6 of the eight-game epic.

"I got way more compliments about that than I ever got criticism," Clarke told the *Toronto Star* in 2022.

Henderson, perhaps still fuming that Clarke asked Van Impe to spear him, later called the hit on Kharlamov "the low point of the series" and likened it to a golfer trying to win a tournament by whacking an opponent in the leg.

In the 2022 interview with the *Star*, Clarke said Henderson called him up and offered a half-hearted apology for what he said.

He told Clarke he made the statement about Clarke's hit on Kharlamov "because I didn't want my grandson doing something like that."

Clarke's response didn't amuse Henderson.

"I said, 'Paul, I have a grandson who plays hockey, too. And he's taught to stick up for his teammates, not backstab them.'"

Henderson hung up on him, Clarke said.

Loyalty Trumps Money

Clarke was baffled by Henderson's lack of loyalty. To Clarke, loyalty was paramount to being part of a team.

It is why he turned down a much more lucrative contract from the Philadelphia Blazers of the World Hockey Association in 1972.

If Clarke hadn't turned it down, the Flyers may still be searching for their first Stanley Cup in franchise history.

In the summer of 1972, the World Hockey Association came courting Clarke. The new league began the previous year, and it competed with the NHL for players.

Snider guarded against the WHA by offering lucrative contracts. While negotiating with Clarke a few months before the 1972–73 season, they had agreed to a five-year deal worth a total of $500,000, according to Alan Bass in *Ed Snider: The Last Sports Mogul.* At the time, it was considered a very generous deal.

After a few meetings, Snider, GM Keith Allen, Clarke, and his agent had agreed on a figure. They shook hands, and Clarke was told to go home to Manitoba and the contract would be drawn up by the lawyers.

In August, Clarke got a call that the contract was ready to be signed. He traveled from Flin Flon, Manitoba, to Philadelphia and stayed in a hotel for a night. The plan was for him to sign the deal the next day.

The night before the expected signing, while sitting at the Grog Shop—a Center City establishment Clarke described as a place "where you drink beer and eat peanuts and throw them on the floor"—Clarke ran into a former Flyers executive who now worked for the WHA's Philadelphia Blazers.

When he realized Clarke had technically not signed yet, he went to a pay phone to call one of his bosses.

He came back with an offer: $1 million a year for five years if he joined the Blazers and became the face of the team.

Clarke politely declined. He had a verbal agreement with Snider. It didn't matter that it was 10 times less than the amount the Blazers were offering. His word was his bond.

When Snider got wind of the fact Clarke had turned down a much more lucrative offer, he phoned the star center and asked him why he didn't use it as leverage in negotiating with the Flyers.

"Because we had shaken hands on a deal," Clarke said.

"I'll never forget this," Snider said.

And that cemented Clarke's future as a Flyer. In a way, he became Snider's unofficial son. Whenever his brilliant playing career ended, he would always have a job in the front office if he desired.

Clarke, who has held numerous spots in the Flyers' front office since he retired as a player, told his boss he would never renege on their verbal agreement.

"Mr. Snider, you and I shook hands on a deal," Clarke said at the time. "I trusted you were going to pay me. I hope you trusted that I was going to play for you."

Snider was deeply touched.

"And from that point on, I was treated better; he paid me better than Bobby Orr and all those great stars," Clarke said. He treated me so good. Right up to his death."

It was at a memorial service for Snider in 2016 that Clarke showed just how much his former boss meant to him.

During a 1-hour, 50-minute public ceremony at the Wells Fargo Center, Clarke spoke from the heart.

"When I pass and we all pass, we don't know where we're going," an emotional Clarke said. "For me, I really hope when I get there, I get the chance to play one more game in the orange and black for Mr. Snider's Philadelphia Flyers."

Clarke the Dad

As a father, Clarke had no interest in babying his four children. When Jody Clarke played soccer at a Minnesota high school, she followed her dad's directive.

"He had a hard and fast rule: If you're not dead and your leg isn't broken, you get the hell off the field [if injured]," she said. "We were never allowed to lay on the field if you were injured. Ever. I dislocated my kneecap while playing in high school. My kneecap was in my thigh. I got off. There was no laying down. That was absolutely against everything he believed in."

When Clarke attended his kids' athletic events, he parked his car close to the action and watched from his front seat.

He didn't want to detract from his kids by having people run up to him for an autograph or to chat.

"He just never wanted to take away from us," Jody said. "He never wanted us to be on the field and look over and see him with people and not watching us."

Jody said her mom, Sandy, ran things at home so Bobby only had to concentrate on hockey.

"She did everything," Jody said.

Clarke loved hanging out at Rexy's, the team's local watering hole in South Jersey, and loved his beer. But during his playing days, he wasn't a partier like many of his teammates.

He got rid of tension in another way: racing teammate and best friend Reggie Leach to the Spectrum in their Jeeps.

Leach sometimes had his daughter Brandie in his Jeep, while Clarke had his daughter Jody in his vehicle. The girls would stand up on the back seat and hold onto the roll bar. The star players, part of arguably the greatest line in Flyers history, would cross the Walt Whitman Bridge and take the Packer Avenue Exit.

Then it was showtime.

"They'd race and cut and cross while Brandie and I stood up and waved to each other," Jody said, excitedly.

Life was good being a Flyer. Or the daughter of a Flyer.

Humble and Generous

Off the ice, the soft-spoken Clarke was humble and generous.

In 1971, he quietly donated the team MVP money he received from the Flyers Fan Club to assistant trainer Warren Elliott's daughter because she needed a heart operation. It was only $50, but it was the gesture that resonated.

When he won the Wanamaker Award and $1,000 following the glorious 1973–74 season, he gave the money to Bobby Taylor, his close friend and the backup goalie.

"They just lost a baby, and they need it more than me," he told the *Inquirer* at the time.

And when he received offers for commercials or endorsements, he would tell his agent to ask if the company would instead use one of his teammates.

When he played, he would give $500 from Jack Lang (a men's clothing company) endorsements to the trainers, and $1,000 to his coach, Shero.

When Shero asked at the time why he gave more to his coach, Clarke grinned.

"Because you dress like a damn bum," he said.

Shero was not offended.

"I want my sons to be half as good as Bobby Clarke," he said in the 1970s.

Some players from small towns get big heads when they become NHL superstars. Clarke wasn't like that. Even when he became a league MVP, he was still the humble kid from Flin Flon who went about life remembering his small-town roots.

On and off the ice.

"He doesn't realize he's a superstar," defenseman-turned-assistant coach Barry Ashbee once said. "Most hockey players, when they get that idea of themselves, they slow down. He doesn't. He practices more than anyone on the team, and he certainly doesn't have to."

Even after winning a league MVP award, Clarke didn't rest on his achievement.

"He's playing in Philadelphia like he's still back in Flin Flon trying to make the junior team," Ashbee said.

In an interview with the *Inquirer* in 1976, Clarke didn't disagree with Ashbee's assessment.

"When you're 10 years old, you play with intensity," he said. "Just because you get older doesn't mean that has to change."

CHAPTER 6

ONLY THE LORD SAVES MORE THAN BERNIE PARENT

Of all the players who helped the Philadelphia Flyers win consecutive Stanley Cups in the 1970s, Bernie Parent was probably still the most visible in the 2020s.

Whether he was doing charity work in the community, inspiring others at a public speaking event, or being the face of the Flyers when a comment was needed about some development, Parent seemed to be everywhere.

Everybody loved Bernie. He had a magnetic personality, which was even more charming because of his French-Canadian accent. He loved life to the fullest, and he felt like everyone's favorite uncle as he used phrases like "it's a beautiful thing" to describe an endeavor.

When he was a youngster, however, there was no indication he would become famous for his hockey ability.

Growing up in Montreal, the capital of the hockey world, Parent had to wait until he was 12 years old—a lot older than most Canadian kids—until he had a regular pair of skates. Parent was the youngest of seven children. The family had one pair of skates, and Parent had to wait for the skates to be passed down to him.

He put on the skates, joined a local team, and awkwardly took some laps around an outdoor rink. His dream was to play defense.

"I had maybe skated a couple times before, and it took me like 22, 23 seconds to go around the rink," he said.

He skated like he had a piano on his back.

Parent wanted to be a defenseman, but he didn't remind anyone of Bobby Orr.

His coach saw his lack of speed, pointed to him, and announced: goaltender!

Little did he know that it would lead to two Stanley Cups and a Hockey Hall of Fame career.

Parent liked the idea of being a goalie. He had played the position in Montreal's ice-filled streets, sans skates, while playing in pickup games.

But he played those games while wearing boots; he would now have to get adjusted to skates, which, he said, were way too big for him.

Parent remembers playing his first game in skates and allowing 20-plus goals. The coach told him to take a hike.

He used the next couple of months to continue practicing in skates and started feeling more comfortable at around the time the team's top goaltender was injured. Parent's coach reluctantly called him back "in desperation."

"He said, 'You want to give it one more chance?'" Parent said.

Parent's team won that game 5–3. A budding career was underway.

Parent signed with Boston in 1965 and had a good training camp with the Bruins. But the Bruins had veteran Eddie Johnston and promising rookie Gerry Cheevers in the nets, so Parent was sent down to Oklahoma City, where he continued to refine his standup-goalie technique in the Central League.

A short time later, the Bruins recalled him because of injuries, and Parent made his NHL debut by stopping 40 shots in a 2–2 tie against Chicago. Parent was only 20, and it was an impressive first step. He got into 39 NHL games that season, compiling a 3.69 goals-against average and .898 save percentage. Respectable numbers for a youngster.

Parent had similar numbers for the Bruins in 18 games the next season, then was left unprotected in the 1967 expansion draft. Harry Sinden, the Bruins' coach, thought Parent was immature, that he enjoyed life (and beer) away from hockey too much and wasn't focused. He was much higher on Cheevers, who became a Hockey Hall of Famer.

The Flyers made Parent their first choice in the expansion draft. Teams were only permitted to take goaltenders in the first two rounds, after which skaters were selected. Philadelphia took Doug Favell, another Bruins goalie, with their second choice. (What are the odds that, 50-plus years after the Flyers started, the best goalie in franchise history would still be the one they selected first in the expansion draft in 1967?)

Boston was deep in the net, so Parent welcomed being with the Flyers, welcomed the chance at a fresh start.

In addition to Favell, Parent had Boston teammates Gary Dornhoefer and Joe Watson selected by Philadelphia in the expansion draft.

Coming to Philly with players he knew made it easier to switch teams. And trying to help jump-start a new franchise "got you excited," he said years later.

But the beginning had growing pains because the Flyers struggled to attract fans. They drew just 7,812 and 5,783 spectators for their first two home games in 1967–68, wins against the Pittsburgh Penguins and Oakland Seals, respectively.

"And probably 2,800 of them were part of my family," Parent cracked.

Easing His Mind

Parent was a bundle of nerves. As part of his pregame routine, he would eat a big steak, take a nap with his German Shepherd, Tinkerbell, and then wake up and watch *The Three Stooges* to take his mind off the upcoming matchup.

But he would still be wound up and would vomit before each game.

Lou Scheinfeld, the first vice president in the Flyers' history, remembers Parent's nerves getting to him when a fan heckled him before a game in Boston.

"This guy confronts Bernie in the hotel lobby. I'm standing right there," Scheinfeld said. "This guy says to him, 'You're going to get beat tonight. You're going to give up five goals.' And Bernie says, 'Please stay away from me. Please stay away from me.' And I had to get between the two of them. Bernie was shook."

Parent, a classic standup goalie, became a fan favorite, but he was dealt to Toronto on January 31, 1971. It was part of a three-way deal in which the Flyers got Rick MacLeish from Boston. They acquired MacLeish for Mike Walton, whom they got from Toronto, and Danny Schock. In addition to Walton, the Flyers received goalie Bruce Gamble and a first-round draft pick in the Parent trade. (Note: When the trade was made, Lou Nolan, now the Flyers' longtime public address announcer, remembers thinking, *Who's this guy MacLeish?* As it turned out, MacLeish would become one of the greatest Flyers centers of all time.)

When general manager Keith Allen called Parent into his office to tell him about the deal, he explained it was the most difficult trade he had ever made. That didn't pacify the 25-year-old Parent. He had spent parts of four seasons in Philadelphia, and he was devastated by the deal.

So were fans, one of whom wrote a letter to the *Philadelphia Inquirer*'s Frank Dolson, which he printed:

"How come it never fails to happen that whenever Philadelphia has a superstar in its ranks, it trades him away?" the fan wrote. "This time it was Bernie Parent. He got traded away for a couple of unknowns. So, we can officially place Parent with Wilt Chamberlain, Richie Allen, Bob Brown, and others as departed stars from Philadelphia."

After the deal, dozens of signs hung from the Spectrum at the Flyers' next home game, saying how much the fans hated the trade and loved Parent.

In his book, *Unmasked: Bernie Parent and the Broad Street Bullies*, Bernie wrote he "cried like a baby" when he learned he was traded. "I bumped into Mr. [Ed] Snider in the corridor of the Spectrum and he started crying, too."

Snider, one of the Flyers' founders, gave Parent a big hug, wished him well, and said it was just one of those things where they had to trade a good player to get someone with great potential.

"He had tears in his eyes. I had tears in my eyes," Parent said more than 50 years later. "But I understood. I was going to Toronto, and I realized I was going to share duties with my idol, Jacques Plante."

In his heyday, Plante, who in 1959 introduced the goaltenders' mask to hockey, performed like Andrei Vasilevskiy and Igor Shesterkin in the 2020s. He was magnificent, and Parent said the reason he blossomed as a goalie was because of the things he learned under Plante. (Plante's sister, Therese, lived next door to

Parent and his family. Whenever word got around that Jacques was visiting his sister, a starstruck Bernie—who was around 11 years old at the time—and his friends hid behind the bushes just so they could get a glimpse at the standout goalie as he got out of his car and walked toward the front door.)

Little did young Bernie know at the time that one day Plante would mentor him with the Maple Leafs.

Plante worked with Parent on one of his weaknesses—clearing the puck. Plante had been the first goalie to leave the net to clear the puck out of harm's way.

When Plante was in goal, Parent studied every move he made.

At a Maple Leafs practice one day, Parent asked Plante, who was then 41, how he was able to read the shooters so well. He told Parent he studied all of them and had a book on their tendencies.

"The next day, I started putting together a similar book," Parent said in his autobiography. "I found out that Plante had more than one book on the shooters. He kept notes on every arena, how to play the boards in each one and how the lighting affected playing goal.

"Cripes, the old man—he knew everything," he said.

Plante, who died in of stomach cancer at age 57 in 1986, told his protégé to visualize making saves in every type of situation, whether a breakaway, an odd-man rush, a tap-in attempt from the doorstep, or a slapper from the high slot or the point. He prepared Parent, both physically and mentally, to play the most important position on a hockey team.

The Flyers were the benefactors.

Return to Philly

Parent spent parts of two seasons with Toronto, then jumped to the World Hockey Association's Miami Screaming Eagles. The

Canadian taxes took a big bite out of his paycheck, and his wife, Carol, wasn't happy in Toronto.

But the biggest reason Parent jumped to the new league was the fact his salary climbed from $30,000 per season to about $140,000, plus a boat, a car, and a house.

He loved boating and fishing and was excited to be in the warm weather in Miami.

Only he never played there.

The new team was unable to find a suitable arena and the franchise folded before it even played a game. Instead, the team relocated to Philadelphia, of all places.

The Philadelphia Blazers were born. The owners said they would only start the franchise if Parent came aboard.

Bernie consented. He was going home.

"If things didn't work out, I figured I could go back to the NHL," he said.

Things didn't work out. The Blazers usually drew 3,000 to 4,000 fans at the aging Civic Center and, after their first season in Philadelphia, headed to Vancouver. Parent left the Blazers after the first playoff game because of a contract dispute and planned to return to the Toronto Maple Leafs.

But to Parent's delight, the Leafs sent him to the Flyers. In the deal, Toronto got Doug Favell and a first-round pick, while the Flyers received Parent and a second-round selection.

Now *this* felt like a homecoming.

"I never wanted to leave in the first place," Parent said.

In the meantime, his English started getting better, and he became more confident in speaking to people, making his humorous personality come to the forefront.

Earlier in his career, the fast-talking Parent had confused his teammates as he tried to speak English.

"He makes no sense in French, either!" forward André Lacroix said at the time.

But Parent seemed to draw strength as his English improved. No longer was he hurt when a teammate made fun of some of the words he butchered. The mispronunciations lessened, and when he did make a verbal mistake, he was the first one to make fun of himself—unlike in the earlier years, when he was apt to be quieter.

On the ice, Parent put the Flyers at the top. They won the Stanley Cup in his first year back with the team.

The Parents had kept their house in Cherry Hill, New Jersey, which was close to Philadelphia. That made the move even easier.

When he returned, Parent was better than ever in 1973–74, leading the NHL in wins (47), goals-against average (1.89), and save percentage (.932) while playing in 73 games, tops among goaltenders.

On his way to the ice before each game at the Spectrum, he would walk down the hall, reach up, and hit the wall with his finger. That was a signal that he felt he was "on" for the night and ready to play, and it would get a huge roar from the players in the line behind him.

It was Bernie Time.

As it turned out, Parent was the Flyers' missing piece. They rode him to the first Stanley Cup in franchise history.

With the final seconds disappearing in the Cup-clinching 1–0 win over Boston in Game 6 at the going-mad Spectrum, Parent revealed 50 years later, he was petrified he was going to allow a long goal.

Asked what he now thinks about when someone mentions the first Cup, Parent smiled.

"I'll never forget. There's about 10 seconds to go in the game, okay? Against Boston. And all the people are standing up, and they're all pumped. The faceoff is in the Boston end.… Everybody's excited. They drop the puck, and the puck goes to Bobby Orr. I'm looking up at the clock at the same time. And he shot the puck from his own end, and it missed the net by about this much."

Parent held his hands a few inches apart, then added the kicker.

"I never saw it."

If Orr had put the puck on goal, Parent said, the Bruins probably would have scored.

"And we wouldn't be talking today," he said.

After the franchise-altering Cup championship in 1974, captain Bobby Clarke was asked about his celebration plans: "I'll follow Bernie," he said. "Just walk across the water with Bernie."

Parent's 1973–74 and 1974–75 seasons were arguably the best by a goaltender in NHL history. Amazingly, he had a combined 24 regular season shutouts during those two seasons, along with six more in the playoffs. He led the NHL in virtually every goalie statistic in 1973–74 and topped the league with a 2.04 GAA the next season.

Knowing Parent was in the net gave the Flyers a chance to take gambles on offense, realizing if it led to an odd-man rush the other way, the 5'10", 180-pound goalie would bail them out.

He had 12 shutouts in each of the two regular seasons that led to the 1974 and 1975 Cups. He also set NHL goaltender records in the former year for games played (73) and wins (47) in a single season.

"Bernie.... Bernie.... Bernie!"

That was the cry that echoed around the Spectrum during those unforgettable years, back when ONLY THE LORD SAVES MORE THAN BERNIE PARENT bumper stickers seemed to be on most cars in the Philadelphia area.

Penalty-Killing Extraordinaire

Parent's brilliance allowed the Flyers to play on the edge, aware that if they picked up a penalty, their goaltender would thwart most of their opponents' power-play opportunities.

In other words, there were many games he stole during the regular season and playoffs with his acrobatics in the nets.

Parent said the Flyers players, many of whom were free spirits who liked to party, had a love for each other and that it showed by how they protected one another on the ice.

"We were crazy, but we were a family, and we cared about each other," he said. "If somebody would give a cheap shot to one of our players in those days—and it happened a lot, you know—everybody would jump on the ice and remind the guy not to do this. You know what I mean?"

He seemed to enjoy the memory.

"Oh, God. That was fun," he said. "That's the fun we had. That's the family we had. And we protected each other and that was beautiful."

Phillies superstar Bryce Harper often talks about the great Philadelphia fans and how they motivate him to be the best he can be.

Parent feels the same way. He brings up the many times thousands of fans would greet the team at the airport after they returned home from a big playoff win.

"They were a part of us," he said. "I'm very grateful that I was in Philly at the time when we won those two championships."

Happy and Content

As Parent inched toward 80, he was happy, content, and madly in love with his second wife, Gini. They got married on the beach in Avalon, New Jersey, in 2016, and when they are together, you can feel their love and chemistry.

They divide their time between the Philadelphia area, the Jersey Shore, and South Florida, and Bernie is in his glory when he is captaining his 45-foot yacht known as *The French Connection*. Give him a boat filled with family and friends, a good cigar, and a fishing pole, and well, Bernard Marcel Parent couldn't be happier.

Getting to this happy place has been a long and sometimes difficult road. It started when his brilliant hockey career ended with a freak accident six weeks before he turned 34.

In a play in front of the net against the New York Rangers, Flyers defenseman Jimmy Watson inadvertently poked his stick through the right eyehole of Parent's old-school, *Friday the 13th*–style mask, blinding him for a few days.

His sight returned, but it wasn't at the level needed to face 100 mph slap shots.

Having lost his livelihood—and the comradery and routine that went with it—Parent drowned his sorrows in alcohol, contributing to the end of his marriage to Carol.

In an interview with NJ.com's Randy Miller in 2015, Parent, who credits Alcoholics Anonymous for straightening out his drinking problem, spoke candidly about his alcohol abuse. He stopped drinking in 1980.

"Beer was mostly what I drank," he said. "In the beginning, it was tough quitting because you have to change the people you would hang around with because I believe you become who you surround yourself with. I had to change. I had to let go of a lot of good friends, but I also made a lot of good new friends, and I'm a better person for that."

The binge drinking lasted a year. Parent turned around his life and started looking at the positives. He became the Flyers' goalie coach in the 1980s and early '90s, and later embraced the role of team ambassador. If there was a Flyers charity event, Bernie was at center stage with a boatload of amused listeners.

"I love people," he said.

It's easy to see why people gravitate toward him. He has a natural, French-Canadian charm, and he is a gifted storyteller and jokester. Those traits, he said, came from his loving parents and siblings.

Be warm. Be friendly. Don't judge people.

Those are characteristics that Parent says he has always followed.

"Love people," he said, "and when you do that, good things will happen to you."

Parent has been married twice, but in his interview with NJ.com, he could not stop talking about actress Brigitte Bardot ("She was a good-looking broad!"), and he exaggerated about how many trips he'd made to the altar.

"Five times," he said. "My first four wives died of bad mushrooms. Do you know what the fifth one died of? She died of a concussion. She wouldn't eat the mushrooms."

He paused.

"No, no, no!" he said, explaining he was just kidding.

He never runs out of stories. Pick a topic. Any topic. Bernie has a story.

It's always told with a smile and a delivery and timing that would make Nate Bargatze proud.

Parent has had many barriers in his life. There was his drinking, his divorce, the stunning 1985 death of the 26-year-old goaltender he had mentored, Pelle Lindbergh. And in 2018 he and his wife, Gini, were badly injured in a car accident when hit by a drunken driver. They both underwent painful back surgeries and long rehabs.

After the accident, he tweeted a message to fans on Twitter: "Focus on the outcome, not the obstacle."

Parent has become a Santa Claus–like figure to Philadelphians. Always jovial. Always in a giving mood. As a matter of fact, he has dressed as Santa for charity events.

"For me, it's very important to share the love," he said. "The bottom line is to have vision to make life interesting. And you never know where (his message) goes. Somebody who really needs somebody else, and it helps them have a good day. That's what it's all about. It's a beautiful thing."

In 2007 Parent told *Philadelphia Magazine* one of his patented beautiful stories. It wasn't about helping anyone, but it centered on how he enjoys all aspects of life, especially the innocent moments.

"I was in New York six years ago, signing autographs," Parent said. "This girl, 17 years old, has no clue who I am. She says, 'Can I have an autograph for my brother?' I said sure."

She noticed Parent's two Stanley Cup rings.

"This is great! They made them for the parents, too!"

The teenager had misunderstood the inscription on the rings: PARENT.

Parent chuckled.

"So, I got up like a good Flyer and one shot, dropped her," he said with a laugh that could probably be heard from the seashore resort of Wildwood, New Jersey, where he was keeping his beloved boat, to Philadelphia.

At Peace with Himself

Parent is at peace with life and himself. He found it many years ago when his son, Bernie Jr., presented him with *The Secret,* an Australian TV producer's self-help book and DVD that examines how positive thinking is the key to happiness.

Having done the unthinkable—shutting out Boston (1–0) and Buffalo (2–0) in the Cup-clinching wins in back-to-back seasons—also has given him a sense of peace, a sense of pride. He stopped all 30 shots he faced in the decisive win over Boston and denied 32 shots in the memorable victory in Buffalo.

In the waning minutes of the epic victory over Boston, Bernie called over defenseman Joe Watson during a break in the action.

Watson thought the goaltender wanted to talk about some strategy, perhaps something that would contain high-scoring Phil Esposito in front of the net.

"How many broads do you think are watching us right now?" Bernie asked.

He relieved the tension, Watson said, by being himself—a fun-loving guy who happened to be the best goalie on the planet.

More than anyone, Parent was why the Flyers won consecutive Stanley Cups in the 1970s. In a tense Game 1 of the 1975 Finals, he was the reason the Flyers weren't trailing Buffalo. The teams were locked in a scoreless tie after the first two periods.

Buffalo, led by its "French Connection" line of Gil Perreault, Rick Martin, and René Robert, dominated the Flyers over the first two periods, outshooting them 22–10. During one 64-second stretch while the Flyers were in a five-on-three shorthanded situation in the opening period, the Sabres fired seven shots at Parent.

The Flyers gave the Sabres six power plays in the first 40 minutes.

"If he doesn't come up with those two periods, we lose the first game," Joe Watson said. "With all the damn goofy penalties we took, we'd be behind 1–0 in games."

"We should have had four goals in the first period," Perreault said.

The Flyers erupted for four goals in the final period—two by Bill Barber, including an empty-netter—en route to a 4–1 win that, both teams agreed, was stolen by Parent. Bernie was also dominant in Game 2, a 2–1 win that was decided by Bobby Clarke's third-period goal.

After losing two games in Buffalo—including a 5–4 overtime decision in which Parent lost the winning goal in the fog that had engulfed a building that wasn't air conditioned—the Flyers took control of the series with a 5–1 win in Game 5 at the Spectrum. Dave Schultz, of all people, led the offense with a pair of goals, and Parent stopped 23 of 24 shots.

Parent was magnificent as the Flyers closed out the series and won their second straight Cup, defeating the Sabres in Game 6 2–0 at the Buffalo Memorial Auditorium. Bob Kelly snapped a scoreless tie by scoring 11 seconds into the third period, and Bill Clement secured the memorable win by scoring with 2:47 remaining.

Kelly's goal was scored after assistant coach Mike Nykoluk went to coach Fred Shero following the second period and told him the team might need a spark. The game was scoreless, and Nykoluk noted that Kelly hadn't played in a while. "He might give you the energy," he said to Shero.

So, Shero sent Kelly, better known as "Hound" and someone who created havoc with his relentless checking and fearless play, onto the ice to start the third period. But instead of being on one of the lower lines, he was on the top unit with Clarke and Reggie Leach.

On the initial shift of the third period, Leach dumped the puck into the Buffalo zone. Kelly chased it behind the net and took a nasty check from Jerry Korab, a 6'3", 220-pound Buffalo defenseman. Clarke cleverly shielded Korab off the play, enabling Kelly to pick up the loose pick and spin out front. He beat goalie Roger Crozier with a backhander.

No other Flyer has ever scored a Cup-clinching goal on the road.

"By Hound scoring the winning goal, it shows you that anybody can do it," Parent cracked.

It was Parent, however, who was the biggest star of the win. He stopped all 32 shots he faced.

The victory gave each player on the Flyers $15,000. Parent, who won his second straight Conn Smythe Trophy as the league's best playoff performer, preferred talking about the Stanley Cup.

"It's a beautiful trophy," he said. "Nothing like it."

The previous season, hundreds of fans climbed over the Spectrum boards and onto the ice, clogging the Flyers' attempt to skate with the Stanley Cup. This time, no one interrupted them. Clarke and Parent clutched the Cup and their teammates followed as they skated around the ice. In a classy demonstration, the Buffalo fans gave them a standing ovation.

"A beautiful thing," Parent said.

Heading into 2025, it was the last time any team won the Cup with all Canadians on its roster.

Five decades since their last championship, the excitement hasn't left Parent. When he makes appearances, he proudly displays his two Stanley Cup rings, and it's not unusual for him to allow others to try them on and have photos taken. He wants others to feel what they mean to him. And his adopted city.

"What's nice about rings like this," he said, "is that people like Bill Gates, who's worth $100 billion, can't buy it. You have to earn it. That's how powerful winning a championship is."

CHAPTER 7

THE PARADES: FROM 20 PEOPLE TO 2 MILLION TO 2.3 MILLION

THE LOVE AFFAIR between the Philadelphia Flyers and their fans can be summed up in numbers.

When the Flyers were created in 1967, a parade was held in downtown Philadelphia to salute the city's new team.

About 20 people showed up.

"There were more people *in* the parade than showed up to watch it," quipped defenseman Joe Watson, one of the original Flyers.

Seven years later, the Flyers were Stanley Cup champions, and 2 million people were at the "scary" parade in 1974.

The next year, 2.3 million attended the parade to salute the two-time defending champs.

In summary: from 20 people to 2 million to 2.3 million.

Philadelphia had become a hockey city.

"The whole Delaware Valley was our family," said Bernie Parent, the Hall of Fame goaltender.

Most of the Flyers lived in small towns in South Jersey, and after they won their first Cup, many of their neighbors made homemade signs and hung them on their streets to proudly welcome Stanley Cup champion (fill in the blank with the player's name) home.

These transplanted Canadians had a refreshingly unassuming air about them, and they became hometown heroes in both their former and new neighborhoods.

But outsiders didn't understand the hoopla.

After the Flyers won their first Cup on Sunday, May 19, 1974, the wildly crowded parade was held the next day in Philadelphia. A patron at the Bellevue-Stratford Hotel on South Broad Street heard the noise and looked out his window.

He called the front desk to find out why there was such commotion.

"Haven't you been in Philly on a Monday?" he was told.

The late, great Gene Hart, the iconic Flyers broadcaster, used to tell that story with perfect delivery.

But even Hart had to be amazed at Philly's quick transformation into a hockey city.

Before the Flyers arrived, Philadelphia had a short NHL stint, but it was unsuccessful and never built a fan base. The Philadelphia Quakers lasted just one season, compiling an unimaginable 4–36–4 record in 1930–31.

Philly was just a temporary stop as the franchise moved to the City of Brotherly Love from Pittsburgh, which was supposedly going to get the team back when it had a suitable arena in place. (The Pittsburgh Pirates, however, never returned to the NHL, and the league pulled the plug on the Quakers after their one-year fiasco.)

In their lone NHL season, the Quakers averaged just 2,500 fans per home game at The Arena, a tiny building at 46th and Market Streets.

So, when the Flyers got a franchise in 1967, there were doubts about whether the city would support them.

Joe Kadlec, the Flyers' first public relations director, remembers the skepticism surrounding the new franchise. He recalled Ambrose "Bud" Dudley, the former owner of the Eastern Hockey League's Philadelphia Ramblers, saying the Flyers would never get off the ground.

Before the Flyers' first season, a group of team executives, advertisers, city politicians, and others went on a bus trip to watch an NHL game at Madison Square Garden. Kadlec was on the trip, as was Dudley.

"You're not going to draw any more than 3,000," Kadlec said Dudley told the group.

Lou Scheinfeld, who was the Flyers' first vice president, had a different outlook. He, too, was on that bus trip to watch the New York Rangers play the Montreal Canadiens, two Original Six teams.

Scheinfeld had heard whispers from people, including his wife, who wondered if the Flyers would ever become popular.

"My wife says, 'A hockey team in Philadelphia? Why? There's no such thing,'" Scheinfeld said. "I told her, 'That's why it's going to be successful.'"

Watching the Rangers and the lively Garden crowd increased his optimism.

"The game starts, and the crowd is beyond itself," said Scheinfeld, still excited five decades later. "By the end of the first period, I said, 'Holy shit. Wait until Philadelphia sees this.' It was a combination of beauty and brutality. Ice Capades, football, sumo wrestling. You name it. Fights, blood, ice spraying, crashing into the goalie. It was unbelievable. I was drained. I couldn't wait to get back on the bus and get back to Philadelphia. I said, 'I'm going to sell the hell out of this sport.'"

The Flyers, however, had a tough time selling tickets in the early part of their first season. The most expensive tickets were $5.50; the cheapest were $2.

The team's inaugural training camp was held in Quebec City. They broke camp and returned to Philly. Watson, being an inquisitive guy, sat in front of the bus as it carried players back to their cars.

"We're coming over the Penrose Avenue Bridge"—12 years later, it was renamed the George C. Platt Bridge, honoring the Civil War hero—"and on the right-hand side, there's machines grinding up cars," said Watson, a steady defenseman of that era. "I asked the bus driver what the machine was doing. He says, 'Oh, they're grinding up body parts.' So, I say, 'You mean car parts?' He says, 'No, the Mafia gets rid of people, and they put them in their cars and grind them together.' That was my first introduction to Philadelphia.

"What the hell?!"

Welcome to Philly

A few days after being told about the Philly mob, Watson and the Flyers had their 1967 introductory parade in Center City. At the time, Watson wondered if Philadelphia was ready for an NHL team.

Fans in cars honked horns and flashed their middle fingers because the caravan was blocking traffic.

"I'm thinking, *We're not going to be in Philly for long*," Watson said more than a half-century later. "I thought we'd be in Baltimore or Washington in six months."

The players were in convertibles, and "nobody paid any attention to them," said Scheinfeld, who was owner Ed Snider's right-hand man at the time.

Watson said that when the parade got to City Hall, the team was supposed to be welcomed by Mayor James Tate.

"The city wanted to have this thing to welcome us, so we go there, and the mayor doesn't even show up to the event," Watson said. "The mayor doesn't freaking show up. I never forgot that."

Seven years later, the city honored the Flyers for winning the Stanley Cup. Naturally, the subject of the mayor being invisible in 1967 was brought up by Watson.

"Where the fuck was the mayor seven years ago?" Watson asked.

"Hey, don't blame me," said Frank Rizzo, who became the city's boss in 1972. "I wasn't the mayor back then."

They laughed. It was easy to laugh because the Flyers had lifted the city on their collective shoulders.

At the time, Philly and the nation needed a positive.

"We came along at the right time," Watson said. "The Vietnam War had been going on and was just ending, and the city of Philadelphia was in the doldrums, like most cities in the States. The economy wasn't the best. Lots of strikes.... And a bunch of Canadians came down here and made everybody happy."

Before the 1974 parade, Watson wanted to document the celebration. He lived in Lansdowne, Pennsylvania, about six miles outside of Philadelphia, and went to a drugstore to purchase some film.

Watson went to the counter and asked for film. No luck.

"How can a drugstore be out of film?" Watson asked, incredulously.

"Didn't you hear that the Flyers just won the Stanley Cup?" the woman behind the counter responded.

"Oh, they did?!" Watson said.

As he walked out of the store, another woman spotted him. "That's Joe Watson!" she shouted. "That's Joe Watson!"

Watson ran to his car. He had film to buy.

Parade Fun...and Chaos

The parade in 1974, which was held the day after the Flyers edged Boston 1–0 in Game 6, was both joyous and chaotic.

The city didn't expect 2 million hysterical fans who did everything to touch, squeeze, or hug the players. They handed the players beers and other beverages.

"People were all over our cars," center Bill Clement said.

Large groups surrounded some of the cars and rocked them up and down with players and/or family members inside.

The players, their families, and club personnel were in convertibles (or cars with sunroofs) for Parade I and were much more accessible to the crowd. Parade II was more organized, as the players and others were on floats.

"The first parade was fucking terrifying because we're in cars, and they just expected some people on the side of the street all along the way," Clement said. "I had a cigarette. I was burning people's hands to get them off the car if I could. And the mounted police were there. And they were swinging their horses between cars so the next car could get through. I felt it was out of control. I was there with my first wife, and we had no control over what was going on, so it was scary."

Bobby Clarke and his wife, Sandy, had to take their young children, Jody and Wade, home early from the first parade.

"We were getting so mobbed, and my mom felt it was unsafe for us," said Jody, whose father was the team's captain and was swarmed by the fans.

At the time, Sandy Clarke said fans jumped on her husband and threw things at him and her. They were supposed to be "gifts," but they didn't feel like presents. Sandy got hit with a glass mug. Bobby Clarke got hit on the leg with a full can of beer—a memory that was triggered when Eagles general manager Howie Roseman was struck in the forehead by a beer can during the 2025 Super Bowl parade.

Fans pushed at the Flyers star, and the three men guarding him were no match for the thousands of people that wanted to party with him.

Clarke was the first player in the car parade, so that added to the hysteria. That and Clarke being the face of the Flyers.

"It was sad," *Daily News* columnist Stan Hochman wrote about the pawing humanity. "Clarke had given the fans six months of blood and sweat, and the fans had given him 60 minutes of anguish in return. It is a feeble alibi, but this city has had so little to celebrate, perhaps it has forgotten how."

"So, some of the Broad Street Bullies"—he was referring to the fans—"did what NHL teams had tried in vain to do all year, wear Bobby Clarke down."

About 40 people were treated at Metropolitan Hospital for injuries sustained during the parade, including some for fighting. A six-year-old boy, Frankie Hudson, was kicked in the face by a police horse as the motorcade traveled down Broad Street; he underwent several hours of surgery at Methodist Hospital. An ambulance couldn't get through the thick crowd, so poor Frankie, his bloody face covered with a T-shirt, was carried to the hospital about 1½ blocks from where he was injured.

Police said 11 people were arrested during the day—four for disorderly conduct, five for juvenile delinquency, and two for indecent exposure.

Left winger Bob Kelly, recalling the parade 50 years later, said it was a "shock to see how many people were there. Nobody knew what to expect. I mean, just seeing the thickness of the people there. They put [some of] us in moonroof cars. But we were sitting on top of the moonroof, so people were walking right alongside you. I mean, they're pulling at your shirts and jackets and whatever else. It was just crazy, and the drivers couldn't see where they're driving. We're looking out to just a sea of people."

While the players were vulnerable to the fans, they came away realizing just how much they had meant to the city. They came away amazed at how much they were adored.

The parade arrived at its finishing site, Independence Mall, at 2:10 PM—nearly two hours later than scheduled because the influx of people in the streets had slowed the march. About 60,000 fans crammed into Independence Mall, where singer Kate Smith, the Flyers' good luck charm, stood at the podium.

The crowd was pushing toward the stage, and people were armpit to armpit as they tried to move closer.

From the podium, Smith, 65, called for order. "C'mon kids," she scolded. "Let's take it easy. Keep it calm."

The crowd joined Smith in a stirring rendition of "God Bless America," which kicked off the ceremonies. Star goaltender Bernie Parent kissed Kate, and the fans started a chant that echoed through the parade route.

"Bernie, Bernie, Bernie!"

Some players spoke briefly to the crowd, as did Mayor Rizzo.

Dave Schultz drew roars as he stood at the podium, cigarette in his right hand, and held up a T-shirt that read: I CAN BE VERY FRIENDLY.

In his remarks after the parade ended, coach Fred Shero saluted the fans.

"You'll never see anything like this again in your lifetime," he said. "If we'd known they loved us so much, we would have won it in four games" instead of six.

The *Bulletin*, then one of the city's prominent newspapers, explained the day this way: "To describe what can only be called The Parade with any form of analogy is inadequate. There never before has been anything like it in this city. Those weren't all hockey fans out there. Those were just plain people mostly, satisfying a hunger to identify with something good."

For some added context: While the Flyers were captivating the city, crime and the Philadelphia police force were also in the public's eye in the mid-1970s. And not in a good way. In those days—and this was unrelated to the Flyers' victory parades—the number of homicides had more than doubled from the previous decade. In addition, the police were charged with numerous beatings, including twisting and kicking suspects' testicles, according to the *Washington Post*. Court testimony about interrogations that judges ruled illegal showed that suspects had been beaten by police with lead pipes, blackjacks, brass knuckles, chairs, and table legs.

The Flyers provided a welcome diversion to a troubled city.

Parade II More "Civilized"

Clement said the second parade was "very civilized, except we'd been drinking all night. I'm on the back float. The dignitaries are on the front float—Bernie, Clarkie, Ed [Snider], Keith Allen, and the rest."

This time, the players and their families weren't mauled by fans who were able to get right up to the convertibles and hand the Flyers beers or give them hugs. Or (lovingly) throw beers and other things at them.

For Parade II, the players, their families, team executives, and city officials were high off the ground in three flatbeds and were not nearly as accessible to fans. A storm of ticker tape, confetti, and beer showered the flatbeds as they navigated the packed streets.

The crowd was estimated at 2.3 million, according to Joseph O'Neill, the city's police commissioner. His estimate was based on helicopter surveys and reports from police.

"This was not just a parade, but the rebirth of a city," wrote *Courier-Post* columnist Ray Kelly. "And the cynics, who cast aside the bitterness of living in an age called Watergate to stand with the masses in the place of the nation's birth to join Kate Smith in singing 'God Bless America,' knew this to be true."

Mayor Rizzo had similar sentiments. His proclamation read: "The Flyers have rekindled a winning spirit in Philadelphia, which has provided its citizens with a sense of pride and enthusiasm unmatched in any other city."

Teenagers made up a large portion of the crowd, meaning there was lots of "hockey hooky" in area high schools. Again.

Lincoln High in Northeast Philadelphia, for instance, had a 25 percent attendance rate the day of Parade II—Wednesday, May 28, 1975. The school's normal attendance rate was 86 percent.

Across the river in New Jersey, 50 percent of the 1,700 Pennsauken High students were absent—and that seemed like the norm for the region.

Signs were everywhere. Among the thousands of them: KELLY FOR MAYOR and THE CUP IS HERE, NOW DRINK SOME BEER. A nun held a sign that read: GOD SAVES SOULS...BERNIE SAVES GOALS.

The second victory parade had a different route, moving from Center City to John F. Kennedy Stadium in South Philadelphia. At the stadium, where a male streaker (pants in one hand, beer bottle in the other) enlivened the already-raucous crowd by racing around the stadium track in his birthday suit, Parent told the crowd he and his teammates would see them again here next year.

"Bernie" chants echoed around the stadium, which was filled with 100,000 of the goalie's closest friends.

All the players were introduced, and Parent, Clarke, Schultz, and Rick MacLeish drew the loudest cheers. Many in the crowd wore Flyers jerseys, with Schultz's No. 8 the most popular.

During Parade II, Clement was among the many people on the second float, and he had a problem.

"My bladder is about to explode, and I didn't know what I was going to do," he said about 50 years later. "So, there was a service station there. I hopped off the float and went through the crowd and said I had to go."

The guy at the gas station told him the rest room was closed.

Clement pleaded his case. He was recognized and the rest room was opened for him to pee.

The parade hadn't stopped, so Clement had to catch up to his float. Somehow.

Two cops obliged. They put their two billy clubs together as a flying wedge and told Clement to grab the back of their belts. They fought through the crowd, got to the float, and helped Clement hop back on.

Less than a minute later, the parade came to a halt. The stairs unfolded on the first float. Out stepped the player who was the MVP of the Flyers' amazing playoff journey.

Bernie Parent had to take a leak.

He walked up to a row home, wiggling his legs to stop the urge to urinate on the sidewalk.

"This little old lady welcomes him into her home," Clement said. "Then I thought about it. If I never understood the hierarchy of our team, I got it then."

Clement, a low-line center, had to beg and plead to get a gas-station attendant to open his bathroom. Bernie Parent, superstar goalie, got escorted into a family's bathroom.

"I still have this recurring dream of being left behind in the parade, and people throwing coins in this bronze toilet in this lady's home that is now the Bernie Parent shrine," Clement said.

The woman, according to Parent, did have the toilet seat bronzed.

Crazy Times

The '74 parade began at the Spectrum and went through the city. It ended at Independence Mall, the reception site. The parade was especially chaotic on Chestnut and Walnut Streets, as narrow thoroughfares became overloaded with humanity.

There were an estimated 1,000 crowd-control officers; they were no match for 2 million joy-struck people.

"We sat on the back of convertibles," said Carolyn DeSimone, who was married to Rick MacLeish and pregnant at the time. "People are trying to get close, and we're covered in beer because they're throwing it. Not to be mean, but [celebrating]. I'm holding onto Rick because they're grabbing him. People are climbing up the back of the car, trying to get to him."

From a teenager's perspective, the first parade was overwhelming.

Lindy Snider, whose father owned the team, was 14 at the time as she sat in one of the parade cars.

She called it "total chaos. Maybe not chaos. It was more like pandemonium. It was beyond exciting. But there were moments when it felt scary.

"Just because of the sheer amount of people, I thought, *How are we not going to run these people over?*" she said. "And the people were rushing right at us. I thought they were going to turn the whole car over. It took a while to realize that everybody was friendly, that it wasn't violent."

In time, as she examined the people who had painted their bodies orange and black, or painted a Flyers logo on their bare chests, she was able to enjoy the scene and absorb all the love.

"It became joyful and didn't feel threatening," Lindy said. "Even as a kid, I knew this was epic. You cannot forget it. It was a sea of humanity. You couldn't see. And I remember the people hanging from the lampposts and the balconies and knowing the schools had let out. It was like adrenaline" shot through your body. "There's nothing to compare to that. Nothing. Boy would it be fun to experience that again."

Shortly after the Flyers won the 1974 Cup, Bill Fleischman, who covered the team for the *Daily News* at the time, wrote a story about the love affair between the city and the champs.

"Any day a Philadelphia professional team wins a championship is special," he wrote. "Memory fades a little, but I don't recall the city erupting over the Eagles in 1960 or the 76ers in '67 the way they did over the Flyers winning the Stanley Cup.

"Maybe it was the Flyers' underdog role against the mighty Bruins. Maybe it was the Flyers' belligerent style that won a city's heart," Fleischman continued. "Whatever it was, a firm, warm bond had been established between the Flyers and their fans. And when they won the Stanley Cup—after just seven years in the National Hockey League—a city's emotions spilled over like never before."

Clarke marveled at the size of the two parades.

"When so many people come out to cheer you, you feel you're on top of the world," he said. "Maybe that's as close to heaven as we'll ever get."

After Parade II, Coach Shero said he was "the luckiest guy in the world. I've had three lucky days—the day I got married, last year when we won, and last night" when they successfully defended their championship.

The second parade followed a Cup-clinching 2–0 win in Buffalo, with the Flyers scoring both goals in the final period.

Beat writer Jack Chevalier was poetic in his game story for the *Bulletin*, starting his account like this:

"Love is lovelier the second time around;

"Much more beautiful with both feet on the ground.

"And so is the Stanley Cup.

"The fabulous Flyers, playing their game with character and discipline of mature lovers, and led by a romantic Frenchman named Bernard Marcel Parent, won hockey's grandest prize for the second straight year last night..."

Streakers Go Wild

Joe Watson remembers lots of streakers at the second Cup parade, and nude women climbing poles to get a better view. (All told, about 15 people were arrested during the day, though not all were for public nudity.)

"My mother and an aunt came down from Smithers [in British Columbia] for the parade, and they were hiding their eyes," Watson said.

A young woman had a No. 7—in honor of Bill Barber—proudly displayed on one of her butt cheeks.

"She was climbing a pole as we went by," Barber said. "My wife, God bless her, was pregnant at the time with my daughter. It probably wasn't the most comfortable ride for her. God bless her heart." (Barber's wife, Jenny, died of lung cancer in 2001. She was 48, and her husband treasures all the memories he has of her.)

The 1975 parade ended at the since-demolished JFK Stadium. As the floats entered the stadium and drove around the track, young women lifted their halter tops to greet the players.

"So, we yell to one of the drivers, 'Go around again!'" right winger Gary Dornhoefer said.

Parent, the goalie who had shutouts in the Cup-clinching wins in 1974 and 1975, was on a float next to Mayor Rizzo in the second championship parade.

They were waving and interacting with people. Every once in a while, Parent noticed that Rizzo seemed distracted as he glanced up in the air.

"Frank, what the hell are you looking at?" Parent asked.

Rizzo: "I'm looking for snipers."

"Well, you're on your own, buddy," said Parent, who moved to another part of the float.

Broadcaster Bruised

Lauren Hart, now the Flyers' anthem singer, was seven years old at the first parade. She remembers being with her family in the lead convertible. The Flyers wanted her father, broadcaster Gene Hart, to get through the route first so he could address the crowd when the parade ended.

Lauren's younger brother, Brian, was among those in the car, and the parade was a few days before his fourth birthday.

"For years, my brother thought everybody was there to celebrate his birthday," Lauren said.

Lauren sat on the convertible's front windshield during the parade.

"It was just a sea of people, and people out of their minds" with joy, she said. "I was just in awe. You know, I just thought it was the most magnificent thing I had ever seen in my life. Again, there were no barriers, so people were right up on the cars. They're slapping my dad on the shoulder, shaking hands. And at the end of the parade, he was bruised up and down his side from really friendly people who patted him" with congratulations.

Her brother has similar memories.

"I remember the commotion," Brian said. "I remember my dad's arm being shockingly black and blue from his shoulder to his upper arm. There wasn't anything blocking the people. The crowd was right there. And when thousands of people keep slapping your shoulder, you're going to get bruised."

Lauren said "everybody on that parade route wanted to congratulate every single one of those guys. That was just an incredible moment."

She and her brother were also in the second Cup parade.

"They had everybody up higher on flatbeds and it wasn't the same," she said.

But it was still wildly exciting.

Still Heroes

Five decades after they became the city's darlings, the players are still recognized, still adored.

Barber lives part of the year in Florida. No matter. Transplanted Philadelphians find him.

"I'll be walking through a grocery store or wherever, and someone will come up to me and say, 'You're Bill Barber, aren't you?'" he said. "It's amazing that to this day, 50 years later, they still come up to you. It's cool. The fans are just absolutely awesome."

Barber, a Hall of Fame winger who also was the Flyers' head coach in the early 2000s and later worked in the front office, said he "loved playing in Philadelphia because the fans made you accountable. All you had to do was show the effort. You're going to have some games that are better than others, but if you just played with honesty and did the very best job you can, you're going to be loved and respected forever."

The Flyers were also respected because they connected to the people. They were at more charity events than any group of pro athletes in the city. They played in benefit softball games in Southeastern Pennsylvania and South Jersey, drawing thousands. They were regular guys who sat at local pubs and talked about life with people on either side of their barstool.

"They were out and about in the community," said Jody Clarke, Bobby's oldest daughter. "They were so present and so many people knew them or had met them or had hung out with them in a bar somewhere. They weren't distant in an ivory tower. They were just amongst Philadelphians."

They embodied the city's blue-collar makeup, and they never put on airs or made anyone else feel inferior.

"So, you were seeing people you cared about do this," Lindy Snider said of the love affair between the city and its hockey players—and their championships. "And it felt like everybody's win. That parade. It didn't feel like the team won; it felt like we won, as an entire community."

The team had "come to embody the city in a way. They were underdogs," Lindy said. "And to me, it was seamless the way the city saw themselves and the team saw themselves. And I think my dad recognized this very much. Philly is scrappy and we had a scrappy team. Who else would go out and embrace the name Broad Street Bullies?"

The fans loved the nickname, created by Chevalier, who covered the team for the *Bulletin*. Editor Pete Cafone put the nickname in a headline, and it grew to epic proportions.

Around the Philadelphia area, the Flyers' popularity after the first Cup enabled many of the players to be hired as spokesmen for products and services.

Bobby Clarke did advertisements for Jack Lang clothes and Kardon Chevrolet, among many others.

Gary Dornhoefer hammed it up for Alluvium, an upscale housing development in South Jersey. Bernie Parent promoted Industrial Valley Bank. And even backup goalie Bobby Taylor got promotional work, touting the carpet and drapes at Finished Floors.

Rick MacLeish, known as "10 to 2" because of the way he tilted his head like the hands on a clock were at 1:50, posed next to sports cars for the Matt Slap dealership, and Dave Schultz promoted Canada Dry Ginger Ale, Barry's Castle Hair Designers, and men's clothes for Fleet's.

MacLeish, Schultz, Dornhoefer, and broadcaster Hart also promoted Haddon Travel and took vacation trips with fans willing to pay $635 to go to Hawaii for two weeks, or $299 to travel to Puerto Rico for a week.

And on and on.

If you were a Stanley Cup champion Flyer, you were treated like a king—then and 50 years later.

"I was told that within five years after I got out of the game, nobody would know who I am," Schultz once said. "That's not the case. Philadelphia will always remember those Cup years."

At the turn of the century, the *Philadelphia Daily News* ran a special section that polled fans on numerous sports topics, including the city's best sports team, uniform, and nickname.

The 1973–74 and 1974–75 Flyers, their jerseys, and "The Hammer" and "Broad Street Bullies" were among the winners. All won by decisive margins.

Those teams are a huge part of Philadelphia sports lore, and their accomplishments have become more magnified—and more appreciated—as each year passes and the Flyers still search for another Stanley Cup.

And another Cup parade.

CHAPTER 8

FRED SHERO: QUIRKY, CEREBRAL, IMMERSED IN HOCKEY UNTIL THE END

FRED SHERO DIAGRAMMED a hockey play while on his deathbed.

That is the essence of the cerebral coach with the quirky personality. Hockey was his life.

Shero, who coached the Philadelphia Flyers to two Stanley Cups and three straight Finals appearances, died after a battle with lung cancer at age 65 in 1990.

"I visited him the day before he passed," said defenseman Joe Watson, 50 years after the Philadelphia Flyers won their first Stanley Cup in 1974. "And he had a little piece of paper and he's diagramming a play for me. We're talking about life and death [hanging over Shero]. He's on his deathbed and he's trying to diagram a little play for me with a pencil. Wow. Never forgot that."

Shero, who wore thick glasses and was a studious-looking man, was a student of the game. He coached the Flyers long before the Internet, long before VCRs, DVDs, and streaming services were around. So, he'd go down to his basement and listen to an opposing team's game on the radio and fill up his big yellow legal pad with the lines, pairings, goalies, and assorted notes that might help him in the future.

Now, teams spend millions of dollars on elaborate scouting techniques. Shero just needed a pad and paper.

"If you could look inside Freddy's brain, you would find a miniature hockey rink," his wife, Mariette, once said.

Shero was known as "Freddy the Fog." There are two theories as to how he got the nickname.

Theory No. 1: When he played defense for the St. Paul Saints minor-league team, a game was called because of fog in the rink. Shero, however, was bewildered. He claimed he could see the puck. His teammates started calling him The Fog.

Theory No. 2: Shero could seem distant and distracted. He appeared deep in thought when trying to converse with him. Hence, The Fog.

The latter theory applies to his years with the Philadelphia Flyers, and his players loved him like a father. His dedication to coaching and his innovative techniques made his players want to please him.

"I really, really liked Freddy," said Bobby Clarke, the captain and inspirational leader of Shero's powerhouse teams. "He was really an intellect, but you didn't have a close relationship with him because he didn't talk very much.... I think I had a reasonably good relationship with him—as good as anybody's—because I was the captain and got to talk to him once in a while."

Clarke paused.

"But he reached a level of a coach that, when he said something, everybody listened, and everybody tried to do it," Clarke said five decades after Shero directed the underdog Flyers to their first Cup. "It takes a really good coach and a really good man to be able to get that out of 20 athletes, where they all sit and listen and believe what you say and try to do it. He reached that level.

"We don't win a Stanley Cup without Bernie [Parent, the goalie], and we don't win without Freddy."

When Parent won a car for being named the MVP of the 1974 playoffs, he gave the automobile to Shero.

"They know damn well I'll cheat for them. I'll steal for them. I'll lie for them. I'll suffer for them," Shero said at the time.

Doesn't Like the Attention

After the Flyers won their first Cup, Shero said there was a drawback: He couldn't go anywhere without being recognized.

"I can't even go into a bar anymore," he told one of the Flyers' beat writers, Jack Chevalier. "I like to drink in peace."

The coach celebrated the Flyers' first Cup by going down to his finished basement for half an hour to process things.

"I tried to decide what more I could have done for this team," he said.

A week later, he was in Moscow, trying to learn more about the game and studying the Soviet system of training young hockey players.

He even learned about a system where blood was removed from a player's body and reinjected to give them more stamina.

Shero found it interesting, but the system was never used on the Flyers. But he was happy to incorporate several of Russia's drills he learned from famed Soviet coach Anatoly Tarasov.

The coach and his wife, Mariette, spent three weeks in Russia.

"He really respected their style," said Ray Shero, Fred's son, who was the general manager of the Pittsburgh Penguins when they won the Stanley Cup in 2009. "And not just their style, but everything. They were so advanced with their off-ice conditioning and their skill development. Back at Penn's Class of '23 rink, they [the Flyers]...started doing all this training with ropes and stuff. There were a lot of different drills."

Shero would "go to seminars with Tarasov, the famous Russian coach, and get information from him," defenseman Jimmy Watson said.

During tournaments, Ray Shero said, the Russians' pregame drills were a lot more sophisticated than those of other countries.

"The Soviets would be flying around the ice and doing all kinds of different drills, and they were always in motion," he said. "And even in my dad's hockey camps—I would go as a kid—it was the same type of thing. I mean, I don't know how many drills I screwed up. I had no idea where I was going. It was like, what the heck is going on here?"

Flyers forwards Gary Dornhoefer and Bill Clement worked the camps with Shero, Ray Shero said.

The elder Shero would talk about stickhandling, and then pull an egg out of his pocket.

"I'm like 10 or 11 years old, and I'm thinking we're having scrambled eggs or something," Ray Shero said.

The egg was part of stickhandling drills and trying to get the players to develop soft hands.

"If you break the egg, that's not good," Fred Shero told the kids.

The ice got messy.

"He put the eggs out for the campers, and I'm telling you, there was yolk all over the ice," said Ray Shero, smiling at the memory. "I'm chopping the thing up, and my dad's shaking his head."

"A winner makes commitments; a loser makes promises."
—Fred Shero

Fred Shero loved the Russians' training regimen but wasn't impressed with the country when he visited in 1974, saying the atmosphere reminded him of Canada in the late 1930s. "They have lines for everything," he said at the time.

When the Flyers faced the Russians in 1976 at the Spectrum, Shero took extra pride in the matchup. Shero, the son of immigrants who fled Russia and moved to Winnipeg to avoid religious persecution, wanted to show them that his system could conquer the mighty Red Army.

He was right. Shero, using both his NHL and Russian systems, directed the Flyers to a 4–1 win that wasn't as close as it looked. The Flyers controlled all facets of the game from the first drop of the puck.

> "I do not believe you can do today's business with yesterday's methods and be in business tomorrow."
> —Fred Shero

Shero's Atlanta Mystery

Beating the Russians was one of Shero's most memorable wins, but there was one important victory he missed during the Flyers' 1974 playoff run. That was their series-clinching 4–3 overtime win over Atlanta on April 14. Dave Schultz scored the winner as the Flyers swept the quarterfinal series, four games to none, and advanced to play the gifted New York Rangers in the Stanley Cup semifinals.

Shero missed the Game 4 win in Atlanta because he had to fly back to Philadelphia after getting involved in an apparent bar scuffle late on a Saturday night. The Flyers didn't play that night.

"He claimed he walked into a telephone pole," defenseman Jimmy Watson said.

The story Clarke said he heard was this: Someone in the bar said something negative about the Flyers, and Shero went after him. A onetime boxer, Shero suffered a broken right thumb, a gash on his left arm that required six stitches, and several smaller cuts and bruises on his face. His glasses were shattered.

To this day, no one knows what the other combatant(s) looked like.

"Freddy drank lots," Clarke said in 2023, "and supposedly someone was saying something bad about the Flyers and Freddy took offense to it. And he was by himself and gets into a fight and gets beat up."

The next day, there was a meeting in Shero's hotel room.

According to Joe Watson, the room was disheveled. A lamp and phone were on the floor, the couch was on its side. It looked like the fight had continued in his room.

"I was like, *Holy shit!*" Watson said.

His teammates don't remember the room being that way. They remember assistant coach Mike Nykoluk—who would coach Game 4 in Atlanta on Sunday night—leading the meeting. Shero, according to forward Bill Clement, was in his hotel bedroom, door locked, while the players gathered for a meeting in the living-room portion of the coach's suite.

"We were all crowded in there, and Mike Nykoluk went down and got a key from the front desk and went into Freddy's room," Clement said. "Freddy's lying in a pool of blood. He had a huge gash on his arm full of stitches. His face was fucked up."

Nykoluk walked back into the living room.

"Meeting's over, guys," he said. "I've got to get some help for Freddy."

Even Shero's son, Ray, doesn't know the details about the Atlanta incident. His dad never talked to him about it. He also kept it a secret from all the players.

Ray Shero remembers going to church with his mom and his brother, Jean-Paul, and then heading to Philadelphia International Airport to get his dad.

"We picked him up and my mom's driving, which was unusual, because my dad always drove," Ray said. "And I'm in the backseat thinking, *Shit, we're driving over the Walt Whitman Bridge. Mom hates driving over the bridge.* And I'm looking at my dad. He looks like hell. He looked all beat up. He's got a bandage over his eye. I mean, all his knuckles were kind of [scraped]. I was 12 years old, and I don't know why, but I never asked him what the hell happened. If I had a redo today, I would say, 'Dad, what the hell happened?' But I'm pretty sure he would have looked back and wouldn't have told me what happened, trust me."

Fred Shero didn't recall much about the fight, which has also been described as a mugging.

"I remember the word 'animal' upset me," he told reporters at the time.

His memory, he said, was foggy about what had happened.

All that is known is that Shero went for a walk shortly before midnight near the Hyatt Regency Hotel, where the team was staying in Atlanta. Shero frequently took solo strolls late at night on the road, usually with deep hockey thoughts running around his mind.

One report said Shero was assaulted by two men. Shero couldn't confirm or deny it.

He usually got up at 7:00 AM. The morning after his incident, however, he didn't wake up until 11:00 AM. He looked in the mirror and couldn't believe that his face was battered.

He called Joe Kadlec, the Flyers' public relations whiz, and gave him a request.

"Get me some cigarettes and a doctor."

With Shero gone, the Flyers clinched the quarterfinal series in Atlanta with assistant Nykoluk behind the bench. Schultz's overtime goal capped a comeback from a 3–0 deficit.

> "There are three things worth having in this world: courage, good sense, and caution. Forget caution. Let's go like hell!"
>
> —Fred Shero

Trailing 3–0, Schultz gave the Flyers momentum as he pounded Bryan Hextall in a fight. Much later, he won the game by finishing off a two-on-one feed from Clarke.

"I just told the players they should win it for the guy who should have been behind the bench," Nykoluk said after the dramatic victory.

"Mike said we owed the man something," Clarke said, "and obviously we do."

They team boarded a plane and arrived at Philly's airport the next morning, greeted by 3,000 fans.

The previous year, Shero's first season with the Flyers, Philadelphia had missed making the playoffs in painstaking fashion. Gerry Meehan's long shot beat goalie Doug Favell with four seconds left in regulation, costing the Flyers a playoff spot.

"Me and my brother cried when that happened," Ray Shero said. But Fred Shero didn't take that devastating loss home with him. Never showed his sons that, on the inside, he was crushed.

The next day, Ray Shero remembers walking to his fourth-grade class.

"That," he said, "was my 'Welcome to Philadelphia' moment. I'm totally distraught, and some kid in the playground before school starts sees me and yells, 'Hey Shero, your old man and Favell blew it.'"

A few weeks later, Ed Snider and GM Keith Allen met with Shero.

The agenda: What were Shero's plans for improving the team next season?

Shero surprised them.

"I need help," he said.

"What?" Snider replied.

"I need another coach."

Shero left the room. Allen sipped on his coffee and looked at Snider.

"Are you fucking kidding me?" Snider said. "Should we fire this guy now or when he gets home? Or what do we do?"

"Ed, seriously, we've got to give him a chance," Allen said.

Snider: "No one's got an assistant coach? This guy, he needs help. Holy Christ."

But Allen talked Snider into it. Nykoluk was hired. He was the NHL's first full-time assistant and became a big part of the Flyers' success before Shero got the New York Rangers job in 1978 and took Nykoluk with him.

The Rangers got to the Stanley Cup Finals in Shero's first season. He later said leaving the Flyers was the biggest mistake of his life.

Shero as a Dad

Fred Shero was shy and guarded, but not the recluse that some people have made him out to be, Ray Shero said.

"You could be a stranger, and if you struck up a conversation with him, he was very engaging," Ray said. "I've had people come up to me over the years and say, 'Man, I had a beer with your dad.' And I'm like, 'How did you know him?' And they'd say they didn't know him, but the Flyers were in town, and they introduced themselves and talked for two hours."

He would watch Ray's Little League games in Cherry Hill from the outfield fence and was always in friendly conversations with the other parents.

At home, he enjoyed simple things, like reading and gardening. He thought about becoming a lawyer down the road.

Shero was proud of his native city, Winnipeg, and was a highly respected boxer in the Canadian Navy. He would take his sons to Monday-night fights at the Spectrum and watch boxers like Bennie Briscoe, among others.

Earlier in his career, Shero was a scrappy defenseman for the New York Rangers from 1947–48 to 1949–50, and in 1949 he fought the legendary Gordie Howe to a draw. Hockey historian Stan Fischler wrote that he doesn't recall Howe ever losing a fight, "but he didn't win that one."

A man's man, Shero also could be a softy. He was kind and patient around the house, and never pushed his kids into athletics, only insisting that they get a college education.

After home games on school nights, he would return home late and go right to his "sleeping" children.

"I'd listen to or watch the games, and my dad would get home at maybe 1:00 in the morning," Ray Shero said. "I would always try to stay up. And I'm supposed to be sleeping because I had school the next day. But every time he would come in, I could hear the door opening, and of course I pretend I'm sleeping. I was in the first bedroom; my brother was in the second. He'd always open the door, come in and rub my head and give me a kiss and say goodnight."

The boss of the Broad Street Bullies, a man whose face was mangled in a long-ago fight that he took to his grave, also had a sweet, gentle side.

Advice from Clarke

From time to time, Shero leaned on Clarke, the team's captain, for advice.

Example: Game 3 of the 1975 Stanley Cup Finals in Buffalo.

"In warmups, Clarkie's skating beside me and says, 'You've got to have a good game tonight,'" Clement said. "I said, 'Well, I plan to. I'm going to do my best.'"

Clarke: "I'm the reason you're playing. Freddy asked me if he should play you or [Orest] Kindrachuk. And I said, 'Against Buffalo, dress Billy because he's a better skater.'"

Said Clement: "So basically, he told me it was his decision to play me."

Clement had no points and was minus-1 in the game, a 5–4 overtime loss in Buffalo. Kindrachuk replaced him in Game 4, a 4–2 Flyers defeat.

In Game 6, Clement returned to the lineup, which also included Kindrachuk. (Terry Crisp sat out, despite having two assists in the previous game.) With 2:47 left, Kindrachuk set up Clement's tally, giving the Flyers a two-goal cushion in what turned out to be a series-clinching 2–0 win.

Clement said Shero was a one-of-a-kind coach.

"A lot of people say he was quirky; he was a genius," Clement said. "I mean, he was an introvert—very bright, very funny—but he also was a pioneer."

Besides trying to learn all he could and going to Russia to incorporate some of the Soviets' techniques, Shero was the first to hire a full-time assistant and the first to have morning skates, and he and his staff and players watched lots of videotape, which was rarely used as a teaching tool in those days. He liked to show players on a struggling line some videotapes of their shifts and what needed correcting.

"He got credit for being the first guy to watch video" and use it as a teaching tool, Clement said, adding there is more to the story.

"Well, there was an old VCR in the room where the beer was kept," he said. "That's where the warm Schaefer was. Freddy would be in there drinking warm Schaefer beer all day watching tapes, so he deserves credit for that, but there was an ulterior motive."

Shero loved his beer, warm or cold. He kept two things in his briefcase: a yellow legal pad and four cans of Schaefer.

Under Shero, the players who were traded "were the guys who had no discipline and couldn't give a shit about curfew," Clement said. "Freddy wanted athletes he could respect—not demand respect from them, but players who wanted to win."

Shero's defensive system was so good, Parent said, "I could put my stick and my gloves on the net, for God's sake. We never made mistakes because we were good to begin with, but we had a fantastic system we practiced every day. We had five ways to come out of our zone, and we would practice it 30, 40 minutes at the start of each practice. And if someone made a mistake, he wouldn't embarrass you in front of everybody."

"Take the shortest route to the puck carrier
and arrive in ill humor."
—Fred Shero

"He did more in the 10 years he coached than some guys did in 30 years," Joe Watson said. "People never talked about systems in the '70s, but when Freddy came along, he instituted systems."

Watson said when the Flyers won their first Cup, "we had maybe three what you would call superstars on our team; the rest of us were plumbers. Boston had about 10, 12 superstars. But Freddy said, 'Fuck, man. We've got two arms and two legs like everybody else, and may the best man win.' And that's the way we looked at it, because, you know, we weren't great skaters. Our defense was big and slow sometimes. But we had my brother [Jimmy] and Tommy Bladon and Moose Dupont, and they were good skaters on defense. But for the most part, we were just plumbers out there."

Shero, Watson said, told the Flyers if they expertly managed six regions of the ice, they would win. He was referring to the four corners and the two net areas.

"That's what you have to control," Watson said, "and Freddy was right. And we believed whatever Freddy said."

Shero also instructed his players to dump the puck into Bobby Orr's corner as much as possible to wear out the superstar. As the series went on, Orr got worn down. The strategy worked.

Ed Van Impe, the steady defenseman who excelled at clearing bodies from in front of the net, once said Shero didn't make the players fit into his system. Instead, he analyzed the players' strengths and worked out a plan that utilized what everybody did best. "A masterful piece of coaching," Van Impe called it.

Right winger Don Saleski said people are mistaken if they think the Flyers won Cups primarily because of their toughness.

"We won because of our system," he said. "We practiced it over and over and over."

Shero, who went into the Hockey Hall of Fame posthumously in 2013, had a human side with his players.

A deep thinker, he spent 13 years as a minor-league coach before being hired by the Flyers in 1971, and the long bus rides gave him lots of time to develop a philosophy about the game. With the Flyers, he would write notes and slip them to his players, trying to get the most out of them.

"Freddy was the first coach I ever had who didn't try to make us feel like we were subhuman if we lost," Clement said. "Every other coach I ever had knew one style of coaching. And it was always with the whip. Freddy coached with sugar as much as he did salt. I never heard Freddy embarrass one player in front of anybody else. If he wanted to talk to you, he would take you aside. Other coaches would just scream at you in front of your teammates. They didn't give a shit if they belittled you."

Between periods, Shero would point out a mistake and would stretch the truth because he didn't want to single anyone out for their poor play.

"For instance, he would say, 'First it was [Rick] MacLeish, then Clement, then Crisp," Clement said. "He would always name three players that were doing something incorrectly, but there was really only one guy. And you knew when it was you."

Shero allowed his players to keep their self-esteem intact.

"Freddy really loved his players," Clement said. "And that was different than most coaches."

And the players loved him.

"He was 20 years ahead of his time," André "Moose" Dupont, who played for Shero in juniors and with the Flyers, said on the *My Dad Used to Play Hockey* podcast in 2021. "I loved the man. He became a second father to me and was probably the reason I got traded to the Flyers."

"Freddy was a gentleman, and if you got him one on one, he was just wonderful to talk to because of all the knowledge he had," Jimmy Watson said. "He was a trailblazer for the league."

Because he didn't want his players roaming around other cities, Shero held 11:00 PM hotel meetings the night before a road game. "That way, he made sure he got everybody out of the bars," Jimmy Watson said.

Shero also had a dry sense of humor, and he kept his players on their toes.

Cigarette, Anyone?

A handful of the Flyers smoked cigarettes, including Clarke, Reggie Leach, MacLeish, Ross Lonsberry, Dupont, and Clement.

Between periods of home games, many players went into a Spectrum players' bathroom and lit up a smoke.

"Now, Freddy was a smoker as well," Clement said. "But we'd go in there and fire up, and when the door opened, you could see who was coming in."

Cue Brownsville Station's "Smokin' in the Boys Room," which was a big hit in 1973.

The players probably felt like they were in high school, looking out for a teacher to crash their cigarette party.

"Someone would give us a heads-up. 'Hey, Freddy's coming.'" Clement said. "So, we'd throw the cigarettes in the toilet and flush them."

The players would hide in the bathroom stalls, but smoke engulfed the tiny room, which had a hard tile floor.

During one game, Shero went in the smoky room between periods.

"You guys think I'm stupid?" he asked. "You think I really don't know you're in there smoking? For God's sake, go and smoke in the room at the other end of the locker room. You're going to dull your skates in here. Go over to the other room. There's carpet at the other end."

Clement said he and his teammates were expecting to be reprimanded.

"We thought, *Oh shit. Here it comes. He's going to give us shit about smoking.* And he just wanted us to be comfortable and have a seat where there's carpet" to protect their blades.

Clement was asked why the smoking didn't affect their performance on the ice.

"We were the Broad Street Bullies," he cracked.

Clement, known as "Claremont" to his teammates and a deep thinker who subscribed to *Psychology Today* during his playing days, said it's "amazing the punishment the human body can take and still perform. But one of the key elements to being able to smoke and produce in a sport like hockey is its anaerobic demand. It's not really an aerobic demand, although there is that quality. But it's 60 seconds [on the ice] all out. Recover. Or 35, 40 seconds all out. Recover. And I had gifted lungs. I mean, I would smoke all summer, but I quit halfway through my career. Once I left the Flyers, I quit. I would train some before coming to camp, and the veterans would just be screaming at me, 'Claremont, slow the fuck down. You're making us look horrible. Slow down.' They were taking 10 days, two weeks to get in semi-good shape, and I was just ripping around the ice. I could get into shape pretty easily."

Shero Got "In Your Head"

Bob Kelly, a bruising winger who would bounce off players like an out-of-control pinball, said Shero's practices were never boring.

"Freddy challenged us," he said. "Sometimes, he'd write stuff on the board, and it was like, *What the hell does that mean?* And Rick MacLeish was like, 'Can you explain that to me?' But you know, Freddy just had a way of getting in your head. And once everybody got comfortable [with him], Freddy settled in. We were lucky to play as many years together as we did."

Kelly recalled a drill that the team was doing in practice, and Clarke, the captain, challenged him.

"Freddy, this drill makes absolutely zero sense. It's stupid, stupid, stupid."

Shero: "I've been waiting for somebody to come and tell me that."

The drill ended.

Shero rarely got upset. But he didn't like complainers. Deal with it. That was his mantra.

Take the game in the Forum against the Kings in Los Angeles, for instance. The air conditioner wasn't working, and the temperature was in the high 80s at ice level.

"The ice was really slushy and wasn't good at all," Saleski recalled. "We were all complaining about how hot it was."

Between the first and second periods, Shero addressed his players.

"I'm tired of hearing you guys talk about how hot it is in here," he said. "The next guy who complains about the heat is getting fined $500."

"That was a lot of money back then," Saleski said.

When the second period started, Joe Watson was on the first shift. When he came back to the bench, he was sweating profusely.

"Jesus Christ, it's hot in here," Watson said.

The players on the bench looked at Watson and Shero.

Watson, without skipping a beat, made a swift recovery.

"But Freddy," he said, "that's just the way we like it."

Shero once used MacLeish as a "stool pigeon" to make a point to him and his teammates.

MacLeish, a center who in 1972–73 became the youngest player (23 years old) in NHL history to score 50 goals in a season, was a smooth skater with a dynamic wrist shot. Clarke called him the most talented player on the Flyers during their Stanley Cup-winning days.

But MacLeish also could have a lazy streak and would coast during some games.

Shero wanted him to develop better habits—and also wanted his team to not take any shifts off. So, one day prior to a playoff game, Saleski said, Shero walked into the locker room with a pail of water and plopped it on a table. He asked MacLeish to roll up his sleeve and put his hand in the bucket.

"Now take it out," Shero said.

MacLeish complied.

"See the hole that's left?" Shero asked.

MacLeish: "There's no hole there, Freddy."

Shero: "Well, that's how much we're going to miss you when you're gone."

"Freddy was sending a message to the entire team. It wasn't to Ricky in particular," Saleski said. "Ricky was a stool pigeon because he knew he'd fall for it."

The message: no player is bigger than the team.

Shero could also deliver messages in odd ways. Example: the Cup-clinching win over Boston in Game 6 of the 1974 Finals.

The Flyers had a 1–0 lead heading into the third period. Between the second and third periods, Shero walked into the locker room. The players were expecting Shero to make a speech. After all, this was the biggest 20 minutes of their careers, many thought.

Years later, Terry Crisp, a center who was a penalty-killing specialist on that team, said Shero picked up a piece of chalk and thought for about a minute, put down the chalk, and walked out of the room.

"That was probably the greatest non-said speech in history," Crisp told the *Tampa Bay Times*. "When he did that, it did more for our team than the biggest rah-rah speech."

When the players left the locker room for the start of the final period, "we didn't walk out on the ice. We floated," Crisp said. "In Freddy's own way, he said, 'Boys, what more can I tell you? What more can I say? What more can I do.'"

The Flyers won 1–0. Shero's bizarre locker-room appearance worked.

"Win today and we walk together forever."
—Fred Shero's blackboard message
before the Flyers clinched
the 1974 Stanley Cup

Savors Cup in His Own Way

After the Flyers won Stanley Cups in 1974 and 1975, Shero didn't stay on the ice for long. He went into the locker room and quietly enjoyed the championship satisfaction.

The second Cup was won in Buffalo, and as Shero walked from the ice to the locker room, assistant coach Nykoluk asked his boss to stay on the ice.

"Please stay out for the Cup, eh, Freddy?" Nykoluk said.

"The players won it. It's for them," Shero said.

Shero went to a corner stall, sat down next to his briefcase, and patted his jacket pockets in search of a cigarette.

According to the *Philadelphia Inquirer*, he accepted a smoke from a reporter, grabbed a cold beer, and began drinking.

That was his way of celebrating.

Three years ago, in the same locker room and in the final game of his first season with the Flyers, he had sat crying. The Flyers had blown a playoff berth by losing in Buffalo in the season finale. The Sabres scored the game-winner on a long shot with four seconds left.

Shero was crushed. He later called it the worst moment in his career.

Now he was at the pinnacle. The coach of the two-time Stanley Cup champions.

"I felt bad for the players back then," he told reporters about the disastrous loss in 1972. "It was a hard thing for them to have to experience. But I knew then, if I wasn't fired, that we were on our way. I knew then that with the system, we could be champions."

Surprisingly, Shero said he was more satisfied with the second Cup, won in Buffalo, than the first one.

"We proved it wasn't a fluke, and I coached here for three years," he said.

He was referring to his extremely successful three-year stint coaching the AHL's Buffalo Bisons. He directed them to a championship in his last season there in 1969–70. His last two teams went a combined 81–35–30.

But when the Sabres started their franchise the next year, it was George "Punch" Imlach, not Shero, who was hired as their head coach. Imlach had coached Toronto for 11 years and had won four Stanley Cups, so he had lots of credibility.

"I have thousands of friends here. I enjoyed it here," Shero said after the Flyers' title-clinching win in Buffalo. "I come back every summer. I always said I wanted to win a Stanley Cup in Buffalo. I didn't get the chance when the time came in, and I thought I should have had the chance."

Flyers fans are glad he didn't get that opportunity. After all, Philadelphia might still be looking for its first Stanley Cup if Shero hadn't been hired by the Flyers.

As for Buffalo, the "Fog" has not lifted. The Sabres still had never won a Cup as the 2025–26 season approached.

CHAPTER 9

DAVE SCHULTZ: FORMER BRAWLER FIGHTS THROUGH TOUGH TIMES

A LITTLE OVER 50 YEARS AGO, bruising left winger Dave Schultz was part of a Philadelphia Flyers team that shocked the NHL and won the franchise's first Stanley Cup championship.

He was also the NHL's bad boy.

Schultz fought his way into America's consciousness and collected penalties at a record-setting pace.

Oh, and he showed he wasn't just a skilled fighter, wasn't just someone who helped give his teammates room on the ice because opponents feared his physicality.

He scored 20 goals in the regular season in 1973–74, added the game-winner in the Stanley Cup quarterfinal-round clincher in Atlanta, then helped set up arguably the most important goal in franchise history in Game 2 of the Finals in Boston.

In short, Schultz was a vital part of the Flyers' success, and it's no coincidence that the Broad Street Bullies reached the Stanley Cup Finals in three of his four years in Philadelphia. He also became a fan favorite—his No. 8 jerseys were worn by tens of thousands—and even had a hit song, "The Penalty Box," that topped the area's music charts.

All of that, you might suppose, would bring a lifetime of happiness and financial security to a player who was brash on the ice, quiet off it.

It didn't work out that way, however. Schultz went through difficult times after his NHL career ended.

But no one can take away from his important contributions for the Stanley Cup champion Flyers in 1974 and 1975.

"Dave gave us courage on the road," coach Fred Shero once said.

Schultz was the unofficial bodyguard for Bobby Clarke, the team's captain and star center.

"If you took a cheap shot at Clarkie—and many did before Schultz arrived—you paid a price," said Lou Nolan, the Flyers' longtime public address announcer. "Even without Schultz, Clarke played with a fearlessness that was hard to match. With Schultz, he became even more fearless—if that was possible."

Schultz was the face of the Broad Street Bullies. He led the league in penalty minutes in those seasons—he had 472 in 1974–75, which is still an NHL record five decades later—and sent a message to opponents: If you mess with one of our star players, you will have to deal with me.

He was The Hammer, someone whose mayhem on the ice was usually something he envisioned earlier in the day.

He was also a walking paradox: someone who was a skilled fighter...but despised throwing punches.

For Schultz, it was a mental strain to prepare for each game and visualize going to war with an opponent—whether it was Terry O'Reilly, Keith Magnuson, or whomever—in the hours that led up to the contest.

Truth is, Schultz only fought because it was his role on the team.

"Fighting," Schultz said 50 years after the Flyers won their first Cup, "was totally different than me as a human being."

Off the ice, he was soft-spoken and kind, someone who wrote charming letters to his girlfriend (and future wife), Cathy, when he was on the road and working his way toward the NHL.

On the ice, it was if someone pushed an "on" switch, and he became The Hammer.

His eyes would bulge out and the veins in his neck looked like they wanted to erupt. After a fight, he would go to the penalty box "and he was so riled up that you couldn't even talk to him," said Nolan, the public address announcer who sat next to players in the penalty box. "It took him a while to calm down—probably the entire five minutes of his penalty—before he came back to his senses."

Fighting became his art. Schultz would soak his hands in pickle juice to toughen the skin for bouts. Hey, anything to gain an advantage.

Small-Town Roots

Schultz grew up in Waldheim, a tiny, rural town in Saskatchewan that had a population of about 400 when Dave was a youngster. In the 2020s it barely had over 1,000 residents.

"It was a very religious town," Schultz said of his youth. "There were five churches, no bars."

Schultz said "everybody in town read the Bible every day, except my dad, who hated religion. I mean, all my aunts and uncles on that side, they were all Bible thumpers."

His dad, Edgar, who became friendly with the other Flyers' dads when he would visit, was a heavy drinker. (So was Dave after he left hockey.) Dave's grandfather owned a car and tractor dealership and was well known in town.

As a kid, Schultz was reserved.

"If my dad yelled at me, I started to cry," he said.

Schultz smiles softly when talking about his mom.

"She was a wonderful lady. Ukrainian. Her parents couldn't even speak English. In the early 1900s, they were given land to farm to come over from Ukraine."

Schultz grew up in a family that didn't have any modern conveniences.

"Never in my life have I had any money," he said. "We were a very poor family. We lived on a farm. No running water, no electricity, and no indoor plumbing. A two-bedroom house with four kids."

Nearly 50 years after Schultz was one of the key players on a team that gave Philadelphia its first Stanley Cup, the bruising left winger was in a pensive mood.

"I've had quite a life, I guess," he said. "And little of it was good."

After winning two Cups and going to another Final with the Flyers, Schultz was traded to Los Angeles—and he's still bitter about it five decades later. He has been divorced ("dumbest thing I ever did," he said) and gone bankrupt. In 2023 he was gallantly trying to beat alcoholism, attending AA classes.

Life was simpler when Schultz was a youngster and hanging out with his protector, his brother, Ray. They were good hockey players at an early age, especially Dave. Ray was known as "Big Edgar" (after his dad), and Dave was called "Little Edgar."

Kids would pick on "Little Edgar."

"They would tease us, and my brother would do the fighting," Dave Schultz said.

Ray Schultz looked after his younger brother, and he would challenge anyone who picked on Dave. Dave, on the other hand, was never in a fight.

That became wildly ironic because Dave Schultz became the most penalized, brawling player in the NHL. But his penchant for fighting wasn't there when he played junior hockey.

It just wasn't in his nature.

"I was a little chickenshit. Never a fighter," he said of his youth. "I was pretty small until I got to junior, and then I shot up in Grade 9."

Schultz remembers still being bullied at that time and refusing to retaliate.

The left winger said the first fight he remembers getting into—on or off the ice—was when he played for the Salem Rebels in the EHL during the 1969–70 season. Until then, he said, he had been "intimidated very easily." He did well in the fight, so in his next game, he had confidence he could handle himself.

"Some guy ran into one of my teammates, and I went after him," Schultz said. "All of a sudden, people thought I was tough, which nobody ever did before. I got recognition for it. My teammates loved it. Fans loved it."

He started playing with an edge. In 67 games with Salem, he amassed a staggering 356 penalty minutes, along with 32 goals. He became known as Sergeant Schultz.

"I would fight every guy in that league," Schultz said. "And that league was dirty."

While Schultz was starting to make a name for himself in the minors, he was keeping a secret from his family and everyone who was close to him.

When he was 11 or 12 years old, he was molested by one of his Western Canada male neighbors.

No matter how hard he tried, he couldn't get the memory out of his mind.

"That," he said, "will dramatically change anyone."

He paused.

"I never really thought about it until a few years ago," said Schultz, who was 73 when he made the statement, adding he will reveal more details when his book, tentatively called *Hammered by Life,* is published.

He said molestation "can lead to a lot of shit, the drinking, the bad relationships." Schultz said he didn't know how to deal with being molested, and he didn't tell anyone about it until he was 70—nearly 60 years after it happened.

"How much has that affected me? I never really thought about that until a few years ago, but I'm sure it had an impact," he said. "It can fuck up your life."

Schultz was asked if all the fighting he did in the NHL was perhaps because, subconsciously, he believed he was hitting the person who molested him.

"I don't think so," he said. "The molestation lasted only a short period of time."

He said he was talking about it in his seventies with the hope it would help clear his mind and perhaps help someone else who went through a similarly tragic situation.

Longtime Boozer

In the meantime, Schultz was trying to be more proactive with his family. Staying away from booze was his first step.

Schultz was a heavy drinker for parts of four decades after he left the NHL. He wishes he could get those years back and had been sober when his kids were young and impressionable. He said his deepest regret is that he let them down, along with his wife, Cathy.

When Dave was dating Cathy long before he became an NHL villain, she wasn't attracted to him because he played hockey. There were other traits she admired.

"He was sweet, and he could be funny," she said. "Really very funny."

She and Dave would exchange letters when he was on a road trip. It was typical of a young player and the woman he left behind.

"Everybody has the same story," Cathy said. "The guys always had a girlfriend at home. That was the one they ended up marrying really young."

Schultz said he is trying to be a better father and person, trying to develop stronger relationships with his grandkids.

"I'm trying to get to know my grandkids because they don't really know me," he said. "My kids are happy I'm not drinking anymore, but all those years I drank, it took a toll on them.

"You're not a good person when you drink," he said.

Fans Had the Team's Back

Looking back to the championship years with the Flyers, Schultz said, the fans always had the team's back. They were beyond supportive, he said.

And not just inside the percolating, sold-out Spectrum.

"I'd walk into a mall, and within a few minutes, there was a big crowd following me," he said.

The Cup-winning Flyers became rock stars. It sometimes made it difficult to stay levelheaded.

"Fred Shero used to say, 'If your feet are off the ground and your head is in the clouds, you're probably a basketball player,'" Schultz said.

Even 50-plus years after they won the Flyers' first Stanley Cup, people approach Schultz in public places and ask for an autograph or an iPhone photo. Or chat about the Broad Street Bullies days.

That's a nice feeling, he said, but a lot of people ask him to put a fist up. He understands why, and he does it. But it bugs him because he doesn't want to be remembered as just a fighter.

That became evident in a guest column he wrote for the *New York Times* less than two years after he retired from hockey. The story ran under the headline DAVE SCHULTZ: A LETTER TO MY SON ABOUT VIOLENCE.

"I have certain regrets about my position as the hit man of hockey," he wrote. "I became a role model for young players such as yourself.... Pretty soon there were juniors and peewees emulating Dave Schultz instead of Bobby Orr.... If playing hockey means fighting, then take up golf, tennis—anything that stresses skill over simple violence."

After he left hockey, Schultz said one of the best jobs he ever had was as a rink manager for eight years at the Skatium in Haverford Township, Pennsylvania.

Many years later, a man came up to Schultz at the Crab Trap restaurant in Somers Point, near the Jersey Shore, and wanted to reminisce with him about that time. "He was having dinner with his wife, and he said to me, 'Dave, I used to practice hockey at the Skatium; we loved when we saw you there.'"

Schultz smiled. Stuff like that makes him feel good, he said. Much better than when someone asks to have a photo taken with him while he holds up his famous dukes.

Fighter Turns into Singer

While Schultz has had many ups and downs in his life, one of the most unexpected peaks happened when he sang "The Penalty Box" in 1975, and it turned into Philadelphia's No. 1 hit.

Radio stations WFIL and WIBG couldn't play it enough for rabid listeners.

These days, Schultz chuckles at the record and pokes fun at himself as a singer. Even though it was so popular in Philly, he said he only made about $500 when it came out. In the 2020s he was still signing and selling the 45 RPM record on social media, with the help of his ex-wife, Cathy.

The song starts out with a referee's whistle being heard, and an announcer explaining: "Flyers penalty on No. 8, Dave Schultz—two minutes for hooking, two minutes for roughing, five minutes for fighting, and a 10-minute misconduct."

Baby, how long will you keep me in the penalty box?
Baby, I'm wrong, but it's lonely in the penalty box.
I know I broke the rules, but rules are broken by fools.
Baby, how long will you keep me in the penalty box?
Love is like an ice hockey game, sometimes it can be rough.
Girl, you got me so all aflame, I never, never get enough.
You got me charging and holding and hugging, and then you blew the whistle on me.
When are you going to let me go free?
... I know I made you mad, but girl, I ain't all bad.
Baby, how long will you keep me in the penalty box?
Girl, I'm not defending my style, but, girl, you blow my mind.
Every little once in a while, you've gotta leave the rules behind.

Later in the song, Schultz croons:

You've got me hungry for loving, and then you call an offside on me.
Lock the door and then hide the key.

Don't you know how slow go the penalty clocks, with the tickety-tocks in the penalty box.
Baby, how long will you keep me in the penalty box?

Cathy Schultz is still amused by the song's popularity.

"It was the No. 1 song in the area," she said, shaking her head as if she still can't believe it five decades later.

"It was ahead of Elton John's '[Philadelphia] Freedom' song."

Other popular songs at that time included America's "Sister Golden Hair," Alice Cooper's "Only Women Bleed," Captain & Tennille's "Love Will Keep Us Together," Van McCoy's "The Hustle," Harold Melvin's "Bad Luck," Glen Campbell's "Rhinestone Cowboy," and the Eagles' "One of These Nights."

Kal Mann wrote the lyrics for Schultz's song. Mann had co-written the lyrics to Chubby Checker's "Let's Twist Again," Elvis Presley's "(Let Me Be Your) Teddy Bear," and The Dovells' "Bristol Stomp."

Vince Montana, who later helped define the disco-era Philly sound, did the musical arrangement for "The Penalty Box." Montana worked with artists such as The Trammps ("Disco Inferno"), Johnny Mathis, Harold Melvin & the Blue Notes, The O'Jays, The Spinners, and The Stylistics.

Schultz sang the song with far less vigor than he showed in one of his fights. He sang it softly and in a monotone voice.

"I can't sing," he said in 2023. "What I did was, I'd go down to the studio with a six-pack of beer. I'd drink a couple and then start singing."

He even performed on the popular *Mike Douglas Show,* lip-synching the song for viewers. "I actually did it a couple times. Live. Did it with The Dovells, who were good friends with a lot of us," he said.

Mark Stevens, a singer with The Dovells who later married the ex-wife of former Flyers star Reggie Leach, remembers performing with Schultz at various venues, including in Atlantic City. They also did the song together at the Coliseum night club in Voorhees.

"Dave felt comfortable doing it with us," said Stevens, who lives next door to his good buddy, Leach, and his wife near Winnipeg.

It was the uniqueness of the song, not Schultz's voice, that made the record a big hit, Stevens said.

Fans watching Schultz sing "went ballistic. They loved it," said Stevens, whose singing duo retired in 2023, long after it recorded the iconic "Bristol Stomp" and later performed at one of Bill Clinton's inaugural balls.

Stevens became extremely friendly with Schultz when he was the face of the Broad Street Bullies.

"On the ice, he was crazy," Stevens said. "Off the ice, unless we were out drinking with the boys, he was very quiet, very shy. He was not what people thought he would be like."

He said Schultz enjoyed his brief singing career.

"I think he thought it was a hoot," Stevens said. "He gets a chance to hang out with The Dovells. He gets a chance to get up on stage in front of a gazillion freaking people at a casino or another large event, and at that moment, he was a rock star."

Cathy Schultz rolls her eyes when she thinks of her ex-husband singing his hit tune.

"He actually had the nerve to lip sync it on stage in front of actual humans," said Cathy, who is still close friends with Dave. "That's how far the character went."

The character was "The Hammer." No Flyers player was more adored at the time. When Schultz was a guest on a Philadelphia radio talk show in 1974, more than 84,000 busy signals were recorded in 90 minutes.

Seeing her husband—a soft-spoken guy who liked to build model ships, work on the lawn, and put together jigsaw puzzles at home—become so popular as a singer amazed Cathy Schultz.

"It was like, *What's next?* I was like, 'When you tell me you're going to be on a stripper's pole, I'm done,'" she said, laughing at the memory.

Career Skyrockets

Schultz's career rose dramatically after the Flyers selected him in the fifth round (52nd overall) of the 1969 amateur draft. Back then, the draft wasn't as publicized, and Schultz didn't find out he had been selected by the Flyers until he read it in the newspaper the next day.

In his second season with the Quebec Aces in the AHL, Schultz had 14 goals and 382 penalty minutes. The next season (1971–72), he was with the Flyers' new AHL affiliate, the Richmond Robins, and had 18 goals and 392 penalty minutes, along with a one-game call-up from the Flyers.

Along the way, his reputation as a fighter grew. Schultz became a Flyers regular in 1972–73, and like a lot of his teammates, settled in the Roberts Mill Apartments in Maple Shade, New Jersey. The apartments offered a month-to-month lease, which was attractive to the players' families because their visas would expire after the season, and they would have to return to Canada.

Dave and Cathy were married in 1972. Dave was 23; Cathy was 20.

With Dave cracking the Flyers' lineup in the fall of '72, life was good for the newlyweds.

"He was very excited," Cathy said about Schultz getting a full-time role for the first time. "Probably didn't think it was going to last, so it was a pleasant surprise. I mean, the first year we were married, everybody would kid me because I kept a big stack of newspapers in the closet, so that when we got sent down [to the minors], I was ready to pack."

The newspapers were to protect breakable items. But they weren't needed. Schultz was never demoted. He had nine goals, 259 penalty minutes, and a league-leading 20 fights as a rookie, a year that included the Flyers winning a playoff series for the first time in franchise history, beating Minnesota in six games. They would lose to Montreal in the Stanley Cup semifinals, but the seeds to success had been planted.

Cathy Schultz would throw away the newspapers. Her husband was becoming a big part of the Flyers. Philadelphia was where they were going to spend a lot of time.

"It was pretty much a culture shock. I hadn't really been to a [big] city in America," Cathy said. "We had everything we owned in a U-Haul trailer that we had driven from Saskatchewan to here, so we were kind of lost downtown."

They quickly got acclimated. Schultz erupted for 20 goals—it turned out to be the best year of his career—and the Flyers won the Stanley Cup in his second season (1973–74). With Schultz as the fist-swinging leader of the Broad Street Bullies, Philly won the Cup again in 1974–75.

Dave and Cathy bought a house in Cherry Hill, New Jersey. In the summers, they would make the 36-hour drive and stay with their folks in Western Canada. Dave built a family room in the basement of his parents' house. He and his wife would also spend time at her parents' lake cottage.

In the meantime, Schultz had become almost larger than life. There was his tough-guy persona on the ice. There was adulation from the fans, some who wore orange army helmets and paraded around the Spectrum as "Schultz's Army."

There was the unexpected popular record.

"It developed slowly over time, but it definitely became his identity," Cathy said about Dave's fighting.

She thinks that, at the time, Dave enjoyed that identity.

"I think he grew to like it very much," she said. "There was so much adoration."

Schultz, who once had 35 goals in 59 games with the Swift Current Broncos in juniors, said he "could have made the NHL any day of the week" with his talent. "Could I have been as well known as I was? No. The media just took it and ran with it. So, the nicknames came out—The Hammer and the Broad Street Bullies—and that created a lot of publicity."

Cathy had never seen Dave play hockey before they got married. Now, by order of coach Fred Shero, she and all the other wives were told to be at every home game. You must support your man. That was Shero's edict.

"You went to the games unless you were in labor or dead," Cathy said.

She watched her husband brawl on the ice and had to avoid the temptation to cover her eyes.

"Sometimes I felt like it wasn't necessary. I felt like it wasn't him," she said.

She paused.

"And then it *became* him," Cathy added.

Schultz's fight preparation was all consuming.

"I think he came to feel real pressure," Cathy Schultz said, "because before a game, he would say to me, 'I'm trying to prepare myself for so-and-so, who I'm going to have to fight tonight.' Or, 'Who am I going to have to fight tonight?' That kind of thing. So, he thought about it prior to games. Not much discussion about it after games, because it was over. I didn't like him getting hit. I didn't like him hitting people. I used to always think he was going to get hurt. And he used to say, 'The only thing that gets hurt is feelings. Somebody gets their feelings hurt.'"

While Schultz tried to kid about his role as the Broad Street Bullies' enforcer, he would confide to Cathy that he felt pressure each game.

"There was a point where would sometimes say, 'You don't know what this is like when I have to do this,'" Cathy said.

Schultz's most famous fight was his pounding of New York Rangers defenseman Dale Rolfe in Game 7 of the 1974 Stanley Cup semifinals.

While Schultz downplayed the significance of his one-sided win, Shero called it the key to a victory that vaulted the Flyers into their first Cup Final.

With the game scoreless in the opening period, Schultz pummeled Rolfe in front of the New York net. He went after Rolfe after the defenseman had pushed the Flyers' Orest Kindrachuk, who had tried to take the puck away from Rangers goalie Ed Giacomin.

Schultz got in 12 straight punches and, at one point, pulled Rolfe's hair to keep his balance and not fall to the ice. By one count, the 6'1", 195-pound Schultz outpunched Rolfe 17–2. Oddly, no New York teammates rushed to the aid of the 6'4", 210-pound Rolfe.

"The Rangers just watched, and I think that fight spelled the end of them," said Nolan, the Flyers' longtime public address announcer. "That wouldn't have happened with our guys."

Shero said it took something out of the Rangers.

"They didn't do as much hitting after that," he said.

Schultz said the fight "just happened," that it wasn't premeditated and wasn't done to ignite his team.

"We didn't need any spark," he said. "It's Game 7."

In other words, no spark was necessary in a win-or-go-home showdown.

The Flyers eventually won 4–3. They outhustled and outchecked the Rangers and had a lopsided 46–15 shots advantage. Gary Dornhoefer scored two goals, including one that gave Philly a late 4–2 lead and turned out to be the winning tally.

"They won," Giacomin said after the game, "because they were all over us."

Maybe they were inspired by Schultz. Maybe they were just hungrier than the Rangers. Whatever the reason, the Flyers took control after Schultz manhandled Rolfe.

Five decades after the fight, it is still fresh in Cathy Schultz's mind.

"It was very distressing," she said. "I just felt it was super violent and extremely upsetting. There wasn't a proud second there."

After his team was eliminated, Rangers star defenseman Brad Park took a verbal shot at the Flyers.

Park said he was "fed up" with the Flyers' physical style. "I wanted to give it right back, but I decided that if I had to maim somebody to win the Stanley Cup, then it wasn't worth it," he said. "I look around the room and I'm prouder to lose with these guys than I would be winning with another club."

The legend of the Broad Street Bullies was growing.

"Anybody would maim somebody to win the Cup," a laughing Schultz said years later. "[But] I didn't maim anybody. It was just a fight. I felt bad for Dale Rolfe. He wasn't the kind of guy who would drop his gloves by any means. From my perspective, him and Kindrachuk were jostling each other, and I skated over. Rolfe dropped his gloves, and I said, 'I don't know if I want to do this.'"

Schultz cackled.

"Just kidding," he said.

Sad Farewell

Schultz spent four seasons with the Flyers before being dealt to Los Angeles just before the 1976–77 season. The Flyers got second- and fourth-round draft picks in return.

Almost 50 years later, he still had an air of bitterness that GM Keith Allen traded him.

But the NHL had changed some of its rules that seemed aimed at reducing fights. And aimed at the Broad Street Bullies.

In June of 1974, shortly after the Flyers won their first Cup, any penalized player who stalled or complained while going to the penalty box was given an additional two-minute penalty. In addition, a player who fought with tape on his hands (as Schultz did) drew a match misconduct that left his team shorthanded for 10 minutes. There were some other rule changes, including one that gave a player a five-minute major for head-butting.

The changes affected the Flyers more than any team, and meant Schultz was expendable in Allen's eyes.

Cathy Schultz had many of the Flyers players, their wives, and their children at her house for her son Chad's first birthday when she learned Dave had been dealt to Los Angeles. Dave arrived after the party started, having been informed after practice by Allen.

So, Chad's first birthday party turned into a farewell bash for the entire Schultz family.

"It was bittersweet," Cathy said. "We still had some fun…but you're kind of in shock."

She said it wasn't like it is for players in the 2020s, who are financially set for life. Dave Schultz averaged about $50,000 per year during his four seasons with the Flyers.

"We were certainly very comfortable for the time, but we weren't [rich] by any means," Cathy said.

She said players during that time played for pride and for winning the Cup. The money was incidental.

Less than two weeks after being sent to Los Angeles, the Flyers hosted the Kings at the Spectrum. Fans arrived early to greet Schultz with cheers during warmups.

Many brought signs that saluted Schultz, including:

DAVEY—YOU'LL ALWAYS BE THE HAMMER OF OUR HEARTS.

I WANT MY HAMMER BACK, KEITH (ALLEN).

Schultz received applause when he stepped on the ice, but by the end of the game, he was booed because he cross-checked Rick MacLeish—who happened to be one of his closest friends—and slashed André "Moose" Dupont. He also taunted the Flyers as he returned to the bench after a shift.

And, then, Flyers right winger Paul Holmgren beat Schultz in a fight. The fans cheered loudly for the player they called "Homer." There was a new enforcer in town.

The old one, however, would not be forgotten.

"Davey is the player who gave the Broad Street Bullies the personality that the organization carried long after he was gone," Bobby Clarke said. "We had good players, but that personality was a big part of our organization."

Food for Thought

After the trade, Schultz sometimes pondered whether NHL president Clarence Campbell asked the Flyers to deal him and clean up their image. He also believed that one of the reasons he was dealt was because Holmgren was ready to join the team, and besides being a very good fighter, he was a better player than Schultz.

Allen, regarded as one of the NHL's shrewdest general managers and the architect of the Flyers teams that won consecutive Cups, told Schultz he was traded after a practice session.

Schultz had heard the rumors for a while, so he was more disappointed than shocked at the news.

"Why couldn't I have played another four years in Philly?" he said five decades later. "Why would they trade me? What was Keith Allen thinking? Did the league force him? Somebody did."

Schultz said he was puzzled by the answer Allen gave when he asked the general manager why he was traded.

"He said, 'I thought you would get tired of fighting,'" Schultz said. "He knows what's in my head? I'll never forgive him for that. I mean, Stanley Cup Finals, Stanley Cup Finals, Stanley Cup Finals."

He was referring to the Flyers reaching the Finals in each of the last three seasons with Schultz.

Said Schultz: "Logically, three pretty good seasons and then… trade him?"

Nearly a half-century later, Schultz is still hurt by the trade.

"It changed my whole life," he said. "I got traded three times in three years and wasn't making any money."

In earlier years, it should be pointed out, Schultz had warm words for Allen.

Late in Schultz's career, owner Ed Snider wanted to bring him back to the Flyers. He felt Schultz deserved to finish his career with the team he helped win two Stanley Cups.

In Blake Allen's book *Keith the Thief* about his GM dad, Snider's devotion to Schultz was spelled out.

In his foreword, Snider wrote that a few years after the Flyers traded Schultz, he was "pushing and pushing" to bring Schultz back until, finally, Keith Allen erupted.

"You want him so goddamn badly, I'll get him for you," Allen said, according to Snider.

Snider backed off.

"To me, that said, 'You're the owner, but this is against my better judgment,'" Snider said.

Schultz never returned to the Flyers.

When Schultz was inducted into the Flyers Hall of Fame in 2009—a movement spurred by Snider—he thanked Allen in his acceptance speech.

"He drafted me, he saw my talents and my skills, and he sent me to the minor leagues, to the Eastern Hockey League," he said. "It changed the way I played the game."

He played the game with fearlessness, with wide-eyed animation. Schultz would sometimes incite fans as he went to the penalty box after a fight and held his nose. He was either telling the referee the penalty smelled—or telling the fans the player he fought stunk.

Either way, the buildings came alive with noise.

It's not a stretch to say more fans went to hockey games in the 1970s to watch the colorful Schultz than any other player around the league.

Now in his seventies, Schultz remembers how fans packed arenas to watch him and the Broad Street Bullies. So, he is annoyed when he hears comments that he ruined the NHL with his fighting.

"Why would someone say that?" he said. "And they say it all the time."

They don't say it in Philadelphia, of course.

"No, no. Oh, we had great fans," Schultz said. "That was the fun part. And we had a great team, and a great bunch of guys."

Guys who knew they had Schultz to protect them, like his big brother, Ray, did for him while growing up in Western Canada.

Inspired by His Granddaughter

Schultz ended up playing eight NHL seasons, with stops in Philadelphia, Los Angeles, Pittsburgh, and Buffalo.

At 30, he was out of the NHL.

After he retired, the drinking started, and he said it clouded his mind for a few decades.

"A lot of wasted years," he said.

He worked lots of different jobs, including coaching in the minors. Some of the jobs gave him joy, others were done just for the paycheck.

In his seventies, he was living mostly off his Social Security check and a combined $17,000 from an NHL pension ($7,000) and funds from the NHL Players Association ($10,000), he said. He also made a little money from selling memorabilia and speaking engagements, along with a part-time job selling electricity to businesses.

No job brought as much joy as his seasons with the Flyers.

He missed the camaraderie, the laughter, the jokes. He missed being part of a group that had a singular goal.

He also missed Bob Kelly's humor. Kelly was his partner in crime with the Flyers. When Schultz did a standup comedy routine after his playing days ended, a lot of his material came from experiences with Kelly.

"The Hound," Schultz said, "was the funniest guy I ever played with. Personally, I think he knew how to speak better, but he screwed up the words on purpose to be funny."

After hockey, there were some sad times for The Hammer. There was his divorce from a woman he still loved. There was the drinking problem and some business projects that soured.

And there was the tragic death of his beloved granddaughter, Annalise.

Schultz's face becomes animated, his voice gets thick with emotion, and his eyes fill with tears when he talks about Annalise, and how she inspires him and others every day.

She died of brain cancer in 2020 at the age of nine.

Schultz said the heartbreak will never go away for her parents—his son, Chad, and his wife, Jennifer—and their son, Sebastian. Nor will it ever go away for Schultz and his ex-wife, or anyone else in their family.

Because of his drinking, Schultz said, he never grieved Annalise's death until three years after she died.

But he was sober in 2023 and in better touch with his feelings. That spring, he visited his granddaughter's grave for the first time since her burial in 2020.

"Cathy goes all the time and reads her some books," Schultz said of his ex-wife, "...but I hadn't been there."

In 2023 Schultz and Cathy went to Annalise's grave twice in a week, including on their granddaughter's birthday. Schultz told her how much he missed her.

"Annalise was so special, and one of the things that made her so special was her relationship with her dad," Schultz said, tears welling. "They were great buddies. Annalise and her Nanna, Cathy, were also great buddies. That was Cathy's little girl. She used to pick up Annalise from school and do different things with her."

Annalise was the life of a party and was always organizing games and making people laugh. She loved to listen to music, and she lived life to the fullest. She loved baseball, softball, soccer, swimming, and Girl Scouts. She loved playing with her cousins, loved panda bears, loved magic tricks and listening to Bob Marley tunes.

She loved to sing and seemed more attuned to music than sports, said her proud grandfather. "She called me Grandpa—I don't go for this PopPop stuff—and she was a pure joy to be around." Schultz said. "I've got things hanging in my condo that she wrote, and they say Grandpa on the front."

He cherishes those notes and cards.

"When our family would get together for Christmas or Thanksgiving, all the grandkids would put on a little play," Schultz said. "They'd laugh and sing and dance for the adults."

Schultz said those are some of the best memories of his roller-coaster life.

A Half-Century Later, Fans Still in Bullies' Corner

In the 1970s, the Broad Street Bullies "played with emotion, played with physicality, played with urgency," Schultz said.

A half century later, Philadelphia still likes teams that play with that style.

That explains why a few hundred people shelled out $350 a ticket for the Flyers alumni benefit called "Friday Night Fights" on March 8, 2024. The event was sold out, and several former Flyers spoke about their old NHL days. Those players, including Schultz, became known more for their fists and the way they agitated opponents.

The event raised money for Flyers Charities—which supports local families affected by cancer—and at the same time, the fans got to mingle with fans who loved the way the Bullies played the game.

"Sometimes I think the fans appreciated my style more than I did, but that's a whole different topic," Schultz said.

Those in attendance even watched Schultz get on stage and sing—if that's what you want to call it. He sang "The Penalty Box," the song that somehow rose to the top of the Philadelphia charts in 1975. He hadn't performed it in several decades.

But the highlight of the night wasn't his singing. Far from it. The highlight was the former NHL enforcers telling stories to the crowd while videos of their fights were shown on the huge screens at the 2300 Arena in South Philadelphia.

There were clips of former Flyers Schultz, Bob Kelly, Paul Holmgren, Donald Brashear, Craig Berube, Dave Brown, Todd Fedoruk, Riley Cote, and Wayne Simmonds pounding an opponent. One scene showed blood pouring off fearless goaltender Ron Hextall as he took off his helmet and mask. There were fast-paced video snippets of bruising checks that echoed around the Spectrum and the Wells Fargo Center. No matter that most of them had happened at least two decades ago. The people in the room loved them.

It was the third time the Friday Night Fights event had been available to fans, and you could tell they enjoyed the way the game was played back in the day.

"When we first put this event together a number of years ago, we wanted to celebrate old-time hockey and the way it used to be played," Brad Marsh, president of the Flyers' extremely active alumni association, told the crowd.

Marsh said when he was telling folks about the event, he was reminded that "we got treated to some old-time hockey a couple weeks ago."

He was referring to a heavyweight fight between the Flyers' 6'1", 218-pound Nic Deslauriers and the New York Rangers' 6'8", 241-pound Matt Rempe, a bout that was long and brutal. A lot like some of the fights Schultz had with Boston's Terry O'Reilly in the 1970s.

Recalling the Deslauriers-Rempe bout, Marsh said "the place was electric" when the two squared off at the Wells Fargo Center, providing one of the best fights in recent memory. The Friday Night Fights crowd listened intently as Marsh excitedly talked about the memorable matchup.

"When something like that happens in an arena, I wish the suits who run the National Hockey League were sitting in the fricking arena because the whole place was alive, the whole place was electric, the whole place was standing up," Marsh said. "And the buzz continued for the rest of the period."

Schultz added an addendum to that fight: "To me, it was ridiculous that they discussed it in the pregame warmup. It was like they arranged for it to happen," he said. "That never happened to me in all the fights in my career. Every one of them was spontaneous. I would never tell a guy I was going to fight him. What for? I didn't want him to know. I didn't want him to be mentally prepared for a fight."

At the 2024 alumni event, Schultz told the crowd: "If I had to fight a guy like Rempe, who stands 6'8" and weighs about 240, I likely would have taken my stick and separated him from his testicles."

He grinned.

"I'm sort of kidding, but I don't know how you can beat a guy that tall, with that kind of reach," he said. "Give Deslauriers lots of credit for probably winning a decision in that fight.

Schultz was not surprised that the fans at that game felt they saw something special. "Philly fans still love brawls and one-on-one bouts, no question," he said.

The young fans of today weren't around when the brawling Flyers changed the NHL, but they have undoubtedly heard the stories passed down from their parents and grandparents about the Broad Street Bullies.

"To me, that is why toughness and the Philadelphia Flyers are still synonymous in the 21st-century NHL," Schultz said.

Some think Philly fans live in the past too much. Schultz says they appreciate the past but know the NHL has changed immensely over the years.

"From my observations, Philly fans also love watching skilled players," Schultz said. "General manager Danny Brière is trying his best to bring both aspects of the game to Philadelphia. He wants tough guys that also know how to play the game, and he also wants guys with great talent. That's the mix that brought us Stanley Cup championships in 1974 and 1975. Yes, we were a tough team, but we were talented, too. Very talented."

Since the Broad Street Bullies days, the NHL has changed some of the rules—many because of the Flyers—and you don't see as much fighting in today's game. But there's still a place for hard-nosed play and a well-timed fight to serve as a wake-up call.

"The funny thing is, I despised fighting when I played," Schultz said. "You may be shocked to hear that because I was good at it, and it gave me a reputation as the NHL's bad boy. Truth be told, I got much more satisfaction out of scoring goals than dropping the gloves. But I knew my role, and I fought for my teammates. The fans and the media seemed to love it, and it became a vicious cycle. I couldn't escape from it."

As Schultz looks back on it about a half century after the Flyers' glory days, "I shake my head at the guy who wore No. 8—me," he said. "Always fighting. Always instigating. Always being the villain in enemy rinks. What was I thinking? I was a 35-goal scorer in junior, but I turned into a fighting machine in the NHL. Mentally, it was exhausting. I'd look at the next team on our schedule and the fighters on their rosters. Then I'd imagine how I would try to get an advantage when I fought them. My time was spent on mentally preparing for a fight instead of how our line could score some goals in the next game."

Schultz's wife at the time, Cathy, wasn't a fan of her husband's fighting. She didn't like that it became Schultz's identity.

"I remember her telling me after a game: 'I felt like it wasn't you that I was watching,'" Schultz said.

Cathy didn't like him getting hit and didn't like him hitting other players.

Schultz can see where she was coming from. "On one side, I made a pretty good living, won two Stanley Cups for an amazing city, and developed some lifetime bonds. Lots of precious memories, to be sure," he said. "But all the fights have left me wondering if my career would have been different if I concentrated more on playing the game and not antagonizing opponents."

Memories Return

Memories of some of his fights came flooding back to Schultz during that winter night in 2024 when Friday Night Fights was held.

At one point, Brad Marsh—who, along with Lou Nolan, served emcees—mentioned that it was the 20th anniversary of the game between the Flyers and Ottawa Senators that produced an NHL single-game record of 419 penalty minutes.

"That record still stands today, and the way the game is played, it will never be broken," Marsh said. "Once again, that's old-time hockey at its finest, and we're going to celebrate that brawl."

They rolled out video from that game, which was played in Philly on March 5, 2004. There was fight after fight after fight in what turned out to be a 5–3 Flyers win. The seeds for the brawl had been planted the previous week in Ottawa, when the Senators' Martin Havlát received a 10-minute misconduct for swinging his stick at the head of the Flyers' Mark Recchi.

"Someday," Flyers coach Ken Hitchcock said about Havlát at the time, "somebody's going to make him eat his lunch."

Eight days later, the teams had a rematch in Philadelphia. Believe it or not, there were few penalties called until the third period.

With two minutes left in the game, only 22 penalty minutes had been handed out. But a time bomb was ticking.

Loudly.

When Donald Brashear and Ottawa's Rob Ray got into a spirited fight, all hell broke loose. That was the start of a fight line that wouldn't end. Brashear then got into another fight. Everyone on the ice squared off. As soon as one fight ended, another started. Even the goalies, Robert Esche and Ottawa's Patrick Lalime, got into an entertaining bout. It was contagious. Ask John LeClair. He got into his only fight as a member of the Flyers. This was all shown on the video screens at the Friday Night Fights event, and the fans cheered and hooted. They were proud of the Orange and Black, proud that they were a part of NHL history.

All told, there were 21 fighting majors and 20 ejections.

Old. Time. Hockey.

Steve Coates was one of the guest speakers that night in 2024, and he put it succinctly as he warmed up the crowd.

"This is how [the franchise] was all built…on balls," said Coates, a former player who had a 43-year career as a Flyers broadcaster.

Coates said enforcers and tough guys "were so entertaining when they played, so important to the game. They had personality and they're good people. They understand how good the game was.… The NHL is the only company that I know that doesn't give the customers what they want to see—that's hitting and fighting. This isn't the Ice Capades. This a hard game to play. It's got to be played hard; it's got to be intimidating. But that's changed. We're here because all of you like the same thing I love."

Bill Clement, one of Schultz's closest friends, agreed.

"Friday Night Fights and The City of Brotherly Love. Sounds about right to me," he said when it was his turn to speak that night.

On this night, Clement said he wanted to "rewind back to the creation of the Broad Street Bullies."

Schultz said it's always interesting to hear different people talk about that because each person inevitably "brings up a point that stirs some previous memories."

Clement talked about a trade early in the 1972–73 season with St. Louis that brought defenseman André "Moose" Dupont to the Flyers, saying it solidified the Bullies and made them a much tougher team to play against.

But Clement didn't have that impression when the trade went down.

"I always thought he was a roly-poly kind of guy, maybe soft a little bit. That was my impression," Clement recalled in 2024. "And then his second practice with us, we had a scrimmage and… he butt-ended me with his stick right in my lower back. And I immediately went into this kind of mode: 'Why I ought to….' So, I dropped my gloves with him. My assessment of him was so off. He was really freaking strong, and he could throw hands. And he became an integral part of our two Stanley Cups. That was a building block on the Flyers' blue line for years."

That night in 2024, Clement introduced Schultz, who joined him and Moose on the panel. The Hall of Fame announcer said Schultz was "one of the greatest" teammates, fighters, and winners ever.

"I'm not sure how true that is, but it was humbling to hear it," Schultz said.

Clement, however, jokingly knocked Schultz down a peg as he slowly hobbled to the stage.

"You're moving at about the same speed that you skated," Clement cracked.

Schultz managed to smile, "but even that made me hurt because of recent dental work I had done. Ah, if I could only rewind the clock back to my youth," back to the days when the Bullies were the most-adored sports team in Philadelphia.

"That may sound funny to current fans because of the popularity of the Eagles and Phillies. But we were the most popular team in the region back then—and it wasn't even close," Schultz pointed out.

He said Dupont helped the Flyers become even more popular. "He was a team-first guy—like all our players—and he would do anything in his power to give us an edge on the ice," Schultz said.

Crazy Development

Crazily, Moose arrived at the Spectrum the day he was traded and went to the St. Louis locker room. The Blues were facing the Flyers, and the defenseman expected to fight Schultz or Bob Kelly during that game.

But when he got to the room, he learned he and a third-round draft pick had been dealt to the Flyers for Brent Hughes and Pierre Plante. Moose turned around and walked into the Flyers' locker room.

Schultz took one look at him and asked a serious question: "What the hell are you doing in here?"

Moose: "I'm your teammate now."

Schultz: "No, really."

Moose: "Really."

"I didn't know if they were going to accept me or not," Dupont said in 2024.

He was accepted, and the Flyers thrived with him on defense. He was the missing piece, someone who made them much better in the D zone and was a big body who cleared opponents away from Philadelphia's great goaltender, Bernie Parent.

"We already were building an image when Moose got here. He enhanced it," Schultz said.

"I think we represented the blue-collar image that the city had at that time," right winger Don Saleski said.

Moose adapted well to the city and became a very popular player.

"I knew the town was made of hard-working people, and a lot of people had to work two jobs to get by," Dupont, who was 23 when he joined the Flyers, said at the Friday Night Fights event. "And we were a bunch of Canadian kids who came here to make a name for ourselves, too. Not one of us was rich by the time we got to Philly, and it was our way to make money, too. We were like them [the fans]—we had to work hard to achieve what we wanted. That's why I believe the city loved us and we loved the city."

"The fans were always behind us. Hey, they even supported my awful singing. I figured I'd test their allegiance—and their eardrums—by singing 'The Penalty Box' at the alumni event," said Schultz. Clement noted that it was the No. 1 song in the area at the time, and that No. 2 was Elton John's "Philadelphia Freedom."

So, a guy with a bad voice and good fists beat out a man who would win five Grammy Awards and have 35 nominations.

"That's loyalty for you," Schultz said. "That's Philadelphia! If you work hard at representing the city, the fans are in your corner. Even to this day."

Singing the song "was hokey, and I'm not sure if I'll ever sing the song again," Schultz said in 2024. "But it was a fun night, and it was for a good cause, so what the hell."

Stu Grimson, a former NHL enforcer who was one of the guest speakers at Friday Night Fights, said he recently had been watching a documentary called *The Greatest Night in Pop*. It's a nostalgic story about the industry's biggest music stars recording "We Are the World." "So, for six days, I've had this song playing around in a loop in my head: 'We are the World…'"

He paused.

"But I'm so glad to now have that replaced by, 'Baby, how long will you keep me in the penalty box?'"

He drew big laughs with that line.

"I've been cured of 'We are the World...'" Grimson added, smiling. "I'm back in a hockey frame of mind."

Grimson talked a lot that night about how his indoctrination to the league was when he fought Dave Brown, a former Flyer who was then with Edmonton. Brown was one of the league's most respected enforcers. Fighting him made Grimson feel like he belonged in the NHL.

That jostled Schultz's memory because some opponents also said that about him in the 1970s.

"To be honest, that doesn't make me happy. Looking back, I don't want to be remembered as a player who caused havoc on the ice and created fear in others," Schultz said. "I only did it because that was my defined role on a team that had lots of skilled players. To this day, I have never been in a fistfight outside of hockey, and that's something that makes me proud."

Schultz became an outstanding fighter "and it became my identity to a lot of people. But I'd rather fans remember me as a good teammate who chipped in with some key goals and assists that helped us win two Stanley Cups.

"That said, I'm a realist. When your nickname is 'The Hammer,' people are going to remember you for what made you famous."

CHAPTER 10

ED SNIDER: HE BECAME A PHILLY GUY

THROUGHOUT HIS ENTREPRENEURIAL LIFE, Philadelphia Flyers co-founder Ed Snider was a driven man, someone who led the discussions and set agendas. He was also someone who had extreme faith in the people he hired and gave them authority to make critical decisions.

A born leader, he had an innate sense for business and dealings, whether it was with his hockey club or one of his many other ventures.

He was used to calling the shots, used to taking risks, used to getting his way.

Unfortunately, one of his final choices couldn't be fulfilled as Snider, frail from battling bladder cancer, wasn't allowed to come home for his final days.

His weakened body was in Montecito, California. His heart was in Philly.

"He wanted to die in Philadelphia," said his son, Jay.

"When my dad was dying and was in California, all he kept saying was, 'I want to get back, I want to get back to my people, my people, my people,'" daughter Lindy said. "You know, he really missed Philadelphia, and all he wanted to do was come back."

Ed had a private plane and would have had his medical staff and children to assist him on the flight to Philadelphia. But doctors apparently told his wife, Lin, that it wasn't advisable for Ed to travel. Lin thought it was best he remain in California, too. Ed unhappily stayed in his posh West Coast mansion.

Snider, 83, died in his California home with his six children—Craig, Jay, Lindy, Sarena, Tina, and Sam—by his side.

Lindy was there for the last five months of his life, doing whatever she could to make her dad as comfortable as possible. During that time, some of Ed's closest friends visited, including Flyers greats Bobby Clarke, Bernie Parent, and Joe Watson.

About a month before his death, Ed and his fourth wife, Lin, separated and she left the house, said someone close to the situation. Ed initiated the breakup. There were irreconcilable differences, and in Ed's eyes, he didn't like the way the much-younger Lin was taking care of him or handling the medical staff at his home. (Shortly after Ed passed, Lin had a daughter, Everly, through a surrogate, according to a source. She was reportedly conceived with Ed's frozen sperm. Everly's initials are the same as her dad's, EMS.)

Snider made his fortune and lifelong friends in Philadelphia, where he became an iconic figure and perhaps the most beloved sports owner in the city's history.

Though raised in DC, Snider considered himself a Philly guy. The Flyers, of course, were the reason.

"My father was watching the games on TV until it got to the point where he could no longer verbalize, could no longer speak," Lindy said. "But he was tracking the games."

While other owners were routinely booed when introduced, Snider was mostly cheered, mostly adored.

After his death, tributes poured in from around the world. His children issued a statement, saying "despite his considerable business achievements and public profile, he was first and foremost a family man. He never missed a birthday, an important family event, or the opportunity to offer encouragement. We turned first to him for advice in our personal and professional lives."

Snider was also loved and deeply respected by the players.

"He was awesome," former Flyer Jake Voráček said. "He made the decision to bring the team here, and he never regretted it. He really enjoyed it like it was his own child."

Yes, the hockey team was Ed's baby.

"I have always looked at the players who played
for the Flyers as my family."
—Ed Snider

Winning two Stanley Cups and always spending to the maximum for players made him a popular figure, even though some of the contracts he handed out weren't always wise investments. But maybe Snider's most endearing trait was the passion he displayed for his team. He wore his emotions on his sleeve and was someone who cared as much about the team as the fans.

That characteristic became rare as more teams, in all sports, were run by corporations and faceless owners who cared more about profits than wins and losses.

Snider and his first wife, Myrna, created a family atmosphere for the players and anyone connected to the team. That atmosphere was so strong, especially in the franchise's early years, that players, club personnel, and their families felt they were Flyers for life.

Lauren Hart, the Flyers' longtime anthem singer, had known Snider since she was a little girl and attended many games when her dad, Gene, was the team's broadcaster.

"I so loved him," she said about the Flyers' owner.

While Snider was toward the end and staying in his California home, Hart put together a moving pregame tribute to him before the Flyers clinched a playoff berth with a 3–1 win over the visiting Pittsburgh Penguins on April 9, 2016. In a duet that included a video of Kate Smith, she FaceTimed the rendition to Snider. Hart blew kisses to Snider when she ended the song.

The idea to include Snider on the video phone call was Hart's. She called Lindy, her longtime close friend, to get permission to FaceTime with her father. Lindy liked the idea.

"It was just one of those things that comes from the heart," said Shawn Tilger, then the Flyers' chief operating officer of business operations. "It gave me chills."

Hart, who knew Snider was gravely ill, texted Tilger after one of the most emotional performances of her career.

"He never made it to the building, so I thought he deserved all our love," she wrote.

She said it "broke my heart" knowing Snider would never be at another Flyers game. Two months earlier, she had visited him in California. At the time, "there was some hope he might be able to come home."

But Hart soon realized that wasn't going to happen.

"I just couldn't imagine him never being there again," she said. "I just wanted to bring that feeling to him. I wanted to give it to him one more time, what it felt like at the beginning of games."

Steve Mason, the goalie who led a late-season surge that carried the Flyers to a 2016 playoff berth, said their owner was on all the players' minds during the months before his death. Throughout his ownership, Snider would visit with the players in the locker room after home games; he would talk to them about the game or their families and stay connected with them.

"We know he's back home in California watching us," said Mason, who, along with his teammates, visited Snider at his West

Coast mansion while on a road trip nearly three months earlier. "We know he's been tuning in all season long, so for us to be able to come up with a playoff appearance, it couldn't happen to a better person. We're real proud to put on a sweater that he's created."

Lauren Hart said Snider "had such a unique perspective on things. He was just brutally honest. He knew what he wanted and what he didn't want. He wasn't afraid of anything. He was so committed, and his heart was so into it all the time. And I think the city loved the team and loved him—unusually so, because he was the only [owner] who could walk out on the ice and get applause."

Snider was ultra-accessible to the media, knowing they connected him to the fans. Fans also connected with him as they noticed him sitting in his box at home games.

"They saw him in his seat watching the game and reacting to every play," Hart said. "They saw him picking up his phone."

Some of those calls went to public address announcer Lou Nolan, who had an ice-level seat and the inside scoop on a referee's decision that Snider frequently didn't agree with.

"He was interactive all the time," Hart said. "And in the beginning [when the Flyers were at the Spectrum], it wasn't high up in the private suites at the top of the stadium. It was right there with the fans, so you could reach up and shake his hand."

Snider was a paradox. He was a rich man—his estimated worth was $2.5 billion at the time of his death—but he was also a man of the people. He was just as comfortable talking to a fan who sat in the nosebleed seats as he was with a president of a big corporation.

Missed Sharing Cup with His Dad

A University of Maryland graduate, Snider became a certified public accountant and started a wholesale record business before becoming the Flyers' most influential founder. He worked long hours to climb to the top of the NHL mountain. When he got there, unfortunately, he couldn't share it with his dad, Sol, a mom-and-pop grocery-store owner who died 11 weeks before the Flyers won their first Stanley Cup.

Like a lot of sons, Ed felt the need to prove himself to his father, who was a successful businessman in his own right. When Ed worked in his dad's grocery store, he took pride doing even menial tasks such as sweeping and mopping the floors or scrubbing the vegetable drawers.

Snider looked up to his dad, sought his advice. Even as Ed grew older and became entrepreneurial, he longed for his dad's approval. To have his team reach the top and not be able to share it with him, well, it ate at his soul.

"That was a heartbreaker for him," Jay Snider said.

Jay's sister, Lindy, agreed. Lindy said that "decades" after the Flyers were NHL champs, her dad on "numerous" occasions brought up that he wished his dad had seen what had transpired, how Philadelphia fell in love with a hockey team that he had built from the ground up.

"There were many times he said how much he regretted that his father didn't get to see what he had built," she said. "He didn't get to see his success, the pinnacle. And at that point in '74, the pinnacle was winning the Cup. It haunted him; it upset him. And it came up many times over the years.

"I don't know what would prompt it," she said, "but sometimes if we were just reminiscing, you could really tell that it weighed on him. His dad was lovely. Like a really warm, affectionate man. Everybody loved him. He was just a really lovable guy."

Even so, Ed sometimes felt his father could be distant to him.

"I remember my dad saying to me that sometimes he felt his dad respected his friends or his peers more than him," Lindy said. "And that's why I think that him not seeing my dad's success weighed on him."

She said most fathers and their sons have an interesting dynamic.

"I think most sons are always wanting to prove something to their dads," Lindy said. "I think it meant very much to him for his father to see what he had created. I don't think he thought his parents truly understood this [hockey] business, and what it was and what it meant. And I think it was very painful for him that his dad missed this."

Ed's doting mom, Lil, was appalled the first time she saw an NHL game. She wasn't sure what she should be watching as she sat next to her son, the Flyers' owner.

She watched the repeated back-and-forth action, with each team taking the puck and losing it, and wondered what the heck was going on. She also watched the physical style of play and was puzzled by it.

"Eddie, what kind of business is this?" she asked.

Jay Snider laughed at the memory of his dad telling him the story. His grandmother, Jay said, "was so old world that all she cared about was her family. I'll tell you, though, he got his business head from her."

Playing to the Crowd

Ed Snider was highly competitive in everything he did, whether it was in the business world or playing tennis or pinball.

He also was a showman.

Jay Snider recalled sitting next to his father during an uneventful game. The arena was quiet. Ed Snider didn't like that.

"It was February, and those were the dog days of the season," Jay recalled.

His father looked at him and gave him a nod that said: *Watch this.*

"I've got to get the crowd going," Ed told his son.

The referee missed what, in Snider's eyes, was a penalty against the Flyers' opponent.

Time for the owner to wake up the sleepy crowd. Lights. Cameras. And...action!

"He starts going crazy," Jay said. "He starts screaming, jumping up, and going nuts. And the whole crowd comes alive. They watched him, and then the whole place goes nuts."

Snider looked at Jay and winked.

Most of Snider's antics, however, weren't premeditated. They came from the heart. Nolan, the public address announcer, experienced Snider's real anger, and naturally, a referee was the cause of it.

Lou was sitting in his familiar spot by the penalty box when Ed called him during his first year as the public address announcer during the 1972–73 season.

Ed never called if he agreed with a ref's call. He'd only phone Lou if he disagreed and wanted clarification. Lou was at ice level and was privy to the calls before they were announced, and he was often given details that were not announced to the crowd.

Lou would frequently appease Ed, telling him the call looked strange to him, too, and that he understood his boss' ire.

In one game, there was a huge brawl, and Bob Myers was the ref. He skated over to Lou so he could announce all the penalties that were being handed out, the iconic announcer said in *If These Walls Could Talk: Philadelphia Flyers.*

Myers was there for a while, figuring out the slew of penalties. The phone rang. Lou, who was in the middle of Myers' explanations, picked up the receiver.

"Just a minute, Ed," Lou said. He put down the phone because Myers wanted to finish and get the game restarted.

Myers finished. Lou picked up the phone. His already-fuming boss sounded as if he was going to erupt.

Flyers co-founder Ed Snider blows out his birthday candles while in his office as his right-hand man, Lou Scheinfeld, watches. The two became inseparable during the Flyers' heyday in the 1970s. (Photo courtesy of Lou Scheinfeld)

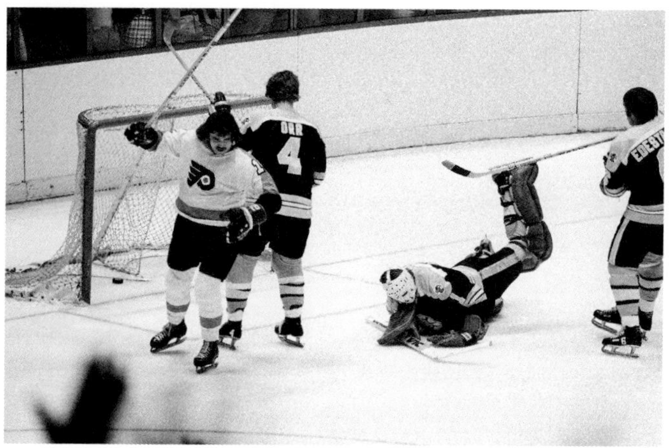

Rick MacLeish (left) celebrates in front of Boston's Bobby Orr after the Flyers center helped set up Tom Bladon's power-play goal in Game 3 of the 1974 Stanley Cup Final. MacLeish was called the Flyers' most talented player by captain Bobby Clarke. (AP photo)

Flyers enforcer Dave Schultz and Boston's André Savard get into a fight during the 1974 Stanley Cup Final. Schultz scored 20 goals in the regular season, tallied a series-clinching playoff goal against Atlanta, and offered physical protection for the Flyers' main scorers throughout the year. (Photo by UPI/Bettmann/Getty Images)

With fans emptying onto the playing surface, Bobby Clarke (left) and Bernie Parent skate around the Spectrum ice after the Flyers won their first Stanley Cup on May 19, 1974. At right is Bill Barber. (AP Photo)

Ed Snider and his wife, Myrna, sit in a convertible and mingle with the fans during the Flyers' victory parade in 1974. Myrna Snider was a caring person who created a family atmosphere for the Flyers, their wives, and their families—and everybody who worked at the Spectrum. The Sniders ran the organization like a "mom and pop" store. (Photo courtesy of the Philadelphia Flyers)

Bob Kelly, placed on the top line for the first shift of the third period because of assistant coach Mike Nykoluk's hunch, snaps a scoreless tie as he beats goaltender Roger Crozier in Game 6 in Buffalo in 1975. It proved to be the winning goal as the Flyers captured their second straight Cup 2–0. (AP Photo)

Ed Snider and Rick MacLeish celebrate after the Flyers captured the Cup. MacLeish was the NHL's leading point producer in the 1974 and 1975 playoffs. (Photo courtesy of the Philadelphia Flyers)

Bob Kelly (left) and Bill Clement party with champagne, beer, and cigarettes after the Flyers became the NHL's best team. Kelly and Clement were important role players for the Flyers in their two championship seasons. (Photo courtesy of the Philadelphia Flyers)

How sweet it is! Ed Snider and broadcaster Gene Hart light up victory cigars after a Cup win. Hart introduced hockey to Flyers listeners and became a Hall of Fame broadcaster. (Photo courtesy of the Philadelphia Flyers)

Clarence Campbell (left), the NHL commissioner, hated the Flyers' fighting style and became their arch enemy. He went to the locker room and tried to give the team a pep talk before it faced the Soviet Red Army in 1976. The players thought he was a hypocrite and wanted no part of him. (Photo courtesy of the Philadelphia Flyers)

Flyers center Orest Kindrachuk (left) and defenseman Joe Watson show how much the Stanley Cup means to them on the plane ride back from Buffalo following their 1975 championship. (Photo courtesy of the Philadelphia Flyers)

An estimated two million fans attended the Flyers' victory parade in 1974. This is an aerial view from above William Penn's statue. The parade number swelled to 2.3 million in 1975. (Photo courtesy of the Philadelphia Flyers)

Deliriously happy fans poured into the streets after the Flyers won the Cup again in 1975, beating Buffalo in six games. (Photo courtesy of the Philadelphia Flyers)

Barry Ashbee, whose No. 4 was the first jersey retired by the Flyers, and his wife, Donna, pose with the cherished Stanley Cup. Barry was a central part of the Flyers' defense before suffering an eye injury during the 1974 playoffs. After Barry's death from leukemia in 1977, Donna was a driving force in the Flyers Wives Carnival. (Photo courtesy of the Philadelphia Flyers)

Sandy Clarke, whose husband, Bobby, was the Flyers' captain, finds a comfortable seat—the Stanley Cup—at a championship party at Ed Snider's house. (Photo courtesy of the Clarke family)

The famed LCB Line—from left to right: Bill Barber, Bobby Clarke and Reggie Leach—posed for photographers at Clarke's retirement party in 1984. The line was almost unstoppable. (Photo courtesy of the Clarke family)

Singer Kate Smith, whose rendition of "God Bless America" became the Flyers' good-luck charm, and goalie Bernie Parent celebrate with the fans. Parent was the Conn Smythe Trophy winner as the best player in the playoffs in 1974 and 1975 and had shutouts in the Cup-clinching wins both seasons. The Flyers went 101–31–5 when Smith's pregame song was played or sung in person before a controversial ban in 2019. (Photo courtesy of the Philadelphia Flyers)

Soviet Red Army players walk off the ice in protest of the Flyers' physical play in the 1976 game at the Spectrum. (AP Photo)

The Flyers were so popular in the 1970s that they had their faces plastered on cans of Canada Dry Ginger Ale. Here's an ad promoting the soda by using Dave Schultz on the can. (Photo: Sam Carchidi)

16-Page Special Flyers Pullout

Tonight & Tomorrow
Clear, Sunny

PHILADELPHIA DAILY NEWS

4★
15c Sports

WEDNESDAY, MAY 28, 1975

One More Time!

- City Celebrates: Page 3
- Larry McMullen on 4
- Chuck Stone on 10
- Bill Fleischman on Back Page
- Stan Hochman on 74
- Jack McKinney on 70

The *Daily News* cover after the Flyers beat Buffalo in 1975 and won their second straight Cup. (Photo: Sam Carchidi)

Phillies Shake Slump, Batter Giants – Page 1-C

The Philadelphia Inquirer

Thursday, May 29, 1975

15 CENTS

2.3 Million Cheer for Flyers

Parade Wild as Year Ago

The *Philadelphia Inquirer* front page after the Flyers' victory parade in 1975. (Photo: Sam Carchidi)

Not many hockey players get on the cover of *Time* magazine. Then again, not many players were as special as goaltender Bernie Parent. (Photo: Sam Carchidi)

Left winger Dave Schultz (left) shares a moment with Rexy's owner Pat Fietto, who served as a confidant and father figure to many of the Flyers. The South Jersey bar/restaurant was the Flyers' favorite hangout. Fietto even cashed some of the players' checks. (Photo courtesy of Patrice Fietto)

The Flyers wives, like the players, were an extremely close-knit group and played an important role in the team's success. In this photo, the women are on a ski trip in Colorado. Flyers wives in the photo include Nedina Stephenson (top left), Carolyn MacLeish DeSimone (third from left, top row), Rhonda McCarthy (top row, far right), MaryAnn Saleski (held up in the middle), and Isabel leach (lying on the ground, left). (Photo courtesy of Isabel Leach)

Several Flyers and front-office execs from their Stanley Cup years gathered around the unveiling of the "Walk Together Forever" Statue in front of the Broad St. Bullies pub in 2013. The statue depicts Bernie Parent and Bobby Clarke holding the Cup. (Photo by Len Redkoles/NHLI via Getty Images)

"Lou, there's something you and I have to get straight," Ed said.

"Sure, Ed. What's that?"

"When I call you," Ed snorted, "I want the referee put on hold."

That was Ed, Lou said with a chuckle a half century after the incident. "He just wanted to blow off some steam. Everybody used to kid me that I was on his speed dial from his suite."

The "Death Stare"

One of the things Lou Scheinfeld remembers the most about Snider is what he calls his "death stare."

It was laser-like and felt like it went through the person he was staring at, said Scheinfeld, the Flyers' first vice president.

"But he could be cute. He could be like a little boy sometimes," Scheinfeld added. "There was this time we lost a game, and he was heading down the corridor. And a young female intern said, 'Hi, Mr. Snider. How are you doing tonight?' He said, 'I'm a 4–2 loser. That's how I'm doing!' He screamed at her. So, then he turns to me and goes, 'Oh my God. I've got to apologize to her!'"

Snider felt terrible. He asked Scheinfeld to please find the name of the young woman and ask her to come to his office the next day.

"The next morning, at 7:00, he calls me and asks if I found out her name. So, he had that way. When he was focused, he could run you over.... We used to say he chews metal and spits out bullets. But when he was wrong, he had a conscience."

Snider apologized to the woman.

Snider and His Superstitions

A lot of people have superstitions, but Ed's went to another level. It was a trait he picked up from his father.

There was the time in Maine, where Ed's family had a summer home, that he drove several miles out of his way because of a superstition.

"We live right on a lake, and he's driving there—I think it was with my uncle—and he's on a road that basically rings around the lake," said Ed's daughter, Lindy. "And all of a sudden, a black cat crossed his path."

Ed put the car in reverse, turned around, and drove the other way.

"He drove about 13 miles out of his way because of the cat," she said.

Ed had another superstition, one that is far less known than seeing a black cat. It went like this: If two people are walking down a sidewalk, you must not allow a pole or column to come between the two. To him, that was bad luck.

When the Flyers had their offices on 15th and Locust, Ed and Lindy would sometimes go to lunch together. If Lindy walked on the wrong side of a light pole, Ed would scream at her, "No, no, no! Come back!"

Lindy would have to walk backward, then walk so the pole was not between her and her dad.

Ed also had a lucky jacket he wore for special occasions or big games, a lucky sweater, and lucky cufflinks. (He broke many cufflinks by banging his arms on his Superbox ledge after something went wrong as he watched a game.)

"And he always had a lucky coin in his wallet, which I have now," Lindy said in 2023. "Some of these superstitions probably came from the old country, from his parents. You know, immigrant families have very old superstitions."

Another of Ed's superstitions: Do not put a hat on a bed. Ever.

"That comes from his dad," Jay Snider said. "I'm thinking that signifies death or something. Like the person is gone and the hat [is left]."

"And he has passed these ridiculous things down to us," Lindy said.

She was referring to Ed's six children. (He had another one, a daughter, a few months after he died.)

At Flyers games, Snider was also superstitious.

"If you were sitting somewhere and you moved your seat and all of a sudden the other team started scoring, you had to go back to your [original] seat," Jay said. "Or if you're in your seat and we're scoring, you're not allowed to change your seat."

Ed was "very serious about that stuff," his son added.

"It's awful because we all are superstitious now, too," Lindy said. "We think he was so successful and had such luck that we couldn't argue. I mean, to this day, if someone throws a hat on a bed, I freak out."

At the 1974 Stanley Cup Final, the Flyers had a 1–0 lead over Boston in Game 6 when the head of security approached Snider. Snider was told security guards should be sent near the rink's glass so fans couldn't get onto the ice if the Flyers won and clinched the Cup.

Snider would not "okay" the request. He was too superstitious, figuring if he did that, the Flyers would lose.

They won 1–0 and several hundred fans emptied onto the ice.

No matter. They had won their first Cup. That's all that mattered to Snider.

The players were just as superstitious as their owner.

There were times when captain Bobby Clarke, speaking on behalf of the team, called promotions director Jay Seidman into the locker room to protest about the balloons that were placed on the catwalks high above the ice before a big game. "It felt like a jinx," Clarke said. They hadn't won yet, and he and the team didn't want them in there, didn't want the opposing team to get incentive from them.

"When I walked in, I felt like I was in the Roman Coliseum," Seidman said. "The players would be banging their sticks on the floor. The Watson brothers and [André] Dupont would be telling Clarkie, 'Give him hell.'"

They also didn't like hearing good luck charm Kate Smith practice singing "God Bless America" a few hours before a game during the 1976 Stanley Cup Finals at the Spectrum. It was the fourth game of the Finals against the powerful Montreal Canadiens. Montreal rallied and won 5–3 to sweep the series and mark the only time the Flyers ever lost during the four times Kate appeared in person.

"They didn't want to give the other team any motivation by hearing Kate Smith was there," Seidman said. "Didn't want to give the other team any sort of locker-room fuel."

Seidman said some of the Flyers also thought Kate was getting too much credit for the team's wins.

The Flyers liked Kate a lot, but "there was so much attention given to it," Seidman said about her good luck song.

When the Flyers stopped using the song in 2019, Philadelphia had a 101–31–5 record during games in which "God Bless America" was played or sung in person.

Landing the Flyers

Even though he smoked a few packs of Lucky Strikes a day, Snider probably didn't feel lucky while he and his group were trying to bring Philadelphia a hockey team and there was one snag after another.

Snider had convinced his boss, Jerry Wolman, then president of the NFL Eagles, that Philadelphia needed to put in a bid for an expansion team. After a lot of red tape and countless meetings, Philly was awarded a franchise because Wolman had promised to build the Spectrum.

But in June of 1967, more than a year after Philadelphia beat out Baltimore for one of the NHL's six expansion teams, there was a major problem. The $2 million expansion fee was due, and the Flyers group was still scrambling to secure the last $500,000.

Bill Putnam, a friend of Snider's who was part of Philadelphia's ownership group, and Scheinfeld headed to Montreal to (hopefully) give the NHL its $2 million check and participate in the expansion draft, which gave the soon-to-be-named Flyers some key players who played on the Broad Street Bullies teams in the 1970s.

After numerous calls, the team finally got a bank loan, and a $500,000 check was cut the morning the money was due.

"Remember, there's no fax machines. No computers. No cell phones back then," Scheinfeld said 50-plus years later. "Ed calls me at my hotel room and says, 'I got the money. I'm going to wire it up there well in time.'"

Snider told Scheinfeld and Putnam to go to the Royal Bank of Canada, which was across the street from the NHL's expansion headquarters at the Queen Elizabeth Hotel.

"They go to wire the money," Scheinfeld said, "and there's a blackout on the East Coast."

They were finally able to send the check, which was made out to the National Hockey League. That was a problem, too. It was supposed to be made out to one of the Original Six teams—in this case, to the Toronto Maple Leafs.

"It's a hot June day in Montreal, and we're wearing suits and ties, and we're soaked," Scheinfeld said. "There's this huge median barrier we have to climb over and run up the steps to and down the hall where the NHL was accepting the checks. That's when Bill Putnam looks at the check and says, 'Oh my God. It's wrong!'"

The Flyers needed a new check, this one made out to the Toronto Maple Leafs.

Scheinfeld ran to his hotel room and phoned Snider in Philadelphia. It was the definition of a Keystone Kops routine. Only Snider wasn't laughing.

"I'm having a heart attack here," he told Scheinfeld.

Putnam, the Flyers' first president and a man who then owned 25 percent of the team, had a private phone line and another check—this time made out to the Maple Leafs—was authorized. Scheinfeld and Putnam ran across the street to the bank and got a new check.

"Two sweaty schleppers," Scheinfeld said.

With the check in hand, they ran back across the street "15 minutes before the deadline," according to Scheinfeld. "We run past the Baltimore guys who are standing outside the room, and we hear Clarence Campbell say, 'Philadelphia, you're up.'"

Even before the Broad Street Bullies era, Campbell did not like Snider, Scheinfeld said. "He basically didn't like American hockey" or that six US teams were entering the league.

But the NHL realized it had to expand for TV coverage, along with the expansion fees.

A stone-faced Campbell, unaware of the drama the Flyers had gone through to come up with the money, took the $2 million check and didn't welcome Philadelphia into the league.

"That'll be all," he said.

Scheinfeld, still catching his breath from running up and down steps during a tension-filled day, was dumbfounded.

"I tuned into Jerry Lewis," he said before going into the goofy voice the late comedian used during his zany routines. "Like, do we maybe get a piece of paper or maybe a receipt? I mean, Ed Snider might like something."

Scheinfeld said the grumpy Campbell told him he would get a receipt "'if the check clears, which I doubt.' It was a cashier's check, so we knew it was good."

"That'll be all," Campbell repeated.

Scheinfeld and Putnam walked out and passed the Baltimore group, which had a $2 million check and was ready to pounce if Philadelphia came up short.

"I think you guys are fucked," Scheinfeld told them.

In the hotel lobby, Canadian reporters bombarded Scheinfeld and Putnam with questions about the new team's strategy in the upcoming expansion draft.

Back in Philadelphia, Snider was a nervous wreck. He finally was able to get Scheinfeld on his hotel phone.

"What happened? Did we get in? Did we get the franchise?" he asked.

"I think," Scheinfeld said.

"'You think?' What do you mean, 'You think?'" he replied, incredulously. "I knew I shouldn't have sent you up there."

Scheinfeld: "They did not give us a receipt. But the press is all saying we got the franchise."

When the franchise was officially awarded to Philly, "we figured we'd be a huge story the next day in the Philadelphia newspapers. But the Six-Day [Israeli] War broke out" and the Flyers got little publicity, Scheinfeld said.

It was the start of an up-and-down period for Philadelphia's new hockey team. But Snider, the majority owner, was relieved and in his glory.

His baby was born.

Snider was just getting started. In 1973 he created Spectacor as a management company to oversee the Flyers and the Spectrum. That helped launch an entire industry: private management of sports and entertainment facilities. In the next 20 years, Spectacor grew, as did its impact in the industry, acquiring nearly a dozen related companies. Along the way, Snider started all-sports radio WIP in Philadelphia and PRISM, considered to be the first 24-hour regional cable network to combine sports and movies.

His dad would have been proud.

Ed the Singer

Around the house or in the car, Ed liked to sing, especially to his kids.

"The Sunshine of Your Smile" is one he'd sing to cheer them up if they were upset. "Pennsylvania 6-5000" was also one of his favorites, along with the spoof version of "Down by the Old Mill Stream," and a Jewish parody of the Ohio fight song that included this line: "Don't give Sam Rabinowitz the ball, 'cause he ain't a real Heb, after all."

Ed had a pet name for Lindy that was intertwined with a song he loved to sing. Her full name is Lindy Lou Snider, and Ed would call her Lou-Lou.

He told her the name came from a stripper. Lindy wasn't sure if he was kidding, but Ed's two uncles owned a burlesque club, so he might have been serious.

But after calling her by the nickname he gave her, he would break into song: Paul Robeson's "Mah Lindy Lou."

To this day, Lindy gets sentimental when she hears the song, which starts like this:

> Lindy, did you hear that mockingbird sing last night?
> Honey, he was singin' so sweet in the moonlight,
> In the old magnolia tree,
> Bustin' his heart with melody.
> I know he was singin' of you,

Mah Lindy Lou.
Lindy Lou.
I'd lay right down and die and die,
If I could sing like that bird sings to you,
Mah little Lindy Lou.

Later in his life, Ed became a big Billy Joel fan and loved to sing his songs. He also was fond of the Black Eyed Peas' "I Gotta Feeling," which became the Flyers' unofficial victory song as they surprisingly reached the 2010 Stanley Cup Finals. That season, he would dance to the song as he high-fived the players in the locker room after a win.

And in 2012, when the 79-year-old Snider proposed to Lin Spivak, he had a group of singers come to his table at a swanky Santa Barbara restaurant. They performed another Snider favorite, "Marry You" by Bruno Mars. Snider got down on one knee and proposed to Lin, who was 34 years younger than her future spouse.

Music was always a big part of Snider's life. But none of the songs meant more to him than "Mah Lindy Lou."

A Caring Dad

While Snider had a street-fighter mentality, he was also very cerebral. As a father, he required his kids to read Ayn Rand's *Atlas Shrugged*. In the book, Rand examines "the role of the mind in man's existence" and her views on reaching your highest potential.

Snider had six children (a seventh was born after his death), four wives, and 15 grandchildren.

Because of all his business dealings, especially with the Flyers, Snider's days were filled with long hours. His kids understood when he was unable to attend their sporting events or plays at school. Myrna, Ed's first wife, was usually there, and seeing her lifted her kids' spirits.

Ed would make up for those absences in other ways, and that would galvanize the family. Every summer, for instance, they'd jump in their station wagon and make an eight-hour drive to vacation in Bangor, Maine. Ed was behind the wheel, with Myrna next to him.

At the time, there were also four kids and two dogs in the car. Ed would sing his favorite old-time songs during the drive, trying to get his children interested in the music he enjoyed. Ed, who once sang a song with Barbra Streisand, loved singing. If there was a bar mitzvah or wedding and an open mic, Ed would jump on stage.

The station wagon was his stage on the trips to Maine, which also included word games to fill the time and make the drive seem faster.

"What my mother and father did was create tradition and structure," Lindy said of the idyllic trips to Maine. "And I think that's something emblematic of the Flyers and our organization. That tradition was important—the things you could bank on. So, I think there was a lot of crossover between our family culture and the Flyers. The organizational culture and tradition matters."

As a dad, Ed had good and bad traits. He was loyal to his children, and they knew he was there for them. Always.

"He would drop anything if you needed help," Jay said. "He was the kind of person you wanted in the trenches with you, absolutely. That's a guy you want at your shoulder. Very straight talking, very plain. He didn't beat around the bush and make it so you had to figure out what he meant. He said what he meant and meant what he said. Very loving. Really smart. He had the ability to cut through problems and issues and get to the heart of it."

Sometimes, that could be difficult for a son, a daughter, or a friend who didn't necessarily want to hear the truth, Jay said.

"You might have all this stuff you're trying to avoid about yourself or a situation," he said. "But he would cut right through to it so you couldn't squirm your way out. There was nowhere to go. He had you pinned down."

On the flip side, Ed had a volatile temper.

"That made it hard to approach him sometimes," Jay said. "When do you approach? You had to think about it. It wasn't just an open door at all. He was quite self-absorbed. Not an egomaniac or anything, but his needs came first in his mood."

And if he gave you The Look, you knew an eruption was about to take place. "It was like, you are going to listen to what I have to say," Lindy said. He never stayed angry at his kids, but when he got mad, "it was like a roar," she added. "Scary."

Even in talks with his children, Ed the street fighter would surface.

When Lindy was a young girl, she came home from school and told her dad she was being bullied by another girl. Ed didn't pick up the phone to call a teacher or the principal. Instead, he told Lindy to take matters in her own hands.

Or fists.

"The next time she says something [mean] to you, just punch her in the nose."

That was Ed's fatherly advice.

"He never would want me to hurt somebody else," she said, "but you had to have a backbone. I think that was clear in who he was as a person...and in how he conducted business. He had a backbone; he had guts, and he was willing to take risks."

Later in her life, Lindy started dating Kenny Linseman, a Flyers center who was nicknamed "The Rat" because of the way he agitated opponents.

One night, Lindy and Kenny got into a heated argument at a bar-restaurant. Lindy didn't want to stay. She called Ed.

"Can you pick me up? I'm so mad at him that I have to leave."

Ed jumped in his car and made the 25-minute drive downtown to pick up his “Lou-Lou.”

But while Ed was driving toward Center City, Lindy and Kenny had worked out their differences.

“There were no cell phones back then. I couldn’t call him and tell him to turn around,” Lindy said. “He gets there and we go outside and I tell him we made up. And he looks at me and says, ‘Honey, I’m glad, and I want you to always call me anytime there’s a problem.’”

When Lindy and Kenny began dating, they hid it from Snider. Lindy and her sisters were told by their dad that they were not allowed to date the players. It was absolutely forbidden.

“So, we dated on the sly,” she said, smiling at the memory.

At the time, Lindy was attending the University of Pennsylvania and living at home for a while. Kenny would pick her up at a designated spot away from the house so Ed couldn’t see what was happening. When they returned home, Kenny would drop her off toward the end of the driveway.

“One night, it’s really late and Kenny is dropping me off, and as we pull up, we’re a little bit away from the house and you see the door open and my father comes rushing out,” Lindy said. “He’s coming right for the car, and he looks like he’s going to explode.”

Ed walked over to Kenny’s side of the car and whipped his door open.

“Get out,” Ed said.

Kenny expected to be chastised. Or maybe he would be put on the trading block?

“Come in and have a drink,” Ed said.

There was a sigh of relief from the two people sitting in the front seat.

“Come in and have a drink,” Ed repeated. “I’m a father first and a boss second.”

"Lou-Lou" could barely contain her smile. She had her dad wrapped around her finger.

Hiding Financial Problems

Snider shielded financial difficulties from his children, who were not aware he had major problems putting together the $2 million franchise fee for the Flyers. Or the other business issues that constantly emerged.

"We never knew," Lindy said. "That's the amazing thing. And look, I'm sure my mother was also living under the stress."

He also shielded his children from his feud with his onetime close friend, Jerry Wolman.

"Dad kept his mouth shut most of the time," said Jay Snider, adding that his father didn't want to burden his children with the Wolman feud or business matters. 'Just don't get into a farting contest with a skunk.' That's what he would say. So, he just sucked it up all these years and didn't even want to acknowledge it."

Lindy said before the Snider-Wolman war brew, her family was extremely close with Wolman.

"As kids, we knew Jerry Wolman, well, like an uncle," she said.

Snider and Wolman were among the Flyers' founders. The seeds of their breakup were planted when Snider, who was the Eagles' vice president and treasurer, was fired by the Birds' owner, Wolman, on the night of the Flyers' first-ever home game in 1967.

Wolman made a fortune in the construction business, but he started leaking money because his building of the John Hancock Center in Chicago had a faulty foundation. Cash-strapped, Wolman eventually exchanged his shares of the Flyers to Snider and Snider's brother-in-law, Earl Foreman, for their shares of the Spectrum.

Snider's relationship with Wolman "was never repaired," Lindy said. "It was sad because they had been friends as young men in DC before Dad ever even came to Philadelphia. It was sad that business had wiped that relationship away."

While Ed masked financial problems, he didn't hide his feelings on how his team did on the ice. He took the results home with him. If the Flyers won, he came home in a giddy mood. If they lost, he was mopey.

When the Flyers lost, he was "almost despondent, and it was hard to get his attention," Lindy said. "His mind was on the team. *What's going on? How can we fix things?* That kind of thing. I always like to joke that if we wanted a little extra money or a raise in our allowance, we approached him" after a win.

"I Lived for Those Calls"

Snider's love for his children and the Flyers were constants in his whirlwind life.

In the final months of his life in 2016, Ed still got the utmost joy from his hockey team as the players worked toward securing a playoff spot. He would get a call from Brian Roberts after each Flyers win. Roberts was chairman and CEO of Comcast Corp., the Flyers' parent company.

"No matter how sick or how much pain Ed was in, he wanted and needed to talk about the Flyers," Roberts said shortly after Snider's death. "Ed lived for those wins. I lived for those calls."

He loved the Flyers so much that Roberts went back to his days as a young hockey fan when he eulogized Snider.

"When I was a kid, every game ended—and Ed, I'm thinking of you now—with the great Gene Hart saying, 'Good night and good hockey,'" Roberts said. "And if I may add, 'Good life.'"

CHAPTER 11

THE BOSS' RIGHT-HAND MAN

Lou Scheinfeld wasn't just Ed Snider's right-hand man. He was also one of his closest friends, his confidant, and his drinking buddy.

Together, they helped build the Philadelphia Flyers and the Spectrum from the ground up. They were involved in a dramatic, last-minute payment to secure the franchise—and just seven years later, in 1974, watched the Flyers do the unthinkable and win the Stanley Cup.

Seven years. That was the quickest time in NHL history for an expansion team to win a Stanley Cup, a record that stood for 49 years. In 2023, the Vegas Golden Knights won the title six years after their franchise was born.

Scheinfeld, a former *Philadelphia Daily News* City Hall reporter who had a knack for breaking important news stories, and Snider, a man with an entrepreneurial spirit, were an unlikely duo.

But they became the best of friends for numerous years, sharing secrets, vacationing together with their wives, and helping to make the Flyers brand known around the world. (Snider always asked friends and workers to let him know if they saw a Flyers jersey while in a foreign country. He took pride in spreading the team's logo around the globe.)

Snider liked Scheinfeld's dogged newspaper work and felt comfortable around him. When Snider was vice president of the NFL's Philadelphia Eagles, he asked Scheinfeld if he wanted to work in the team's public relations office.

Scheinfeld declined.

"I love being a reporter," Scheinfeld told him.

He liked the idea of "making or breaking" someone, liked the chance to "put the bad guys away or save the good guys."

Snider understood. He and Scheinfeld began hanging out, going to dinners, drinking together at bars.

Scheinfeld began writing about Philadelphia trying to get an NHL franchise. Along the way, he turned down other job offers from Snider. He was later asked if working for the hockey team—if a franchise was awarded to Philly—might interest him.

"If you get the franchise," Scheinfeld told Snider, "I'm in."

And so, Scheinfeld and Snider became intertwined when the NHL welcomed Philadelphia and five other expansion teams in 1967. Scheinfeld would help run the Flyers and the new arena, the Spectrum. He was named vice president of the team and the arena.

When they needed to relieve some stress, the two men occasionally smoked pot (Snider called it "candy") together in their Spectrum offices, Scheinfeld said, and they became inseparable. They could speak bluntly to one another without worrying about hurting the other's feelings.

Scheinfeld called the duo Flash (that was him) and Cash (that was Snider). Snider, who grew up in Washington, DC, knew the business world. Scheinfeld knew Philadelphia and had his hand on the city's pulse. Their relationship had its ups and downs, but at the core, they deeply trusted one another and valued each other's opinions.

In his book, *Blades, Bands, and Ballers,* Scheinfeld talked about his love of the Spectrum, a building he named, and the fascinating stories behind it.

The Spectrum was where the Flyers would eventually become the hottest ticket in the city. It was an intimate, loud building that, along with the Broad Street Bullies, brought fear to opposing hockey players; it was the building that created a rebirth for Kate Smith's monumental singing career, a building where the Flyers won their first Stanley Cup in 1974.

The arena also hosted the NBA's 76ers, concerts, and other events. Scheinfeld, who became the Spectrum's president, was responsible for keeping things in order.

"Think of it like planning a big wedding, only you've got 20,000 guests coming," he wrote years later. "And another wedding tomorrow and maybe on Saturday, and two more on Sunday.... What could go wrong?"

Oh, just a few things. Like a portion of the Spectrum's roof blowing off—twice. Like a ticket scandal fueled by an employee. Or a near-riot ensuing because there weren't enough giveaway T-shirts for half the fans.

Common Upbringings

Scheinfeld and Snider learned the value of hard work at a young age. Both witnessed it firsthand. Snider's parents started Snider Quality Market, a grocery-store chain, in Washington, DC. Scheinfeld's parents operated Al's Variety Store for 51 years in the Brewerytown section of North Philadelphia.

Scheinfeld was 30 when he was lured by Snider (then 33) from the *Daily News.* At the time, Scheinfeld had never attended an NHL game, but his drive, smarts, and personality endeared him to Snider.

In the fall of 1966—11 months before the Flyers would make their debut—Scheinfeld traveled to Madison Square Garden to watch his first game in person: the Montreal Canadiens vs. the New York Rangers.

As he observed the action, he sensed Philadelphia fans were going to love the game and the atmosphere in their shiny new $6 million arena.

He pulled out a notebook—he was still a reporter at heart, after all—and wrote down some observations.

"A bare-knuckled combination of football and figure skating," he scribbled. "Beauty and brutality. Muscle and skill. Flashing blades, iconic uniforms, romantic names. No timeouts. No time to catch your breath. And blood. Lots of blood!"

Philadelphia, Scheinfeld thought to himself, *is going to enjoy the hell out of this.*

It didn't start out that way, however. Ticket sales were slow, very slow, during the franchise's early days. That was somewhat expected, but nonetheless disappointing. Philly was a basketball and football town in the fall. It would take time for hockey to take root.

On top of that, two exhibition games had to be canceled, Scheinfeld said, because the boards surrounding the Spectrum ice weren't installed yet.

"The boards were in Brooklyn being finished. They were maybe 95 percent done," Scheinfeld said 50-plus years later. "But the unions went on strike there, so we couldn't get the boards.... We made a few calls. Money changed hands, and the union [took the bribe and] decided to take a break from picketing around midnight and leave the doors open."

The Flyers sent two tractor trailers to Brooklyn, picked up the boards, and took them to a South Philly shop to be finished. They were installed at the Spectrum. Crisis averted.

In the meantime, Snider was running himself ragged. He ran the Eagles during the day and worked with the Flyers' staff on hockey and arena projects at night.

Scheinfeld was hoping for 10,000 fans at the Flyers' home opener October 19, 1967, against Pittsburgh. Instead, only 7,812 attended the game, won by the Flyers 1–0 as Bill Sutherland scored the lone goal and Doug Favell blanked the Penguins.

"I'll bet 3,500 tickets were comps," Scheinfeld said.

Earlier in the day, Jerry Wolman had fired Snider from the Eagles. Wolman, the Eagles' owner, went to Snider's house in Wynnewood. Snider was shaving, and as he looked into the bathroom mirror, he saw Wolman staring at him.

Wolman: "I came to talk to you so we could get this settled."

Snider: "Fuck you and get out of my house."

Wolman told Snider he was fired. He felt Snider had been disloyal to him. Wolman, cash-strapped because his building project in Chicago had a faulty foundation and was losing millions, wanted to keep the Eagles. So, he reportedly tried to get Snider and others to sell their Flyers and Spectrum shares to an Arab sheik. The Flyers apparently would then be sold and relocated before ever playing in Philadelphia.

Snider was among those who declined. Eventually, an unhappy Wolman had to sell his shares of the Flyers for Snider's shares of the Spectrum.

Snider was stunned by his firing, but in retrospect, it may have been the best thing that ever happened to him. His attention was now solely on the hockey team.

With the Flyers, Snider had an eye on everything, and it spanned from the players' performances on the ice to the comfort of the Spectrum seats. Every detail mattered.

"Ed was the type of guy that could get in a revolving door behind you and somehow come out ahead of you," Scheinfeld said. "I mean, he was sharp. Smartest man I ever met in my life. Resourceful. He could 'will' things to happen. He really willed this thing to happen."

He was referring to the birth of the Flyers.

Early Attendance Woes

The Flyers struggled at the gate early in their first season.

Back in October of their maiden season, the Flyers drew 7,812 (Pittsburgh), 5,783 (Oakland), 10,859 (for Gordie Howe and Detroit), 4,708 (California again), and 4,203 (Minnesota) in their first five home games. That gave them an average of 6,673 spectators for that span.

It was far below what the team—which played a defensive style of hockey that wasn't exciting to watch—needed to average to break even: 12,000 or so fans per home game.

The early months of the inaugural season were filled with apprehension—and that was before sections of the Spectrum roof blew off. Twice.

Howard Baldwin, the team's first ticket manager, remembers the struggle to fill the seats.

"I'm sure it was scary for the owners—Ed, Bill Putnam, and Joe Scott. But they had a lot of guts," said Baldwin, who later enjoyed great success in Hollywood and was nominated for a Best Picture Oscar in 2005 as a producer for *Ray,* a film about rhythm and blues musician Ray Charles. "Scary as hell. I know Eddie had the box-office statement hanging on the wall in his office to the day he died. It had my signature on it and a $13,000 gross gate" from an early game. "That's pretty low."

Scheinfeld offered some perspective.

"When I was there in 2011, the gross was $4 million a game," he said. "That includes concessions, parking, and tickets."

Part of Scheinfeld's job was trying to find radio and TV sponsors during the Flyers' inaugural season.

The Flyers had yet to resonate with the public. As far as name recognition, they weren't in the same stratosphere as the Phillies, Eagles, or 76ers. Heck, they were far behind the teams in Philly's famed Big 5—the St. Joseph's Hawks, Temple Owls, LaSalle Explorers, Penn Quakers, and Villanova Wildcats.

"We were scrambling. We didn't have a lot of money," Scheinfeld said. "I'm calling people to be sponsors, and..."

A lot of them had no idea the Flyers were the city's new NHL team.

Scheinfeld was persistent.

"Would you like the be a sponsor of the Flyers?"

"Breyers? Breyers ice cream?" came one response.

"No, no, no. The Flyers hockey team."

"What's Flyers hockey? Are you talking about the Friars Club?"

This wasn't going to be an easy sell.

"A lot of people thought we were going to fail," Scheinfeld said, "and we wanted to prove them wrong."

Contributing to the low attendance was the fact that the media didn't exactly swarm to Flyers games. The *Inquirer*, Scheinfeld said, told him they wouldn't give the Flyers a lot of coverage until they began drawing home crowds of at least 10,000 on a regular basis.

"And they wouldn't cover away games at that time," he said. "Some of the reporters went on their own with us on the team [flights]."

Scheinfeld recalls the team paying WCAU to broadcast the third period of games on the radio.

He knew it was imperative to stir interest by having games on the airwaves.

"We had to be one of the Big Four," he said, referring to the Flyers and the three established pro teams in town at the time. "It's like it is right now with the Union [soccer team] in Philadelphia. You've got the Big Four and the Union."

WCAU executive Jack Downey, who later opened the popular Downey's Drinking House & Eating Saloon in Philadelphia, told Scheinfeld it would cost the Flyers $35,000 if they wanted the third period of their Sunday games on the radio.

Scheinfeld agreed...with a provision. WCAU had to include the Flyers on its billboards that were spread around the city, promoting the logos of the Phillies, Eagles, and 76ers.

Downey agreed.

"The first time I saw a billboard that had us on it, I cried," Scheinfeld said. "I said to myself, 'I think we're going to make it. I think we're damn well going to make it.'"

Eventually, 61 of the Flyers' final 68 games were broadcast on the radio. Even though it was only the third period of games, the added exposure paid dividends.

Gradually, attendance picked up, aided by Joe Scott's brilliant idea. Scott, who had built one of the world's largest beer distributorships and owned 15 percent of the Flyers, helped draw fans and cultivate youngsters to become dedicated to the hockey team.

"Joe was connected to a lot of private schools on the Main Line," Scheinfeld said. "He would go to the schools and give tickets away."

A student got in free, but there was a catch: They had to bring a ticket-buying adult with them.

"We started getting thousands of people from this, and then they would tell other people, and it was fantastic," Scheinfeld said. "Joe Scott was a bull. He was 60 and I was 30—and he wore me out."

During those early days, the Flyers tried just about everything to try to generate interest in the new team in town, including monthly luncheons with fans at the Spectrum's Blue Line Club, along with table-hockey tournaments at local playgrounds. Some Flyers players would attend the luncheons, and some would show up at the table-hockey tournaments.

"Anything to drum up interest," said Jay Seidman, who headed the Flyers' promotion department at the time.

Turning Point with Fans

In the Flyers' 1967–68 debut season, Baldwin said the turning point in the attendance battle was February 3 and 4. More than 50 years later, he still had the dates etched in his mind. They were that important to him when he was a young ticket manager.

On those dates, the Flyers hosted Original Six teams Chicago and Toronto. They beat those opponents 5–3 and 4–1, respectively, before sellout crowds. Scalpers were reportedly getting $10 for tickets that cost $3.25.

The Flyers would soon have to play home games on the road for a while because sections of the Spectrum roof blew off as winds reached nearly 50 miles per hour. Nevertheless, they were becoming a part of Philadelphia's consciousness.

Earlier in their inaugural season, Joe Kadlec, the team's first public relations director, said there was a Monday in which the Flyers received top billing across the *Bulletin*'s lead sports page—above the story on the popular Eagles, who had played the previous day.

"That," Kadlec said, "was pretty exciting. That's when we knew we were on our way."

Still, no one could have imagined that just seven years later, the Flyers, who had become widely known as the Broad Street Bullies, would be the most popular team in Philadelphia.

By far.

The Kate Smith Phenomenon

When Scheinfeld was the Flyers' vice president of business operations in the Spectrum's early years, the Vietnam War was raging. Many people opposed the war, and that led to disrespectful behavior—or indifference—when the national anthem was played before Flyers home games.

"People were unhappy and unpatriotic at the time," Scheinfeld said, adding that many fans sat and talked while the national anthem was being played. "People are eating and smoking and hardly anybody was standing. It pissed me off."

Scheinfeld approached his boss, Snider.

"Listen, I wonder how people would react if we took the national anthem away from them?

"What the hell are you talking about?" Snider responded.

Scheinfeld: "I'm thinking about playing something else."

Snider: "Are you crazy?"

In the next weeks, Snider forgot about the discussion and got involved in more important hockey matters.

But Scheinfeld went on a mission. He was determined to find a song that would inspire the fans. He listened to lots of novelty songs, but none hit home. Finally, while browsing through some dusty records at a store on South Street, he found a song that seemed perfect: Kate Smith's rendition of "God Bless America" from Carnegie Hall.

Scheinfeld had a sound engineer play the song through the Spectrum speakers on a night when the building wasn't in use. When Smith bellowed the last part of the song—"home sweet home"—Scheinfeld got chills.

This song might just work, he thought.

"The building is dark and empty. I asked him to play it several times," Scheinfeld said. "I go up to the last row upstairs.

It sounds fantastic. When she hits that 'from the mountains to the prairies,' I'm like, *Oh my God*. The building is shaking and there's nobody in it! I said, 'This is it.' I felt like Kramer [from *Seinfeld*]. 'This is it!'"

The sound technician converted the record to a reel-to-reel tape.

"That was our high-tech system back then," Scheinfeld said.

Scheinfeld saved the tape's debut for December 11, 1969. The Toronto Maple Leafs were in town, and "it was what I called a money game," he said. "We were facing a big team, and it was being telecast all over Canada and North America."

That night, the public address announcer informed the crowd to please rise and join Kate Smith in singing "God Bless America."

"There was this buzz," Scheinfeld said. "Some people are saying, 'What? What are they singing?' There was some cursing. It was like, 'What the fuck?' And you could hear the buzz."

Snider was furious when he heard it and cursed out Scheinfeld in his Superbox.

"Spittle's coming out of his mouth," Scheinfeld said.

"What the hell are you doing?" Snider asked.

Scheinfeld explained he had told Snider he was going to change songs. Snider wasn't amused.

"I didn't think you were crazy enough to actually do it," he said between expletives.

But a funny thing happened before the game ended and the Flyers beat the Maple Leafs, 6–3. Fans walked by Snider's suite between periods and told him how much they liked the song.

After the game, Snider searched out Scheinfeld.

"You son of a bitch. I don't know how you did it, but you pulled it off," he said.

The Kate Smith era was officially born.

Before Smith's recording was played, the Flyers had won just one of their previous nine games. Her song became the team's good luck charm.

Kate's first live appearance before a Flyers game was in the home opener in the 1973–74 season, a 2–0 win against the Maple Leafs. Seidman, the team's promotions director, had worked with her agent for a year while trying to get her to the Spectrum.

"I was in my early twenties and worked on special projects—and Kate Smith was one of them," Seidman recalled more than 50 years later. "It was a long, slow process, and she probably came because I bugged her agent so much. I would never take no for an answer. If they said, 'Call back in two weeks,' I'd call back in one week."

It also helped that Kate had an uncle who lived in West Philadelphia, and he had been sending her newspaper clippings about her being the Flyers' good luck charm. Kate became intrigued.

The agent said he might be able to work it out "as long as you don't insult me with an offer," Seidman said. "Being a young kid who didn't know much about money, I put out an offer that was insulting."

As Seidman recalls, the original offer was $2,500. The agent wanted $25,000. The parties agreed on $5,000.

"It was a tremendous thrill for it to come through," Seidman said.

The singer was hesitant to perform because the dress she packed was wrinkled, and no one in the Spectrum could find an iron. Disaster was averted when Scheinfeld's secretary called an aunt who lived four blocks away and she ironed the dress.

Kate's second live appearance at the Spectrum was May 19, 1974, the day the Flyers won their first Stanley Cup. When she walked on the ice, she was greeted with a five-minute standing ovation.

"To this day," she said at the time, "it remains the greatest ovation I ever received. It was the greatest thrill of my career."

After Kate sang "God Bless America" before that historic game, Boston Bruins stars Bobby Orr and Phil Esposito tried to alter the jinx she seemed to put on opposing teams. They shook her hand and presented her with roses.

The fans booed.

According to those who worked at the Spectrum at the time, Kate left the ice and said to a security guard, "Wasn't it nice of the Flyers to give me flowers?"

She apparently believed the Flyers were behind the Bruins' gesture.

When told it was, in fact, the Bruins who were responsible for the flowers, she was stunned.

"Whaaaaat?!" she said.

She picked up the roses and tossed them into a trash can.

The Flyers' win that day gave them a 37–3–1 record when "God Bless America" echoed around the Spectrum before games. Before the plug was pulled on Kate's voice in 2019, the Flyers had amassed a 101–31–5 record—a staggering .737 winning percentage—when the song was used.

The song helped rejuvenate her sagging career. Smith, who at one time was so popular that she had her own weekly TV and radio shows, even made four personal appearances to sing the song before Flyers games.

KATE LIVES! bumper stickers became popular in the Philadelphia area.

In a 1974 interview with *Goal Magazine*, Smith was asked what the publicity from her Flyers connection did for her career.

“First and foremost, five PR men could not have gotten me the publicity and coverage in papers all over the country,” she said. “I had front pages in Philadelphia. It was at least a half-million dollars’ worth of publicity. I did not go to the Spectrum for that. What is so wonderful about it is the fact that it’s connected with a wonderful sport.”

Smith died at age 79 in 1986 from diabetes complications, and Snider was one of her pallbearers. So, she and Snider, who died in 2016, did not know about the controversy that surrounded the singer in 2019.

The statue that was erected of her and placed near the Wells Fargo Center was covered in a black tarp. The Flyers, following the lead taken by the New York Yankees, said some songs Smith performed in the 1930s contained “offensive lyrics that do not reflect our values as an organization.”

Smith performed two songs in the ’30s that contained racist, anti-Black lyrics. A fan brought those songs to the attention of the Yankees, who had also played Smith’s rendition of “God Bless America.”

The Yankees removed the song from their musical lineup. The Flyers followed. They canceled the video duet of Smith singing with Lauren Hart performing live. They also covered the statue and removed it.

“I’m very sad and disappointed,” Scheinfeld said at the time. “I think the whole thing could have been handled differently.”

He said covering up the statue was a mistake and that the Flyers rushed to judgment without researching the facts. “When you make a knee-jerk reaction, you can’t take it back.”

Covering the statue, he said, “was grotesque.” He said if Snider was still alive, the statue would not have been covered or removed.

“He had a lot of courage, and I think he would have taken some time to think about it and talked to his people about it and get a feel from the fans," he said. "This thing happened 80 years ago, and it's even questionable about whether it's satire or not. Paul Robeson, the great Black singer, sang it, so there's a lot of extenuating circumstances. I don't think there was any time given for an intelligent discourse."

A local Black Lives Matter activist, Asa Khalif, had called for the Flyers to remove the statue. He said other activists had also expressed anger to the team over Smith's work through social media, emails, and phone calls for more than a year.

In a statement, Paul Holmgren, who was then the Flyers' president, said, "We cannot stand idle while material from another era gets in the way of who we are today."

The Flyers said some songs Smith performed contained "lyrics and sentiments that are incompatible with the values of our organization and provoke painful and unacceptable themes."

The *Philadelphia Inquirer* ran a story on a long-forgotten radio speech Smith made in 1945, one in which she passionately attacked racism and bigotry. She called them "diseases that eat away the fiber of speech."

The newspaper pointed out that there were two 1930s songs that were racially charged—one believed to be a satirical jab at racists, the other performed in a movie—and questioned whether Smith sang them only because she was following her bosses' instructions.

It was also mentioned that Smith was honored in 1945 for fighting racism, and that she gave many African Americans their big break on her TV show.

No matter. The Flyers didn't change their stance. They kept Smith's statue in storage close to the Flyers' arena.

Goodbye, Spectrum

Scheinfeld and Snider were close for several decades, though there was a falling-out period when they didn't speak to each other for nearly 16 years. They reunited when Snider called Scheinfeld in 2008, asking him to return and help close out the soon-to-be-demolished Spectrum.

Snider wanted Scheinfeld to give the venerable building a "proper sendoff. No one cares about that building more than you," Snider told him.

Scheinfeld was supposed to develop a final-year celebration for the building. But the more he got involved, the more he wanted to keep it open. He reached out to people to see if they wanted to make it a sports museum, a small-event venue, or a movie or TV sound stage.

There were no takers.

So Scheinfeld and his staff began the process of selling almost everything from the building, including seats, floorboards, signage, and even urinals. More than $3 million of memorabilia was sold.

When the Spectrum was about to be torn down in 2010, Snider attended the tributes but left before the wrecking ball hit the building. It was too painful to watch.

"Do it without me," he told public relations man Ike Richman after many speeches were made about what transpired during the Spectrum's magical era.

"We can't," Richman protested. "This is your baby."

Snider hopped into a car and off he went, refusing to watch the bricks topple.

Fans had some glorious memories, however. Scheinfeld said it was "fulfilling" to hear the heartfelt stories of people who purchased memorabilia because the Spectrum meant so much to them or their family members. Some talked about their first date there, or their first game, or first concert. Some said they met their future spouse at one of the building's events. Some relived the Flyers winning the 1974 Cup by upsetting Boston.

The stories were endless.

One woman bought her dad a pair of seats—the same two he had used for 40 years after being an original Flyers season-ticket holder. He had retired to Florida, and his daughter said he sits in one of the seats during every Flyers game he watches on TV. "He's so happy, he cries," the woman told Scheinfeld.

That, he said, "tugs at your heart."

Just like the building he named and used to operate.

Snider the Womanizer

While Ed clearly adored his children, he didn't have the same loyalty to the women he married. He was married four times, and he wasn't discreet about some of his extramarital affairs.

"It was constant," said Scheinfeld, admitting he also was a philanderer back in the day. "And he didn't cover his tracks."

Scheinfeld described Snider as the Don Draper character in the hit TV show *Mad Men.*

"Ed was a very, very sharp dresser. Everything was custom made," Scheinfeld said. "A very stylish, classy guy. When he walked into a room, you knew it. You just felt electricity coming off this guy. He was so intense, so focused, and he had a certain air about him. He could be very friendly. He would walk around and say hello to everybody."

Snider wasn't good at hiding his extramarital affairs, Scheinfeld said. "Let me put it this way. He didn't cover his tracks well. He had a Flyers-orange Corvette with F1 on the license plate. He had a girlfriend on Naudain Street."

The Center City street was so narrow that cars could barely fit on it.

"He would park half on the pavement, and half on the street," Scheinfeld said. "And cars couldn't get by it. I said to him one day, 'I see you were over [at] what's-her-name's house last night.' He says, 'How did you know?' I tell him, 'Your car is parked right outside her door, for Christ's sake.' Like I said, he didn't cover his tracks too well. And he was a bad liar. He would look down [when lying] and not have his facts straight. There might be lipstick on his shirt. Yeah, that might be a hint."

Ed asked his wife, Myrna, to have an open marriage, Scheinfeld said. "He wanted to see other women. She found out he was fucking around," Scheinfeld said.

Even though they were married at the time, Scheinfeld said he and Snider felt like they were bachelors in the summer.

"Look at the two of us," he said. "My wife is at the beach all summer, and Myrna is in Maine all summer. He and I are left to our own devices."

They bedded as many women as they could, he said.

"Don't forget, this is the late '60s, early '70s," Scheinfeld said. "Free love, pot. Pantyhose hadn't been invented yet. Girls are still wearing silk stockings with garters, and there was free love every night. I mean, no bras. They're burning their bras, and he and I succumbed to the sirens of the street."

According to Scheinfeld, the end of Snider's first marriage came on the other side of the Atlantic Ocean.

"Ed buys this boat, the Centra, this big 105-foot boat with a crew," Scheinfeld said. "The boat was in Europe with Myrna, and Ed flies over."

At this point, Myrna was very aware of her husband's indiscretions.

"Myrna had heard all about his peccadilloes and even spoke to some of the girls that he had seen from their social circles," Scheinfeld said. "And she was disgusted with him."

Ed knew it. He tried to appease her.

"He'd go out and buy her $1,000 earrings and all this shit," Scheinfeld said. "Myrna and I were dear friends until she died [of lung cancer in 2014 at age 78]. She would say, 'Look, he's trying to buy me and pulling all this shit.' And she was straight [with me] because if anybody was going to mess with her, it would've been me—and I never did because I loved her like a sister. She was the best, the absolute best. One of the best women I've ever met in my life."

When Ed traveled to Europe and met Myrna on the boat, he noticed she was making the captain appetizers and drinks and bringing them to him.

"Ed tells me this after he gets back," Scheinfeld said, adding that Snider "got a little pissed" at all the attention his wife was giving the captain. "He confronted her, and she says, 'Well, I'm doing what you're doing.'"

She then told her husband she was having an affair with the captain.

"He goes nuts," Scheinfeld said, telling Snider's side. "Now his story is that he jumps off the boat, swims to the shore. They weren't that far off the shore. Somehow, he gets a change of clothes and flies home. Her story is that he insisted that they take him to the dock."

The Sniders got divorced in 1981.

In 2001 Myrna married the sea captain, Martin Thomas. They sailed around the world for several years, sometimes with family and friends.

Ed ended up marrying three more times after he divorced Myrna, a woman whose caring way created the feeling of family among the Flyers players and their wives and children during the franchise's early days.

"Everybody loved Myrna," Scheinfeld said. "Just a wonderful person."

Friendly. Funny. Caring. That's how most people describe Myrna.

"She was absolutely extraordinary for the growth of the franchise because that rubbed off on everybody," said Baldwin, the Flyers' first ticket manager.

CHAPTER 12

GENE HART: BELOVED BROADCASTER HAD "WARS" WITH A BROAD STREET BULLY

Gene Hart was the Philadelphia Flyers' beloved broadcaster during their golden years; he was someone who educated the fans, many of whom were unfamiliar with hockey when the franchise started in 1967.

His excitement reached a crescendo when the Flyers were peppering the net with shots, and "He shoots, he scores!" became a repeated phrase from Cape May to Conshohocken...and everywhere in between.

It was probably Hart's favorite phrase. But he had a slew of them, and he used them with vigor and perfect timing, like Tom Hanks delivering a memorable line in a movie.

"Gene performed. He didn't just do play-by-play," said Bill Clement, a center on Philadelphia's two title teams and later an analyst for the Flyers and ESPN. "As a result of his desire to perform—and he seemed to be a born performer—his call was almost theatrical at times. And that's what separated him from everybody else."

As the 50th anniversary of the Flyers' first Stanley Cup approached, Jimmy Watson said Hart was a big part of creating such a huge fan base.

"He was really instrumental in helping hockey grow in the Philadelphia region," said Watson, a rookie defenseman when the Flyers won the Cup in 1974. "He actually took it on himself to be an educator to the fans about the game. So, he would explain offside, icing, the penalties, things like that. The fans were learning as they went along, and they really came to love and respect Gene for that."

When the Flyers started, many fans thought icing was something atop some of their Tastykakes, not a frequent term used in hockey.

"He loved the Flyers," said Gary Dornhoefer, an invaluable right winger during the team's glory days and a man who later was in the broadcast booth with Hart. "I mean, they could do no wrong. Let's face it. When you work for a team, you're almost like a cheerleader. And if you're not, you get reprimanded."

Dornhoefer remembers a member of the Flyers' brass criticizing him and Hart "for getting too excited when the opposition scored."

They were told to calm themselves down. Such is the life of a sports broadcaster.

Hart had a magical voice that could go up and down like a roller-coaster, depending on the situation on the ice. He could make a scramble in front of the net sound just as exciting as a game-winning goal.

"They POKE at it; they JAM at it. It's LOOSE IN FRONT," he would tell fans in a voice that started in a matter-of-fact tone and then reached a crescendo as, for a split second, he realized a goal might be in the making.

He was known as the "Voice of the Flyers" for more than two decades, but Hart was knowledgeable in all facets of life. He could talk with authority about Russian culture or the opera—just as comfortably as he explained why Bobby Clarke had such a high plus-minus rating.

"Gene was almost bigger than life," Watson said, "and he had a little bit of an ego. He liked to show off and exhibit how smart he was to everybody. But he was an encyclopedia of information. You could ask him basically anything, and he would come up with the answer. And if he didn't know it, he would get an answer for you."

Hart, who always seemed to have a Coke in his hand, had a playful sparring partner on the Flyers, Bob "The Hound" Kelly.

They would frequently take verbal jabs at each other. Hart would tell the left winger his IQ matched his uniform number (9). Kelly would tell the broadcaster if he skipped meals for a month, he'd still be overweight.

Flyers plane trips and bus rides were always entertaining because of Hart and Kelly.

"They would go at it pretty good," Watson said, mindful that the "combatants" respected and loved each other to the core but took pleasure in the art of busting chops.

"You'd get arrested today for some of the things we did back then," Kelly said as the 50th anniversary of the Flyers' first Stanley Cup approached.

One day, shortly after the Flyers boarded a flight in the 1970s, Kelly asked the stewardess if he could make an announcement over the plane's loudspeaker.

She agreed.

Kelly grabbed the mic and disguised his voice.

"Excuse me. Mr. Gene Hart? Mr. Gene Hart? Could you please identify yourself?"

Hart, who was nicknamed the "Great Pumpkin" by Kelly, sheepishly raised his hand.

Kelly went back to the mic.

"Mr. Gene Hart? Can you please stand up?"

Hart had no idea what was going on. Annoyed, he unbuckled his seatbelt and wiggled his chubby body to stand up in the tight space.

Kelly had Hart right where he wanted him.

"Momentarily, sir, we will be around with a seat belt extender," he cracked.

The players roared.

Kelly, his teammates, and the staff deeply admired Hart. But, hey, a good prank is a good prank, and Kelly had pulled it off at 30,000 feet.

"We used to just bug each other," Kelly said. "It was in our DNA. It was like, who could get the last jab in?"

An Ornery Side

Hart was playful and had an ornery side. And, oh, how he loved the Flyers. Say something negative about the Orange and Black and it lit a fuse.

During the 1973–74 season, for instance, Chicago was battling the Flyers for first place. Chicago coach Billy Reay kept predicting his team would catch Philadelphia in the standings.

In the process, the coach took a jab at Flyers wingers Dave Schultz and Don Saleski. Actually, he showed Schultz the ultimate disrespect by not even knowing his correct name, calling him "Schwartz."

Schultz was known for his fighting, but he scored 20 goals that season. When the left winger collected a hat trick in a 4–2 win over the New York Rangers on January 3, Hart sent the following telegram to Reay in Chicago, according to John Brogan, who then worked in the Flyers' public relations department:

"Schwartz scored three tonight."

Signed: Don Saleski.

Hart was just getting started.

In his next game at the Spectrum, Schultz again scored a hat trick, this one against Minnesota.

Hart sent another telegram.

"Schwartz did it again!"

Signed: Don Saleski.

In the Flyers' next Spectrum game, it was Saleski's turn to shine. The lanky right winger scored the lone goal in a 1–0 win over Atlanta.

Hart knew what he had to say in his next telegram.

"Saleski did it tonight!"

Signed: Schwartz.

Lauren Hart's Memories

Lauren Hart, Gene's daughter, is an accomplished singer. She performed for President Bill Clinton's inauguration and did songs for TV series and movies. During Flyers home games, she inspires the crowd with her stirring rendition of the national anthem.

As a little girl, she wouldn't attend Flyers home games that ended late because she had school the next day. But she vividly remembers lying in bed late at night and determining whether the Flyers had won or lost in an unusual manner.

If the door in their South Jersey home opened and she could smell her dad's cigar smoke drifting upstairs to her bedroom, that meant he was happy, and the team had won.

If the door opened and she soon heard classical music from a record, that meant her dad was in a more pensive mood. It also meant the Flyers had lost.

"He was silent, but there was opera music playing, like a tragic event had just happened," Lauren recalled with a soft smile nearly five decades later. "He mourned every single loss, and he [celebrated] every single win."

Gene looked at the games differently than most people. He had a much deeper view.

"He always said that hockey and this team was a metaphor for life," Lauren said. "It was the good guys and the bad guys. The triumphs and the tragedies of people. The camaraderie, the enemy, the heroes."

NYC to South Jersey

Gene Hart was born in New York City and moved to South Jersey at a young age. He played baseball, a sport in which he excelled, and football at Pleasantville High, close to the Jersey Shore, and then attended Trenton State College, where he earned his teaching degree.

When he got out of the Army in 1957, Hart officiated football, baseball, and basketball games. He later began broadcasting high school games while still maintaining his day job as a New Jersey history teacher.

The Flyers were looking for broadcasters when they landed a franchise in 1967. Hart had little experience, but he submitted an audition tape.

Hart had gone to Madison Square Garden with a cassette recorder to make the tape as he watched a New York Rangers game.

He started the Flyers' first season as their public address announcer. Early in the season, however, he became their radio voice.

The Flyers had hired him partly because he was inexpensive, and they didn't have a big budget.

They would hire a more "known" announcer when they could afford it. That was the theory. But Hart had other plans.

Hart, who was known for his intense preparation and research before games, quickly assumed the play-by-play duties, and he lasted 29 years with the Flyers, with many of his broadcasts simulcasted on radio and TV.

His machine-gun delivery was perfect for hockey, and he did more than 2,000 Flyers games, including Stanley Cup Finals in 1974, 1975, 1976, 1980, 1985, and 1987.

Hart's son, Brian, was at most of the home games during the Flyers' glory years, sitting beside his dad in the press box. He also traveled to several of the road games that were drivable and attended many West Coast matchups when Philly played there after Christmas.

"I'd carry his briefcase into the press box," said Brian, who also tagged along with his dad when he called horse races at Brandywine Raceway, located in Wilmington, DE, in the summer.

When he was about 12 years old, Brian traveled with his dad and the Flyers to Western Canada. After a game in Edmonton, Brian got into an altercation with a fan as he was walking to the Flyers' team bus.

"Back then, Canadian crowds were usually very sedate; it's a much different game experience than games in the States," Brian said. "It was a very intelligent crowd, and they knew the game very well, but they were quiet."

Some of the folks in this Edmonton crowd, however, were more boisterous than usual.

After the game, Gene Hart and most of the Flyers were already on the team bus as Brian walked to the vehicle, planning to sit next to his father.

Edmonton Oilers fans pushed the bus and rocked it, Brian said.

An adult male fan shouted expletives at the Flyers and pushed him, said Brian, who returned the favor. With the players and Gene Hart watching through the bus windows, Brian and the

Oilers fan got into a shoving match. A security guard approached, and the fan disappeared into the crowd.

"I'm horrified because you're supposed to be unobtrusive and be on your best behavior," Brian said. "You're not supposed to cheer [from the press box], let alone get into a fight. For a second, I'm thinking, *I really fucked up*."

Brian's fears were unfounded. As he walked onto the bus, the players cheered for him. He became an honorary Broad Street Bully.

"Way to go," said one of them.

Another player patted him on the back as he sheepishly walked to his seat next to his dad.

Brian laughed at the memory.

"That's when I learned that fighting can be a good thing," he said.

Gene Hart didn't give his son any grief.

"The players loved it, so he loved it," Brian said.

Personal Touch

Hart, who called his listeners "friends" while on the air, incorporated a sense of humor and his personal touch into broadcasts, which he ended with his trademark: "Good night, good hockey."

The son of a Hungarian acrobat (his dad, who produced shows) and a former Viennese opera singer (his mom), Hart was a natural storyteller, and he had plenty of tales to tell from the variety of jobs he worked over the years. He had been a car salesman, a bill collector and repo man, a rock-and-roll disc jockey. He had also been a teacher, a water clown, and a dolphin-show emcee, among other things.

Hart's family once operated the famous water circus on Atlantic City's Steel Pier. He became part of a diving clown act known as

Binswanger Bathing Beauties. While working there by the Atlantic Ocean, he met his future wife, Sarah Detwiler, who was diving on horses on the Boardwalk at Steel Pier.

As bizarre as it now sounds to animal-rights activists, a horse would run up a long, carpeted ramp while the rider waited at the top, 40 feet above. The "diving girl" rider would mount the horse, and they would jump into an 11-foot tank before pushing off the bottom to spring back up.

This was during Atlantic City's heyday, when big stars would perform at Steel Pier, including Frank Sinatra, Ricky Nelson, and the Rolling Stones.

Hart's future wife was a star in her own right; she would jump with her horse into a big tank of water, a popular attraction that lasted from 1929 to 1978.

"But it was well-padded," Sarah recalled. "It had all kinds of foamy stuff all around it, and the horses would never get hurt. Scientifically, the horse could not miss the tank. It was perfectly safe."

Sarah had other jobs. She met Gene when she was working a Steel Pier basketball stand on the Boardwalk, where you could win salt-water taffies or packs of cigarettes by making baskets.

Showing people how it was done, Sarah was shooting hoops one day and "all these kids started running toward a very tall person" who was tossing shots next to her. "I beat him by one basket, and I found out later who it was," she said.

A guy named Wilt Chamberlain.

Because of the way the hoops were set up, "you couldn't put any arc on the ball," Sarah said. "You had to hit the rim and get it in that way."

Chamberlain "stomped off a bit" after she beat him.

So, Gene Hart married the woman who once won a shooting contest against arguably the greatest player in NBA history.

A Budding Hockey "Annonser"

Gene grew up in New York City in the 1930s and became a die-hard Rangers fan. As a kid, he worked on Atlantic City's Steel Pier during the summer and kept notes and autographs in a satin-covered book. Some of the autographs were from notable performers like Abbott and Costello, Eddie "Rochester" Anderson, Betty Grable, Harry James, Eddie Cantor, and Kate Smith.

The book also included a spot to predict his future, Gene recalled in *Score! My Twenty-Five Years with The Broad Street Bullies.*

There was a part in the book that read: "I want to be when I grow up…"

Gene, who was around eight years old at the time, finished the sentence with HOCKEY ANNONSER. (He added his spelling had improved since that entry.)

Little did he know that it would take nearly 30 years to fulfill his destiny—and with a team that wouldn't exist until 1967.

Gene's family moved to South Jersey in 1941. They settled in Absecon Highlands, about 15 miles from Atlantic City.

Country life didn't agree with Gene. He was a city kid, used to taking the subway to go to the Polo Grounds or Ebbets Field. The Rangers, Brooklyn Dodgers, and New York Giants (in both baseball and football) were his teams, and he would listen to as many games as he could on the New York radio stations.

He loved hockey more than any sport, and he became even more hooked when his dad took him to New York in 1944 to see his first Rangers game in person. It was an epiphany of sorts. When he was in high school and college, he would take the 250-mile round trip from South Jersey to Madison Square Garden to watch his beloved (and then-awful) Rangers.

Gene also began listening to *Hockey Night in Canada* broadcasts done by the legendary Foster Hewitt, who unknowingly became an inspiration to Hart.

Hewitt did the first hockey broadcasts in the 1920s for the Toronto Maple Leafs. "He was the man who created the vocabulary for a hockey broadcaster," Gene wrote in his book, which was co-authored with Buzz Ringe.

In February of 1958, Gene made his broadcasting debut, working a Trenton High basketball game for WOND radio. At the time, no one knew it would be the start of a legendary career. He later became the high school radio voice for football and basketball games played by the Atlantic City Vikings, Ocean City Red Raiders, and Pleasantville Greyhounds—never getting paid more than $15 per game, and even having to pay for gas and expenses out of his pocket.

But most important to Gene was the fact he was learning his craft, which included handling the equipment, doing commercials, and keeping statistics. He was also gaining poise and confidence on the airwaves.

While continuing to broadcast high school sports, Gene had several other jobs. At various times, he worked as a sports car salesman, the operator of an FM music station, and a teacher. He then worked in South Philadelphia at Aquarama Aquarium, a Marineland-type exhibit that included a whale and dolphin show. (It was located across the street from where the Spectrum would be built.) Gene served as an announcer and assistant public relations director, hosting several shows a day.

Still, his lifetime ambition was to become a hockey announcer, and when he learned in 1966 that a Philadelphia group consisting of Jerry Wolman, Ed Snider, and Bill Putnam was landing an NHL team, Gene snapped to attention. The Flyers would start in 1967–68, and Gene needed to get some experience broadcasting hockey games.

Trying to get hockey interest in the area, the Flyers sponsored the Jersey Devils at the Cherry Hill Arena, and he ended up broadcasting the third period of their home games on WKDN, the Camden radio station where he was doing some high school games.

By broadcasting Devils games, Gene got to know some key Flyers personnel, including Keith Allen, who was their first coach. He also became friendly with Stu Nahan, who was broadcasting Eagles games and working on a children's television show as Captain Philadelphia. (Nahan became the original play-by-play voice of the Flyers on channel 48.)

Gene was determined to impress the Flyers. With help from the New York Rangers' public relations staff, he was able to tape his broadcast of the second period against the Boston Bruins at Madison Square Garden.

Boston won 2–1 behind a young goaltender named Bernie Parent. Young defenseman Joe Watson also aided the Bruins' win.

Hart made the audition tape and presented it to the Flyers. By then, Nahan had been hired to do the TV games. Gene was hopeful he would get a call to be their radio voice.

On one hand, he had great hockey knowledge. On the other hand, he had little experience broadcasting the sport.

Finally, he got a call from Putnam, who was then the Flyers' president.

"Bill asked me if I'd like to be the P.A. announcer for the Flyers' home games," Hart wrote in *Score!* "At first, I felt a little bit as though I'd won a consolation prize in a beauty contest."

But he quickly became thrilled "to be involved with sports, especially hockey at the major-league level."

He called it his "lifelong dream. And, now, suddenly, here I was in the National Hockey League, along with Parent and Watson and the rest of the people acquired by the Flyers in the expansion draft."

Early in the Flyers' first season, Hart, then 36, heard an announcement that the team had signed a deal to broadcast games on WCAU radio.

Hart was despondent. He had never been informed, so he assumed someone else had been hired as the Flyers' radio voice. Maybe it would be the well-known Bill Campbell, who had done Phillies, Eagles, and (Philadelphia) Warriors games. Maybe it would be someone from Canada who had hockey experience.

So, Hart was not in a good mood when he received a call from Nahan, the Flyers' TV voice.

Nahan told him the Flyers would have the third periods of most of their remaining games on the radio.

"I heard," Hart replied.

"You don't sound very excited," Nahan said.

"Should I be?" Hart replied.

"Sure, you're going to do them."

Hart, who had broadcast high school football games while standing in the rain, was flabbergasted.

His wife, Sarah, was by his side. She saw her husband's smile lengthen and was curious as to what was happening.

Gene covered the receiver.

"I'm a star!" he said, beaming proudly.

"All our lives are intertwined forever because of that phone call," Lauren Hart said 50-some years later.

Poking Fun at Himself

In his book, Hart said the Flyers didn't have a lot of money in 1967 to hire a big-name, high-priced announcer, "so for the time being, they penciled in the native local high school sports guy from South Jersey, despite his being fat, unknown, and one of the world's worst dressers."

He was paid just $50 a game but didn't complain because he felt he had a bright future.

"I was blessed by being at the right place at the right time," he said.

Left unsaid: he worked hard to be in the "right place."

In his first game, the man who as a youngster wrote he wanted to be a HOCKEY ANNONSER, did the third period at the fabled Forum in Montreal. Only the third periods were broadcast because the Flyers didn't have many advertisers in those days.

Hart prayed the Flyers wouldn't be getting blown out by the time the November 4 game went on the air.

When the third period started, however, it was the expansion Flyers who were leading the Canadiens 2–1. Former Canadien Leon "Cheesie" Rochefort scored the only two goals of the third period, giving him the first hat trick in the Flyers' young history.

The Flyers won 4–1 as Parent made 33 saves. It was their first victory over an Original Six team, and Hart was feeling exhilarated when he phoned home after the game and talked to Sarah.

"How was it?" he asked.

"It was," she said, "like a symphony."

The first of many.

Huge Following

Hart did radio and TV from 1967–68 to 1994–95, and he created a huge following because of his frenetic style and his ability to make the listener/viewer feel they were in the arena with him. He painted pictures with his words, and he did it so well that he went into the Hockey Hall of Fame in 1997, the winner of the Foster Hewitt Memorial Award.

Lauen Hart said the Flyers players were like brothers to her dad, and that could be felt in his passionate broadcasts. "They were his family," she said. "He loved the game, and he loved those guys as much as anyone can love anything."

In 1999 Gene died at a hospital in Camden, New Jersey, where he was being treated for severe dehydration and an infection following chemotherapy to treat a tumor. Wayne Fish, who covered the Flyers for the *Bucks County Courier Times*, captured Hart perfectly in his eulogy:

"A man of the arts, a cultural type.

"Conversant in Pavarotti, but just as comfortable hanging out with guys like [former Flyer] Lou Angotti."

Fish drew laughs and nods from the 3,000 or so people who attended the mostly somber ceremony at the Flyers' arena.

Gene made hundreds (thousands?) of memorable calls, but the most famous one was in the closing seconds of the Flyers' Stanley Cup–clinching 1–0 win over Boston on May 19, 1974.

"Ladies and gentlemen, the Flyers are going to win the Stanley Cup! The Flyers win the Stanley Cup! The Flyers win the Stanley Cup! The Flyers have won the Stanley Cup!"

Years later, Flyers owner Ed Snider said he still got goose bumps when he listened to Hart describe the final seconds.

"It will go down in sports history," Snider once said, "as one of the greatest broadcast moments of all time."

Flyers fans would agree.

But Hart almost wasn't in the booth to make the most famous call in franchise history.

Snider was always one of Hart's biggest supporters and the two men were close. But a few years before the Flyers won their first Cup, Snider was furious that Gene mixed up some names during a game the owner watched. He voiced his displeasure to his right-hand man, Lou Scheinfeld.

"Gene Hart is calling the wrong people," Snider said in the angry phone call.

"Well, he's way up in the ceiling calling the games," Scheinfeld replied.

"He's saying it's Bob Clarke, and it's Bill Clement," Snider said. "I've had it with him. I want him fired."

The next day, Snider strolled into work near 11:00 AM. He liked to sleep late and work late.

"What's going on?" he said to Scheinfeld.

"I'm interviewing new announcers," Scheinfeld said.

"What for?"

"Well, I fired Gene Hart."

Snider's eyes bulged.

"What?!!! You did what?!!! Are you crazy?!!"

"You told me to," Scheinfeld said.

"You listened? Since when do you listen to me?" Snider asked.

Scheinfeld smiled softly.

"Look, I didn't fire him," Scheinfeld said. "I never even called him."

Snider was relieved.

Scheinfeld knew how to read Snider, knew he was just venting when he complained about Hart the previous night. He knew that, deep down, Snider was a big fan of Hart's work.

Hart would have an illustrious career with the Flyers and would become a broadcasting icon in the city. If they ever built a Mount Rushmore of Philadelphia sports broadcasters, you know it would include Bill Campbell and Harry Kalas.

You also know it would include Gene Hart, a man who played a huge role in making the Broad Street Bullies become a part of Philadelphia's sports lore.

CHAPTER 13

FLYERS CHILDREN: THEIR INNOCENT AND AMUSING PERSPECTIVE

THEIR FATHERS BECAME FAMOUS, but the children of the Stanley Cup champion Philadelphia Flyers didn't look at them that way. They looked at them as dads who had cool jobs that took the kids to the bottom level of the Spectrum.

It was their playroom, of sorts.

"It was magical," said Lindy Snider, whose dad, Ed, was one of the franchise's founders.

In the bowels of the Spectrum—an unassuming oval building that percolated with excitement during Flyers games—they played hide and seek under the stands while navigating hundreds of stacked chairs and chased the cats who chased the mice. It was where the kids got into lots of mischief and liked to go into the locker room and erase the messages that cerebral coach Fred Shero had scribbled on the blackboard.

Thankfully, Shero's most famous message—"Win today and we walk together forever"—was never wiped away. But some of the girls not only erased other messages, but proudly wrote their names on the blackboard—naïve to the fact they were identifying themselves as guilty.

"We used to write weird messages on it all the time," Jody Clarke, daughter of Bobby and Sandy, remembered nearly five decades later. "And then we'd write our own names."

Ah, the innocence of youth.

Whereas Shero sent a code of conduct that the wives needed to follow, he did no such thing for their children.

"He did try to make his son, Ray, and Jamie Leach [a future NHL player who was the son of Reggie] and my brother, Wade, look after us," Jody said. The boys wanted no part of it. Instead, they were glued to the practices or games.

"They watched on the ice, and we'd wreak havoc and go play in the locker room," Jody said.

Eventually, the boys would make their way to the locker room and help themselves to some equipment.

"I used to steal Rick MacLeish's sticks all the time," said Ray Shero, who many years later served as general manager of the Pittsburgh Penguins and New Jersey Devils. "He scored 50 goals one year and he probably would have scored more but I'm guessing he ran out of sticks."

Ray Shero remembers Marcel Pelletier, a onetime Flyers player personnel director who played a key role in helping build the team's Stanley Cup championships, telling him and the other kids that if they ever got bored, they could go into his Spectrum office.

To this day, Shero doesn't know if Pelletier, who died in 2017 at age 89, was kidding, but he took him up on his offer one night.

"So, we're beating the California Golden Seals like 10–1, and I'm getting so bored, right?" Shero recalled five decades later. He went to Pelletier's office and innocently opened some of his drawers. One of them had a stack of *Playboy* magazines.

During intermission, Ray Shero's mom met up with him and asked her teenage son if he was coming back upstairs to watch the rest of the game. "And I'm like, 'Maybe, Mom. Maybe.'" Shero said.

The Kids Felt Protected

The sons of the players and of the team's executives always felt like the Flyers had their backs.

Jay Snider, one of Ed's three sons, remembers sitting with his brother, Craig, during a 1974 playoff game in Boston. "We were maybe a row or two behind the team's bench in the year we won the Cup," he said. Jay was 16 at the time. "The Bruins' fans were throwing coins at us and hitting us in the head."

A shouting match ensued, and a security guard came down to restore order.

"After the game, [Flyers winger] Bob Kelly comes down and says, 'What was going on behind the bench with you guys?' I didn't know he saw us back there," Jay Snider said. "He's serious, and he says, 'I was ready to climb over the glass.' True story. He wasn't fooling around. He was actually watching what was going on, this confrontation. So, you don't even think they're seeing this stuff, or their heads are going to be somewhere else, but he had his eyes on us."

They were all together in this, all part of the Flyers family, all part of the Broad Street Bullies.

Years later, Ed Snider kept that family together by hiring numerous former players and putting them in different roles—some in the front office, some as club ambassadors, some on the coaching or scouting staffs.

"Once a Flyer, always a Flyer," was his motto, Jay Snider said.

Back in their early years, the Flyers and their families had a closeness that was created by Ed Snider's first wife, Myrna. She was the person who helped put together a Christmas party on the ice each year. The players' kids skated, drank hot chocolate, met Santa Claus, and opened presents she had purchased for them. She also bought presents for the players and their wives, among others.

"Everybody in the organization was a part of it. People that worked in the ticket office would be skating on the ice with the team. It was a big family event. That's what it felt like," said Jay Snider, who at 25 became the Flyers' president in 1983. "This organization was so bonded. It didn't matter whether you were a player, a GM, or a ticket seller. Everybody knew each other and loved each other, and enjoyed getting to actually spend time together."

"And at that time, everybody was at everybody's house. We all lived close by," said Lauren Hart, whose dad, Gene, was the Flyers' broadcaster in those years. "All the families were interconnected. They all lived in the same neighborhoods," mostly in South Jersey, a short ride from where the Flyers played across the Walt Whitman Bridge in South Philadelphia.

Several of the Flyers and their families would eat Sunday dinners at each other's houses or spend the holidays together.

"We were all like family, because our [real] families were all up in Canada," said Kerri Barber Dean, whose dad, Bill, was the Flyers' star left winger at that time.

Jody Clarke said the players' kids were "bubble-wrapped in our own way. We were insulated by each other. Every year after Christmas, all the wives would throw their kids in an RV, and we'd all be on our way to Killington" while the players went on a road trip. Ski trips to Killington or the Poconos were common for the families the players left behind.

Play Time for the Players' Children

Before home games, the team's brass, such as Ed Snider, Fred Shero, and Keith Allen, and their wives would meet in the director's lounge and have a buffet dinner. Their kids would eat dinner and do their homework in the room. When they were done, some would play imaginative games and some would play street hockey in the hallways on the Spectrum's bottom level. Ray Shero, Blake Allen, Craig and Jay Snider, among others, would have to stop the game and move their net as the players filtered into the locker room.

The players' wives had their own lounge, a nondescript room where they ate dinner, and some stashed the leftover booze into the drop ceiling for future use.

Jody Clarke, Tina Snider, Kerri Barber, Kendra Kelly, Brandie Leach, Danielle MacLeish, and the other younger kids would play hide and seek under the stands. There, they would find cats who looked weak and in need of a good meal, so the kids would sneak back to the lounge and take some chicken, steak, and other items to feed their "pets."

The kids weren't at all the home games. Most of the younger ones stayed home if a game was played on a school night.

"Wade and I would wait for the schedule to come out every year," Jody Clarke said, referring to her brother. "And we'd circle all the afternoon games and the games that fell over our school holidays because we knew we'd go to them."

Like Jody, Danielle MacLeish Stewart, whose late dad, Rick, was one of the Flyers' stars during their heyday, is among many of the players' children who have fond memories of running around the Spectrum's vast basement during the 1970s and 1980s, or dancing on a stage at Ovations bar-restaurant in the arena.

The players' kids "were like all a part of our families because most of us didn't have [an extended] family around here at the time," Danielle said. "Kerri Barber was like my sister.

"All the kids knew the Spectrum inside and out," Danielle said. "They knew all the little crevices and hiding spots. I mean, we were pretty much let loose while practices or games were going on. We didn't have much supervision; it was like, *Just find something to do*."

Cecilia Baker, who worked in the ticket office, was an unofficial babysitter, and the kids gravitated toward her. When a game wasn't being played, they would wander to the Spectrum's third level, which was added in 1972 and increased the seating capacity from 14,646 to 17,007, because it was a cool hiding spot.

"We got in trouble for being all the way up top," Danielle said.

Dads Needed Their Rest

All of the players' children remember they were instructed to be quiet at home during game days so their dads could take an afternoon nap, a ritual that still occurs in the 2020s.

"My mom would put a note on the front door, 'Do Not Ring Doorbell,'" recalled Kerri Barber Dean. "And she'd make us as kids take naps. And no kid wants to take a nap, so I used to dread game day because of that."

The players reacted to the game results differently. Some came home and stewed after a loss. Some were more talkative and engaging after a win.

Some were more even-keeled, and you couldn't tell if the team had won or lost by their demeanor.

Rick MacLeish fit that category, according to his daughter, Danielle.

"My dad was a man of very few words," she said, adding she didn't know her father was famous until she became a teenager. "I couldn't tell the difference between how he acted after a win or a loss. He didn't show a lot of emotion."

She said one of the memories she has of watching her dad play was seeing a brawl and MacLeish "skating around on the outside. He wasn't part of it. And I was like, *What the heck. Come on, get in there!* And he was just skating around and not a part of that."

MacLeish, who was a good fighter in the rare times he got into an altercation, was one of the league's best scorers and probably knew he was more valuable on the ice than in the penalty box.

"An Amazing Grandfather"

Danielle was asked what she wanted people to remember about her dad, who died at age 66 in 2016 after battling meningitis, and kidney and liver problems.

"He was a kind, good-hearted person," she said. "He was an amazing grandfather."

She paused, overcome with emotion. Her four-year-old son, Tyler, died in 2007.

Several days a week, Rick would babysit/hang out with Tyler while Danielle worked. They would go to ice skating lessons, hockey games, and do other things together. To those close to Rick, he was a quiet person who seemed more comfortable being around kids than adults. Tyler would spend the summers at his grandfather's house in Ocean City, New Jersey, and Rick took him on a memorable trip to Disney World.

Rick MacLeish and his wife, Carolyn, had two daughters, Danielle and Brianna, and later got divorced.

"He finally got his boy, so they were super, super close. And that destroyed him," Danielle said of Tyler's death.

She and her husband have two teenage daughters, Rylie and Jayden.

The girls, she said, got her dad's athletic genes, especially when they play soccer.

Danielle said her youngest daughter, Jayden, has her grandfather's unassuming personality—on and off the soccer field.

"She plays soccer the way he played hockey," she said. "Very effortlessly. When I watch her play, I'm like, *Oh my God*. Some people used to get annoyed with my dad because it didn't look like he was trying very hard. And that's exactly how she plays. She doesn't have to put in an all-out effort, and she plays amazingly."

Her dad played with a coolness as he smoothly skated and whipped one of his trademark wrist shots, which became his No. 1 weapon. He knew when to turn things up a notch on the ice. It was a style that produced 349 career goals (328 with the Flyers) and made him one of the leading scorers in franchise history.

Coincidentally, Kerri Barber Dean says her son, Cameron, has a lot of the traits of her dad, Bill, who became a Hockey Hall of Famer.

Cameron plays baseball at Missouri Western State and is "the spitting image of my dad," said Kerri, who worked primarily in the marketing department for Comcast SportsNet Philadelphia from 1997 to 2008. She now lives in Kansas City with her husband and two sons. "My son is an unsung hero, like my dad was.... He's a catcher, so he's kind of a leader on the team, but he doesn't do it in your face. He's a behind-the-scenes player who leads by example. His coach called him a throwback. I watch him and I'm like, *Oh my God. That's my dad.*"

She said Cameron's mannerisms "are just like my dad's—the way he walks, the looks that he gives."

Kerri has fond memories rooting for her dad and the Flyers, though she has mixed feelings about the 1980 Stanley Cup Finals, when they faced the New York Islanders.

She was five years old at the time, and her dad had promised her a bike if they won the Cup.

"I remember my mom had a bunch of the wives over to watch the game," she said of Game 6 in the thrilling and controversial 1980 Final. "They lost, and the wives are crying, and I'm sitting on the floor crying. I'm crying because I'm not going to get my bike."

The next day, however, her dad "took me to get a bike anyhow, bless him. It was pink and it had a little Petunia Pig bell on it. It's crazy the things you remember."

Kerri was born at the height of Flyers mania in Philadelphia. It was less than three months after the Broad Street Bullies won their first Stanley Cup in 1974, and she has been told stories about her mother vomiting at their first championship parade because she was ill during her pregnancy. "She told me she was sicker than sick that day," Kerri said.

When she was born in Philadelphia's Methodist Hospital, Kerri said, she later learned that scores of people visiting the hospital walked up to the glass and pointed at her like she was royalty. All because she was the daughter of Bill Barber, Stanley Cup champion.

"My mom told me all these old Italians were coming in just to get a glimpse of you!" she said. "She was kind of touched by it. And she told me that after they won the second Cup, there were people camped out on our lawn at our house in Somerdale [New Jersey]."

They were celebrating that their neighbor, one of them, was a national hero.

Lasting Bonds

Bill Barber and Rick MacLeish, who was mostly a loner, were close. So were their wives, Jenny Barber (who was 48 when she died in 2001 of lung cancer) and Carolyn MacLeish. The bonds continued with their daughters as Danielle MacLeish and Kerri Barber became best friends. Ditto Jody Clarke and Brandie Leach. Those players' daughters are still best friends today, long after some of them had erased coach Fred Shero's blackboard poetry to the players.

That unbreakable bond was a common theme of the Broad Street Bullies. The players were close and remained that way. The same could be said for their wives and their children.

It made for one big loving family, and that feeling remained in the 2020s.

It turns out when Shero said, "Win today and we walk together forever," he wasn't just talking about the players, coaches, and team executives.

Unknowingly, he was also talking about the players' wives and their children.

CHAPTER 14

BARRY ASHBEE: FLYERS' "DEN FATHER"

One of the Philadelphia Flyers' most respected men during their championship days was Barry Ashbee, a no-frills defenseman who wasn't on the ice when they won Stanley Cups in 1974 and 1975.

But he was always on the Flyers' collective minds.

In '74, Ashbee suffered a scary injury deep in the playoffs, ending his playing career. The next season, he was an assistant coach for the Flyers when they won Cup II.

Fifty years after the Flyers won their first Cup, the players from that team talked in reverential tones when they mentioned the defensive-minded player who was fondly known as "Ash Can."

Ashbee, then 34, was hit in his right eye while blocking a deflected Dale Rolfe shot during the 1974 Stanley Cup semifinals against the New York Rangers. He never played again. The vision in the eye was reduced to about 15 percent, closing his late-blooming career. He had registered a team-best plus-53 ranking in the 1973–74 regular season.

"I'm not bitter," Ashbee told reporters. "Some people strive 60 years or so to achieve certain goals in life and never make it.

I got what I wanted when I was 34—a Stanley Cup. I had thought of being on a Stanley Cup winner since I was seven."

Ashbee sat with Ed Snider in the owner's Spectrum box when the Flyers beat Boston in Game 6 1–0 to win the 1974 Cup.

When the game ended, Ashbee had tears streaking down his cheeks; they were tears of joy.

"Don't write me up as the great tragic figure," he said at the time. "Right now, I'm the happiest man alive."

Coach Fred Shero asked Ashbee to be one of the club's assistants the next season, and he agreed to give it a shot.

Overlooked in Minors

Ashbee toiled in the minors for 10 years—the last seven with the AHL's Hershey Bears—before becoming an NHL regular with the Flyers in 1971 at age 31. He became one of the team's best defensemen—and one of the most respected players in franchise history. He was someone who thrived on hard work, someone who proved he should have been an NHL regular much sooner.

Stunningly, Ashbee was diagnosed with leukemia in 1977 and died about a month later at age 37.

In his eulogy, captain Bobby Clarke talked about what Ashbee meant to the Flyers.

"It took an incurable blood disorder to quell a spirit that the loss of one eye, a spinal fusion, torn ligaments in his knee, and a pinched nerve in his neck could not dampen," Clarke said. "Barry never gave in to the luxury of exhaustion or pain."

Years later, Clarke called Ashbee the "strongest guy I've ever seen mentally."

Ashbee was so beloved that his No. 4 became the first number retired by the organization.

Each year, the best Flyers defenseman is named the winner of the Barry Ashbee Trophy. Donna Ashbee, Barry's wife, or her son, Dan, frequently made the presentation.

Ashbee epitomized the toughness of the Broad Street Bullies. Like Ed Van Impe, he prided himself on clearing the crease in front of goalie Bernie Parent. Like Van Impe, he played with a mean streak.

"No Gray Area"

"He was a warrior," said Hall of Fame left winger Bill Barber, who was near Ashbee when he was struck in the eye in the defenseman's final career game. "I looked up to him as a leader, like a father-type image. When he told you something, you took it to heart. There was no gray area."

Right winger Don Saleski called Ashbee a "salt-of-the-earth, old-school, blue-collar guy. He came up the hard way and finally made it to the NHL. He was a good family man and a hard-nosed hockey player. Tougher than nails. We spent a lot of time together, and he was probably my best friend on the team back then."

Barber said Ashbee was great taking younger players under his wing, perhaps because he had a lot of practice in the minors. He also knew when to offer constructive criticism.

"If he wrapped a puck around the wall, you better get it out or you heard about it when you got to the bench," Barber said. "He had that rugged side to him, but it rubbed off on the younger guys and the team itself that you've got to be accountable. No excuses. No gray. [It was] black and white. Simple as that."

Before the eye injury ended his career, Ashbee had overcome two bad knees, and painful back and left shoulder ailments, along with bone chips in his left elbow, and severe nerve damage in his neck that forced him to wear a padded "horse collar" on the ice.

Fans in some opposing arenas chanted "Toilet Seat" when Ashbee had the puck, mocking the look of the collar he wore.

Ashbee didn't let it bother him.

"He had more heart than any man I've ever seen," said Joe Kadlec, the Flyers' public relations director when Ashbee played.

When Ashbee retired, the Flyers surprised him by chipping in and buying him a camper van. Ashbee drove it onto the ice before a practice. They scrapped practice that day and drank beer in the Winnebago. And when the Flyers had some time off before a playoff series, Ashbee took the defensemen down to Atlantic City in the van.

On the way home, everyone in the vehicle was inebriated, defenseman Joe Watson said, as the van crossed the Walt Whitman Bridge.

"The cops are behind us and they saw us," Watson said. "We're bouncing around the fucking bridge, so we get to the bottom of the bridge and the cops stop us. And one of them says, 'What the hell is going on?'"

When they realized the Flyers were in the van, they gave each of them a ride home. They took the vehicle to the Spectrum parking lot.

"It was a different time back then," Watson said five decades later. "Imagine if that would have happened today. Oh, boy. The guns would have been drawn and everything else now."

Grim News

While getting ready to face Toronto in the 1977 playoffs, the Flyers learned Ashbee had a form of leukemia.

The assistant coach told the players he didn't want sympathy, didn't want this to turn into a "Win one for the Gipper" situation.

"You'll win and I'll get better," he told them.

The Flyers rallied past the Maple Leafs in the quarterfinals, losing the first two games and then winning the next four. In the semifinals, they lost to Boston in four straight, a series that ended on May 1 as Ashbee's health deteriorated, causing him to leave the team and be hospitalized.

Eleven days later, Ashbee died.

Ashbee had a profound effect on many Flyers. In a way, he was their moral compass, and when he played, he was like a coach on the ice. He had a particularly strong effect on defensemen Jimmy Watson, Tom Bladon, and André "Moose" Dupont, mentoring them and improving their games.

His death sent shock waves throughout the entire team.

"We didn't play very good," Clarke said of the semifinal loss to the Bruins, one that coincided with Ashbee's health getting worse. "I was lousy. Our whole team was lousy."

Clarke phoned Ed Snider and set up a meeting. He felt he owed him an explanation about the team's sluggish play.

When they met, Clarke offered Snider an apology of sorts.

Clarke: "First of all, I'm really sorry about my performance and the team's performance. You know, with Barry being sick, we just couldn't get over it."

Snider: "I understand, but you don't have the right to use Barry as an excuse. Barry wouldn't want you to use him being sick or him passing to play poorly. You should have known him better. You should have played harder because you lost your friend."

When Clarke recalled the meeting with Snider nearly five decades later, he said it was "one of the things that stuck with me for the rest of my life. You know, don't use that as an excuse to be a shitty player. And we did in that series. The Bruins might have beaten us anyway, but we certainly could have played a lot better. We used Barry's death as a reason for not playing well. And that's not good."

Clarke recalled a story that surrounded Ashbee's death, and it exemplified the man's indomitable spirit, he said.

The end was near and Clarke and other teammates went to the hospital and said their goodbyes. According to Clarke, Ashbee's wife, Donna, and his brother, Don, then entered the hospital room. Barry was given a shot, supposedly of morphine, and was expected to pass away that night.

"And he lasted all night and got up in the morning, grabbed Donna, and said, 'We've gotta get out of this place,'" Clarke said. "That was one tough man."

Ashbee died a short time later, but his legacy is still alive nearly a half-century later.

Acquired in a seemingly minor 1970 trade that sent minor-leaguers Darryl Edestrand and Larry McKillop to Boston, Ashbee can be best described as an Everyday Man. He didn't ooze with talent, so he made his mark by being positionally sound, outworking everybody, and being the quintessential team player.

Outworking Clarke

Clarke was rarely outworked. There was an exception, however, and Ashbee provided one during his playing days.

At the end of practices, coach Fred Shero had his players skate laps. But on this day, he told two of his hardest-working players they could hit the showers before their teammates.

"Clarke, you can go off. You're playing a lot," Shero said. "Ashbee, you're playing a lot, too. You can go off."

Clarke started toward the locker room. Ashbee didn't.

"Luckily, I hadn't gone off yet, because Ashbee says, 'Fuck you, Freddy. As long as my teammates skate, I skate,'" Clarke said, chuckling softly and admiring the memory of his late teammate.

Clarke came back. Like Ashbee, he joined his teammates as they did laps.

"And I never [left] after that. What a great lesson, eh?" Clarke said. "He said if my teammates can skate, I can fucking skate. What a lesson for everybody."

"He was a true, true teammate," Joe Watson said. "He was like all of us—whatever you had to do to win you did."

If Ashbee had lived, many feel he would have become the Flyers' head coach when Shero left Philadelphia and joined the New York Rangers in 1978–79.

"Barry Ashbee was a leader," said Lou Scheinfeld, the Flyers' first vice president. "I can picture him right now, standing up straight, and guys bouncing off him. There wasn't a player on the team who didn't respect him. He was kind. He was a gentleman. He helped so many players get better and led by example."

On or off the ice, Scheinfeld said, Ashbee "carried himself with a certain air of—I don't want to say authority—but of confidence and warmth. Just a wonderful human being, and it was tragic what happened to him."

Ashbee's wife, Donna, died of what the family called a cardiac event in 2021. She was 82.

Donna Ashbee and the players' spouses helped the Flyers Wives Fight for Lives Carnival raise millions for leukemia research and other charities over the years. She said the carnival enabled her family to stay close to the Flyers.

"As a couple, they were giants in our universe," Scheinfeld said. "She was quiet and demure, and they were both always there for the team. They were like the den mother and den father for the team."

Barry and Donna Ashbee were pillars in the Flyers family. They set an example for all future Flyers couples, an example of loyalty and leadership.

CHAPTER 15

THREE-PEAT DENIED, BUT AN EPIC WIN OVER RUSSIANS

A HALF CENTURY AFTER THEIR 1975–76 SEASON ENDED, the disappointment was still fresh for the players on that Philadelphia Flyers team.

"Too many injuries," Hall of Fame left winger Bill Barber said.

When that season started, it didn't take long for the two-time defending champion Flyers to set their sights on their goal: becoming the third team in NHL history to win its third consecutive Stanley Cup. At that point, no American-based team had ever done it.

A few nights after the Flyers' Stanley Cup parade in 1975, owner Ed Snider held one of his lavish parties for the team and their families. (The previous year's party at Snider's house featured memorable Elvis Presley imitations from Dave Schultz and Bill Clement. Thank you. Thankyouverymuch.)

Dress was casual. Very casual.

Most wore Flyers-themed T-shirts that said: WIN IT AGAIN! AND AGAIN! AND AGAIN!

Around the Delaware Valley, bumper stickers were quickly printed. HAT TRICK IN '76! they proclaimed.

Coach Fred Shero told the *Philadelphia Evening Bulletin* that the summer after the Flyers won their first Cup in 1974, "all I did was worry. I was ridiculous. All I could think about was how the team was going to get complacent."

Shero's concerns disappeared when he found out his players had rented a rink in Cherry Hill and were working out before training camp. Captain Bobby Clarke and his just-as-driven teammates never took their eyes off the prize.

After winning again the next season, Shero learned the Flyers were again reporting to Cherry Hill on their own to get a head start on the 1975–76 season.

In other words, Shero didn't have any concerns about his players' desire and work ethic.

"My biggest problem is motivating myself," he said. "Sometimes a guy can be coaching too long and after a couple years, he doesn't work as hard."

Shero didn't rest on his laurels, either. He took a $500 course in motivation the summer before the Flyers tried to bring home Cup III.

"Maybe it will help," he said. "If I make them better people, then we have better athletes."

Shero said the class included 20 different videotapes that "you have to go over five or six times before it really registers.... Maybe I'll improve my team and improve myself. Maybe I'll learn just the one little thing that could possibly make the difference between winning and losing."

The team's 1975–76 roster included the addition of hard-nosed center Mel Bridgman, the No. 1 overall pick in the previous NHL draft. The team was minus veteran defenseman Ted Harris, who had retired to become the Minnesota North Stars' coach.

So, the Flyers had mostly the same crew as the previous season, and they showed there was no complacency in 1975–76 as they collected 118 points—a franchise record that still holds 50 years later.

The Flyers might have won a third straight Cup that season if they weren't missing star players such as goalie Bernie Parent and center Rick MacLeish in the '76 Finals against Montreal. Parent had neck surgery, and MacLeish, who had been the Flyers' top playoff scorer in their two previous runs that ended with them lifting the Stanley Cup, was sidelined by torn knee ligaments.

In addition, Bobby Clarke played on an injured left knee that made it difficult for him to zigzag on the ice, Orest Kindrachuk played with a bad back and was ineffective in the Finals, and Gary Dornhoefer struggled for air during the playoffs because of pneumonia-ravaged lungs.

"We did about as much as we could with all the problems we had," Shero said.

Even if they were healthy, there were no guarantees the Flyers would have beaten a Canadiens team that went 58–11–11 and accumulated a league-high 127 points during the regular season. The Flyers (51–13–16, 118 points) had a dominating regular season as well, along with a 2–1–1 record against Montreal.

The Canadiens swept the Stanley Cup Finals in four games, though it wasn't a cakewalk. Three of the games were decided by one goal.

In Game 4 at the Spectrum, the Flyers had a 3–2 lead before Yvan Cournoyer tied the score with 11 seconds left in the second period. Guy Lafleur and Pete Mahovlich then scored 58 seconds apart in the final 5:42 to give Montreal the Cup with a 5–3 win.

"Somewhere down the line, people will see that we won four straight games—and [think] that it was easy," Montreal goaltender Ken Dryden said after the sweep. "But they will not be more wrong. If you'll notice, we're drinking our champagne sitting down."

In other words, they were too exhausted to stand.

Reggie Leach had four goals in the series and won the Conn Smythe Trophy as the MVP in the entire playoffs. He set a playoff record with 19 goals, giving him 80 if you include the regular season.

But the Canadiens' Doug Jarvis and Doug Risebrough effectively shadowed Clarke. Their persistence—and Clarke's injured knee—contributed to the captain being held without a goal in the series. That made MacLeish's absence even more critical.

The biggest factor, however, was the absence of Parent, who might have altered the three one-goal losses. Parent's backup, Wayne Stephenson, had just a .873 save percentage in the series.

"We ran out of juice the third year there," Barber said. "We were banged up."

It was the first of four straight championships for the Habs. In the series win over the Flyers, Montreal combined swift skating and physical play, with defenseman Larry Robinson providing numerous punishing hits and Bob Gainey frustrating Philly with his checking.

After the Game 4 loss, the fans at the Spectrum stood and applauded. And applauded some more. It was a standing ovation that served as a "thank you" of sorts for an incomparable three-year run that produced two Stanley Cup championships, three trips to the Finals, a 152–47–39 record in the regular season, and hundreds of memories.

It was a standing ovation that thanked the Flyers for erasing the "City of Losers" label that had plagued Philly—and thanked the Broad Street Bullies for giving fans arguably the greatest three-year run in Philadelphia sports history.

Beating Russia and Saving NHL's Image

So, as it turned out, the highlight of the Flyers' season was their epic 4–1 win over the Russians. In fact, Joe Watson said it was the second-greatest victory of his career. To him, it was not as fulfilling as the first Stanley Cup, but more rewarding than the second championship.

The other Flyers said it ranked behind the two Cups, but that didn't diminish the significance of the monumental victory.

"This was the only time that anybody in Canada was cheering for the Flyers," Watson said of the game against the Soviets. "We had to uphold the prestige of hockey in North America. We had to win."

The Flyers restored North America's pride. The Red Army (CSKA Moscow) toured North America and was undefeated in its first three games against NHL teams, including the mighty Montreal Canadiens.

Technically, the Russian players were enlisted in the military, but their only job was to play hockey.

Before facing the Flyers, the Red Army had crushed the New York Rangers 7–3 and Boston Bruins 5–2. It managed a 3–3 tie with the eventual Stanely Cup champion Canadiens.

Russia's final stop was the Spectrum on January 11, 1976. The buildup was enormous. As though it was Game 7 of a Stanley Cup Finals between two teams that hated one another.

Leading up to the game, Lou Nolan, the Flyers' public address announcer, watched a Russian practice with interest.

"They had a bunch of KGB agents watching them, making sure they didn't defect," Nolan said.

At the time, Nolan was also working for PSFS Bank, but he took a few days off to attend the Red Army's practices and "get a feel" for their game.

Nolan remembers Red Army captain Boris Mikhailov walking around the smelly locker room, and he "handed me a Russian pin with their logo. I said, 'Thanks,'" Nolan recalled. "He wanted something in return. I signaled that I had nothing, but I went through my pockets. I had a Kennedy half-dollar and I gave it to him."

Mikhailov seemed thrilled with the souvenir.

Nolan walked out to the hallway to talk to someone. A couple minutes later, Mikhailov saw Nolan and pointed to him. And a group of Russian players came over to Nolan, giving him pins and hoping to get a Kennedy half-dollar in return.

"I got the interpreter and explained to them that I would get the coins, but that I had to go to the bank to get more," Nolan said. "I went to PSFS, my bank, and got a couple rolls of Kennedy halves and got more pins in exchange. You would have thought they struck gold because they were so happy with the trade."

A short time later, Nolan found out a KGB agent took all the Kennedy coins away from the players.

"Back in the days of the Cold War, [John] Kennedy and [Nikita] Khrushchev weren't exactly on good terms," Nolan said of the respective US and Soviet Union leaders, "so I guess the agent thought it was insulting for them to have the half-dollars. But later on, I managed to give some of their players more Kennedy halves. I wonder if they ever made it home?"

Snider Feels Disrespected

The day before the big showdown, all the players were introduced at a Spectrum luncheon. Snider had learned some Russian words from broadcaster Gene Hart and had planned to use them. But he felt the Soviets were being disrespectful at the goodwill luncheon and spoke briefly, omitting the Russian welcoming phrase he had practiced.

When Flyers defenseman Ed Van Impe was introduced, the Russians pointed and sneered at him, according to left winger Bob Kelly. Van Impe was older (35) and heavier than his teammates, and the Russians mocked him for it.

The Russians, composed primarily of players who had dominated international competition, nodded when Dave Schultz was introduced. They whispered to each other, probably saying that this was the guy who liked to fight and antagonize opponents.

"At one point, Schultz stood up and just glared at the Russians," Jimmy Watson said almost 50 years later. "He just fricking glared at them, and he scared the hell out of them because the next day, I had some friends who were staying at the stadium Hilton. They were in the lobby, and they said when the Russians came down to the lobby to get ready to go to the game, they all looked like they were frightened out of their minds."

Driving to the game, Shero thought about how he wanted things to unfold as he chain-smoked Lucky Strikes on his way to the Spectrum.

"We're in a weird position," Shero said prior to the showdown. "All year long, people keep telling us that we're bad for hockey, bad for Canada because we're too rough. Now we're supposed to save the game for the NHL, for Canada, for everyone. Hah! For the first time, we're the good guys."

Before the matchup, Clarence Campbell, the NHL president, went into the Flyers' locker room to give the players a pep talk. This was the same man who had looked like he was about to vomit when he handed the Flyers their Stanley Cups. Campbell and the league's "Big Cigars" despised the Flyers' intimidating style, and they made rule changes after the 1973–74 season that seemed targeted to Philadelphia.

Clarke said Campbell's disdain for the Flyers motivated the team.

"We knew he didn't like the Flyers," Clarke said, "but he helped us by not liking us. Great. Fuck him."

Campbell was critical of the Flyers fighting too much and occasionally going into the stands after fans who threw things at them.

"But that was kind of dumb on his part," Clarke said of Campbell's criticism. "When you think about it, everywhere we went, we filled buildings. I mean, he should have been thanking us."

Early in the 1974–75 season, a little over five months after the Flyers had hoisted their first Cup, Clarke was ultra-critical of Campbell. This was after the NHL had suspended Kelly and Don Saleski for six games because of an early-season melee in Oakland. The bench-clearing episode led to an NHL record 232 penalty minutes.

"I think it's time Campbell got out of there and they get somebody in who can do a decent job," Clarke said at the time. He called the suspensions "ridiculous."

The *Philadelphia Daily News* splashed the story on its back page under the headline: QUIT, CLARKE ADVISES NHL BOSS.

"You wonder who's running the league," Clarke told reporters after the suspensions. "Kelly was our leading scorer at the time, and they got him out of there without a hearing. He was guilty until proved otherwise" in the NHL's eyes.

Clarke asked reporters Campbell's age. He was told the NHL president was 69.

"Isn't 65 the normal retirement age?" he replied. "He's a little overdue. No commissioner in any sport is that old."

So, when Campbell gave the two-time defending Stanley Cup champion Flyers a pregame pep talk before the 1976 game against the Russians, the players couldn't wait until he left.

To a man, they thought he was a hypocrite.

Here was a man who had chastised their style and repeatedly fined them for incidents (Snider picked up the tabs), and now he was imploring them to show the type of hockey that was played in North America.

"He came in and said we have to win for the preservation of the National Hockey League and its reputation and all that stuff," Kelly said. "And it was like [the Flyers were thinking], *Get the fuck out of here. We'll do what we have to do*. And we did."

Gary Dornhoefer remembers the situation more specifically. He said Van Impe used f-bombs and told him to leave. "You have a disdain for the Philadelphia Flyers, and you don't tell us what to do," Dornhoefer said Van Impe told the NHL president.

"The league office didn't like us, obviously," Joe Watson said. "But we kept the league alive" by drawing standing-room-only crowds in NHL cities. "We probably helped them keep a lot of people working because, goddamn, they're fining us every freaking game, you know? It was like we were bringing money into the coffers for the league itself."

Added Watson: "We were not well-liked, and we didn't care. I used to feel sorry for [general manager] Keith Allen because every time something happened, Keith would have a goddamn meeting with Clarence Campbell on the phone. And Keith would say, 'Well, just tell us what we owe you, Clarence, and we'll send you something.' But [in reality] you owe us more money."

Watson laughed.

The league should have paid the Flyers, he said, "because we were an attraction. We really were."

"Play Your Game, Fellas"

Before the game, which was dubbed the Cold War, Scotty Morrison, the head of NHL referees, entered the Flyers' locker room. "He told us, 'We're going to let you play today,'" said Jimmy Watson, Joe's younger brother.

Referee Lloyd Gilmour also poked his head into the locker room, and he shared similar sentiments.

"Play your game, fellas," Gilmour said.

The message: Don't be afraid to play like you usually do—with a physical edge.

The Flyers played a relentless and physical style and were the kings of the North American hockey world. The pass-happy Russians used finesse and creativity to become the best of Europe.

"This happened during a period of time when the NHL was aways considered to be the top league in the world," Jimmy Watson said. "And all of a sudden, the Russians were coming in and putting a dent in those thoughts and creating doubts. Our pride was at stake."

Watson said he was more nervous to play the Russians than when he played in the Stanley Cup Finals.

"Leading up to the game, I don't think I slept for two nights," he said of the Cold War matchup.

"I think it's going to be the highlight of my life," Shero said as the game approached. "If we win, I'm going to be sky high. If we lose, I think it'll be worse than dying."

The day before the confrontation, the Flyers practiced at the Spectrum. The Russians sat in seats and watched.

The Flyers had three players repeatedly skate down the ice as linemates. The first time, they had one puck. They later carried two pucks, and "eventually we'd have three pucks and we're all trying to pass it to one another while maintaining possession of the puck [coming your way]," Jimmy Watson said. "Pucks are going all over the place. And we're all thinking to ourselves, *Holy shit, the Russians must be wondering: How the hell are these guys in first place?*"

The Soviets went to a movie theater to watch *Jaws* on Saturday night, believing they would continue their win streak the next afternoon. But the Flyers played with precision and coasted to the 4–1 victory while holding a 49–13 shots domination. Bill Barber and Rick MacLeish each had nine shots.

"The reason we beat the Russians was Freddy," said Saleski, who had seven shots and an assist in the game. "He had a game plan; he had it figured out. Everybody was getting beat because they were chasing the Russians all over the ice. We played almost like a soccer game. No chasing. Let people come to us. We frustrated the crap out of them, and then we threw a little bit of physical play at them."

Shero, who years later called it the "biggest game in Flyers history," confused the Russians by stacking the neutral zone with his players and not allowing the visitors into Philadelphia's zone.

"They get the opening faceoff and made maybe five or six passes on their side of the red line," Dornhoefer said. "But they didn't improve their position."

"They couldn't understand what we were doing," Joe Watson said

The Flyers had much more muscle than their opponents.

"One thing about the Russians at that time, they didn't have upper-body strength, so you could win battles in the corners," Dornhoefer said. "And they didn't want to shoot the puck into the zone; they wanted to carry it in, and we really stood them up at the blue line. We played aggressively like we'd do in any other game, and I think they were totally frustrated because they couldn't gain the blue line and carry it in."

It wasn't until the third period that the Russians started to dump the puck into the offensive zone. "But they couldn't win battles. I mean, they didn't have an [Alex] Ovechkin who is as strong as a bull," Dornhoefer said.

Joe Watson said that before the game Shero told them: "Boys, they have the Iron Curtain in Russia. We're gonna show 'em the

Iron Curtain in North America. I want the defense to stand up at center ice and challenge them when they come down. And our forwards drop in behind and pick up any loose pucks we can get, and we'll go the other way. And when they're coming at us, we'll be going the other way."

The Flyers controlled the game from the outset.

"So eventually, what happened was that the Russians start shooting the puck in our zone," Watson said, "and they never shot the puck into the zone" when they played their style. "They always carried it in. But they couldn't penetrate our line, and they started dumping and chasing it. And our guys would get back there quickly and try to get the puck out as quickly as we can."

The game became infamous for what happened with 8:39 left in the first period.

Until then, the Flyers had most of the scoring chances, but the game was scoreless when the Russians walked off the ice. They were protesting a hard hit by Van Impe, who darted out of the penalty box and, as the Soviets tried to break out of their zone, knocked down Valeri Kharlamov, the Red Army's best player.

"He ran into my elbow," Van Impe deadpanned.

The Cold War got colder.

Van Impe said Kharlamov exaggerated his pain and "rolled around looking dead." He added that "if he had done that to me, I would've just gone to the bench." No penalty was called by referee Lloyd Gilmour. The Russians couldn't believe it and went to the locker room as the Spectrum erupted in boos.

Dave Leonardi, who had become a fixture at the Spectrum with his clever, homemade signs, held up a placard in the crowd: TELL IT TO THE CZAR.

Hart, the Flyers' broadcaster, understood the language and heard Russian coach Konstantin Loktev calling the Philadelphia players "animals" after the team left the ice.

During the 16-minute delay, Flyers captain Bobby Clarke addressed his teammates.

"Fellas, listen. Stay calm, stay together," he said. "They're pulling bullshit here. They're going to come back."

The Russians returned when Flyers owner Ed Snider threatened to not pay them if they didn't finish the game.

"Their attitude softened when the subject of money came up," said Frank Torpey, director of NHL security.

"The Russians cried 'uncle,' and it wasn't Sam," wrote the Associated Press' Ralph Bernstein.

When play resumed, the physical Flyers continued to dominate. It was a shooting gallery in front of legendary goalie Vladislav Tretiak. Just 17 seconds after the game re-started, Reggie Leach gave the Flyers a 1–0 lead, scoring on a power play that was called on the Russians for leaving the ice and delaying the game.

"We had so many great chances," Joe Watson said, still proud of the shorthanded tally he netted to give the Flyers a 3–0 second-period lead. "I wasn't a goal scorer, but I could have had three goals that game. I hit Tretiak twice off the shoulder with shots, and then I snuck one in in the second period."

The low-scoring Watson said Shero later told him he had "set back Russian hockey 20 years" by finding the back of the net.

Flyers (Usually) Hated Around NHL Cities

The Flyers were hated around the NHL because of their bullying tactics and their success.

A few days before the Russian showdown, the Flyers were playing in Toronto, and something strange happened.

"I remember getting on the bus in Toronto and people were wishing us good luck against the Russians," Joe Watson said. "This was in Toronto, where they hated us, and I was kind of shocked by this. But it meant so much to us. It was like we had to win at all costs. It was the only time that anybody in Canada was cheering for the Flyers. We had to uphold the prestige of hockey in North America. We had to win."

Besides Leach and Watson, MacLeish and Larry Goodenough scored for the Flyers in the victory. Backup goalie Wayne Stephenson, playing because Bernie Parent had a pinched nerve in his neck and was on a Jamaica beach, made 12 saves.

Philadelphia's penalty kill was sensational, allowing a total of two shots on the Russians' seven power plays.

BRING ON THE MARTIANS, said the sign held by Leonardi.

The win gave the Flyers a 44–3–1 record when Kate Smith's rendition of "God Bless America" was played before games.

"We got telegrams from all over Canada, all over the United States after we beat the Russians," Joe Watson said. "We got letters from all over the world. Australia. New Zealand. In fact, my first wife's parents lived in Stuttgart. They had never watched a hockey game in their life. And they watched that game. And in Russia alone, 100-some million people watched the freaking game.... That's just like the Super Bowl. That's a lot of people."

The normally subdued Shero gloated after the convincing win.

"Yes, we are the world champions," he said. "If they had won, they would have been the world champions. We beat a helluva machine and 99 percent of the National Hockey League didn't think we could do it."

The Flyers' dominance in the game was overshadowed by the Van Impe incident. Russian newspapers showed a cartoon of oversized, Neanderthal Flyers players carrying big clubs as they skated down the ice.

Snider proudly kept a copy of that front page on display.

PHILADELPHIA FLYERS TRY TO START WORLD WAR III was one of the headlines around the world, Dornhoefer said.

The *New York Times* blasted the Flyers.

The *Times'* Dave Anderson wrote: "In their patriotic contribution to the Bicentennial celebration, the Broad Street Bullies, alias the Philadelphia Flyers, alias the Stanley Cup champions, dissected the touring Soviet hockey team Sunday 4–1 and upheld the Spectrum's reputation as the cradle of licensed muggings."

Continued Anderson: "The triumph of terror over style could not have been more one-sided if Al Capone's mob had ambushed the Bolshoi Ballet dancers. Naturally, it warmed the hearts of the Flyers' followers, who would cheer for Frankenstein if he could skate."

Anderson's *New York Times* colleague, Robin Herman, was also unflattering.

"After the 17,077 spectators finished a sonorous rendition of 'God Bless America,' the Flyers charged onto the ice brandishing their sticks and gunning for the Russians' top players," he wrote. "From the beginning, it was a game of intimidation. The Flyers began with the unethical and finished with sound, defensive hockey, bringing the Soviet Central Army team to its knees. But the overall series had been decided last week and so this contest was a simple grudge match."

Loktev, the losing coach, downplayed the defeat.

"One game doesn't decide anything," he said.

He also said the Soviets had "never played against such animal hockey."

In a way, Joe Watson said nearly five decades after the game, "I felt bad for the Russians. They were so hated, you know. The country itself is so hated."

Irony of ironies: In 2017 Watson and a group of Flyers alumni went to Russia and played a three-game goodwill tour. They got to meet Russia's president, Vladimir Putin, who plays hockey and has a rink at his opulent residence.

"Putin didn't play against us, but he was very good to us," Watson said. "He really was. I talked to one of the security guards, and he said you had to play hockey to be a security guard for him. He had five security guards, and they get up at 5:30 in the morning and play hockey three days a week with him."

Perhaps some of those guards were ancestors of players who fell to the Flyers in a 1976 confrontation that, at least for one game, had most of North America cheering for Philadelphia.

Even the NHL's sour-faced president.

EPILOGUE

50 Things You May Not Know About the Broad Street Bullies and Other Flyers Teams

1. During their Broad Street Bullies days, the Flyers were given bonuses for certain team accomplishments. Defensemen, for instance, earned $200 per shutout—or $2,400 for the 12 times Bernie Parent blanked an opponent in 1973–74. Those D-men each also earned $100 for each game in which the Flyers allowed just one goal.
2. Bobby Clarke was fond of pulling out his fake teeth and putting them in the drink of the unsuspecting person sitting next to him at a bar.
3. Gary Dornhoefer said if he had to do it all over, he doesn't think he would be a hockey player, noting his quality of life has not been good because of all his injuries. He has had eight hockey-related surgeries since retiring. "While I was playing, I loved every minute of it...but now when you get to be my age, it's not pleasant when you wake up in the morning" in pain, he said.
4. Ed Van Impe used to have a funny observation about winger Bob Kelly: "He's the only guy to go offside on a breakaway."
5. Dornhoefer is a pet lover. As of this writing, he and his wife have three greyhounds, five cats, and eight parrots.
6. Ed Snider almost fired broadcaster Gene Hart during the team's early years. Hart went on to become a Hockey Hall of Fame broadcaster.

7. Fred Shero, the brilliant coach of the Flyers during their heyday, took painful losses to heart. After the Flyers were denied a 1972 playoff berth because Buffalo's Gerry Meehan scored on a long shot with four seconds left in the regular season finale, Shero said he felt "the same way I did when my mother and father died."
8. In their first season, only the third periods of their games were broadcast on the radio because the Flyers had a difficult time getting sponsors.
9. Kate Smith, whose "God Bless America" became the Flyers' good luck charm, almost didn't make her first appearance on the Spectrum ice because her dress was wrinkled, and she was reluctant to perform in the 1973–74 season opener against Toronto. The Flyers were paying her $5,000, but team officials couldn't find an iron in the Spectrum. As the start of the game approached, one of the front office's secretaries arranged to have her aunt iron the dress in her South Philadelphia home. Crisis averted. (By the way, Smith's agent wanted her to sing some of her new songs before a game, but the Flyers nixed the idea.)
10. After Smith walked out on the red carpet and sang before the Cup-clinching win over Boston in 1974, Bruins coach Bep Guidolin was not a happy camper. "That bleeping song, that bleeping carpet, that bleeping organ. They turned this thing into a bleeping circus," he said.
11. Fitz Dixon, one of the Flyers' owners, was furious that the team was always fighting in the 1970s and asked Ed Snider to change things so a more dignified product was created for the fans. Snider didn't pay attention to his request.
12. Though he was good at it, Dave Schultz hated to fight. He finished with 2,292 career penalty minutes, the equivalent of 38.2 games.
13. Schultz collected as many points (three) as Boston superstar Phil Esposito in the 1974 Finals.
14. After some home games, Ed Snider would sometimes go into his office with his right-hand man, Lou Scheinfeld, and smoke a little weed.

15. Lou Scheinfeld started playing "God Bless America" at some home games because fans were being disrespectful when the national anthem was being sung. This was during the time when the unpopular Vietnam War was raging, and people were disenchanted with the government.
16. Bernie Parent was the only goalie the Flyers used in all 17 of their 1974 playoff games. He had a 2.02 goals-against average and .933 save percentage. In leading the Flyers to the 1975 Cup, he played in 15 of the 17 playoff games and had a 1.89 GAA and .924 save percentage.
17. Enforcer Dave Schultz scored 20 goals in the 1973–74 regular season and led the Flyers by connecting on a staggering 21.1 percent of his shots.
18. When the Flyers won their first Stanley Cup, they had 11 regulars who were 24 years old or under: Bill Barber (21), Tom Bladon (21), Bobby Clarke (24), Bill Clement (23), André Dupont (24), Bob Kelly (23), Orest Kindrachuk (23), Rick MacLeish (24), Don Saleski (24), Dave Schultz (24), and Jimmy Watson (21).
19. At 34, Barry Ashbee was the oldest Flyer during the 1973–74 season. He led the team with a plus-53 rating. Bobby Clarke was second at plus-35.
20. The Flyers won the '74 Cup even though right winger Bill "Cowboy" Flett failed to score in the 17 playoff games. He was replaced by Reggie Leach the next season.
21. Reggie Leach had 45 regular season goals in 1974–75, then added eight in the playoffs. The Flyers acquired him at the urging of captain Bobby Clarke, who played with Leach on the Flin Flon Bombers. In his second season with the Flyers, Leach erupted for 61 goals, then added 19 more in the playoffs. He led the NHL in both categories.
22. Center Bobby Clarke said the man who served as his mentor was someone who played a different position—defenseman Ed Van Impe. He liked the way Van Impe carried himself and guided

the team with his unselfish play. Clarke replaced Van Impe as the Flyers captain in the second half of the 1972–73 season.

23. At the time, Clarke was the youngest captain in NHL history at age 23.
24. How much did Philadelphia need the Flyers to become a great team in 1973–74? Well, Philly was known as the "City of Losers" before that season. The 76ers were coming off the most embarrassing season (9–73) in NBA history. The Eagles were trying to rebound from a 2–11–1 season, their fewest wins since 1940. The Phillies? They were headed to their third straight last-place finish.
25. Coach Fred Shero used to send a letter to the players' wives, telling them the code of conduct that was expected of them. Hockey was his life. On his deathbed, he diagrammed a hockey play to Joe Watson.
26. Ed Snider was with the Flyers and Eagles when the hockey team was about to start its first season. Jerry Wolman fired him as the Eagles' vice president on the same day the Flyers were about to play their first home game in franchise history.
27. After Philadelphia's penalty-filled 3–1 victory in Atlanta on January 3, 1973, the *Bulletin*'s Jack Chevalier sent a story in which he called the Flyers the "Blue Line Bandidos." A few hours later, he instructed copy editor Pete Cafone to change it to the "Bullies of Broad Street." Cafone shortened it to "Broad Street Bullies" so it would fit in the headline. An iconic nickname was born.
28. Howard Baldwin was the Flyers' first ticket manager. He later was chairman of the Pittsburgh Penguins, owned the Hartford Whalers, and became a major player in Hollywood, producing numerous movies, including the Oscar-nominated *Ray*, *Sudden Death*, and *Mystery, Alaska*.
29. The Flyers players were an extremely close-knit group off the ice. Their wives were just as close. They went to all the home games, and most of them gathered at each other's homes to watch the

away games together. Some of the wives even vacationed together when the players were on a road trip.

30. When he was nearing his death, Ed Snider was still thinking about the Flyers. "I can't believe I'm going to miss his career," he said about Shayne Gostisbehere, then a promising young defenseman.
31. The Flyers were considered the seventh team in the running for the six expansion franchises. That changed when Jerry Wolman said he would build a 15,000-seat arena in Philadelphia, putting the team ahead of Baltimore.
32. The franchise fee for the Flyers was $2 million before their first season in 1967. In 2021 the franchise fee for the expansion Seattle Kraken was $650 million.
33. For their inaugural home opener in 1967, the Flyers drew just 7,812 and one front-office official estimated that half the people had comp tickets.
34. Joe Scott, who then owned 15 percent of the Flyers, greatly helped the team's attendance grow in their first season (1967–68). He offered free tickets to many schools on the wealthy Main Line if the student was accompanied by a paying adult. A slew of those spectators liked what they saw and returned to future games.
35. Perhaps the biggest turning point in enticing fans to attend games in Year 1: The Flyers scored back-to-back home wins over Original Six teams Chicago and Toronto in early February.
36. Getting swept in four playoff games and being pushed around by St. Louis in 1969, the Flyers' second season, is what convinced Ed Snider that his team needed to get bigger and tougher. After that, the Flyers started drafting players like Dave Schultz, Don Saleski, and Bob Kelly.
37. The Flyers had two dominating lines in the Cup-winning 1973–74 season. The second line—Rick MacLeish (32 goals) centering Ross Lonsberry (32) and Gary Dornhoefer (11 in an injury-limited season)—combined for 75 goals that season. The top unit—composed of Bobby Clarke (35), Bill Barber (34), and Bill Flett (17)—combined for 86.

38. Myrna Snider, Ed's first wife, took the players' wives under her wing and created a family atmosphere that made everyone comfortable. Some teams had a big-business feel to them. Not the early Flyers. Myrna went out of her way to make everyone feel important.
39. Several Broad Street Bullies said the acquisition of unheralded defenseman André "Moose" Dupont was a key part of their success.
40. After the Flyers were eliminated by Montreal in the 1973 Stanley Cup semifinals, Bobby Clarke held a players-only meeting and told his teammates they were close to becoming an elite team. He implored them to stay in shape during the summer "because we have a chance to do something special."
41. Barry Ashbee, a salt of the earth guy, was like an older brother or father figure to many of the younger players. "When he told you something, you took it to heart. There was no gray area," left winger Bill Barber said.
42. Dave Schultz had 472 penalty minutes in the 1974–75 season, an NHL record that is likely to stand forever.
43. In 1972–73 Rick MacLeish became the youngest player in NHL history (23) to score 50 goals in a season.
44. During Game 3 of the 1975 Finals, it was 90 degrees inside Buffalo's Memorial Auditorium, causing fog and forcing the game to be delayed 11 times.
45. After the Flyers won their second straight Cup, coach Fred Shero didn't want to get complacent, so he spent $500 on a summer motivational course, trying to bring home another championship.
46. As a youngster, Snider was bullied by anti-Semitic kids in his DC neighborhood. Some believe that played a part in him putting the Broad Street Bullies together. Said Snider on the Broad Street Bullies days: "Everybody hated us. We loved that."
47. In the '74 Finals, Boston's Wayne Cashman had a series-leading 41 penalty minutes—three more than Schultz.

48. Bobby Clarke said the team's hangout, Rexy's in South Jersey, put the Flyers in their comfort zone. "It was on our way home; it was a working man's bar and restaurant. Just worked perfect for us," he said.
49. During the Flyers' first season in 1967–68, the cheapest tickets were $2, and the most expensive ones were $5.50.
50. Early in his career, Gene Hart was the radio voice for high school football and basketball games played by Atlantic City, Pleasantville, and Ocean City. He later became a Flyers broadcasting legend.

Whatever Happened to the Bullies?

Most of the Flyers from their championship teams in the 1970s grew up in small Canadian towns, and most stayed in the Philadelphia area—South Jersey was their most popular spot—after they retired from hockey.

Here are the Flyers who were on either the 1974 or 1975 Stanley Cup champs during the playoffs—many were on both teams—and an update on them:

Barry Ashbee: The rugged defenseman, regarded as one of the best leaders in franchise history, died of leukemia in 1977 at age 37. After an eye injury ended his playing career, he became a Flyers assistant and was apparently being groomed to be their head coach someday. His No. 4 was retired.

Bill Barber: The Hall of Fame left winger became a Flyers assistant and head coach and is now a senior advisor with the club. Barber's goal in Game 4 of the 1974 Finals was one of the most important tallies in franchise history. Barber, who lives in South Jersey and Florida, still holds the Flyers record with 420 career goals.

Tom Bladon: The defenseman possessed a cannon shot on the power play, and later owned a Tim Hortons restaurant in

Edmonton, where he lived. In a 1977 game against Cleveland, Bladon became the first defenseman in NHL history to collect eight points (four goals, four assists) in a game.

Bobby Clarke: Known as the ultimate captain and the face of the Bullies, he became a Hall of Famer and later served in many capacities with the Flyers, including general manager. He still holds numerous Flyers records, including most points in a career (1,144), and is a senior adviser with the club.

Bill Clement: The former center is a Renaissance Man. After retiring from hockey, he was a Flyers and national broadcaster, an author, an actor—he appeared in *All My Children*, and did a slew of commercials—and motivational speaker. He resides in Waynesville, North Carolina.

Bruce Cowick: A scrappy player, he played in eight playoff games for the 1974 champs. After he retired from hockey, Cowick became a police officer for 28 years in Victoria, British Columbia, which is where he still resides.

Terry Crisp: The hustling little center was an unheralded but key player on the Bullies and was a superb penalty killer. Crisp spent 60-plus years in hockey, winning a Cup as the head coach in Calgary and later broadcasting Nashville Predators games.

Gary Dornhoefer: After hanging up his skates, "Dorny" spent time as a Flyers broadcaster, a golfer, and a devoted caretaker to dozens of animals. The lanky right winger, a two-time All-Star who was a terror in front of the net, also served as a Flyers ambassador for many years.

André Dupont: Many Flyers from their championship teams said the acquisition of Dupont was a major part of their success. "Moose" scored a critical goal in Game 2 of the 1974 Finals, keying the win in Boston. After his playing days, he was a junior coach, a scout, an owner of a sporting-goods store, and a consultant to a hockey agent.

Bill Flett: Nicknamed "Cowboy," the bearded right winger scored 43 goals in 1972–73, his first season with the Flyers, before managing 17 goals in his second season, when the Flyers won their first Stanley Cup. He battled alcoholism and died in 1999 of liver failure at age 55.

Larry Goodenough: "Izzy" played in five playoff games for the Flyers in 1974, contributing four assists. The defenseman became a Flyers regular in 1975–76 and later was the hockey director at the Bucks County Ice Sports Center in Warminster, Pennsylvania.

Ted Harris: The defenseman brought veteran leadership to the 1974–75 team; it turned out to be his final year because he became the Minnesota North Stars' coach the next season. The five-time All-Star won five Cups—four with Montreal, one with the Flyers. He later managed a South Jersey paint store.

Bob Kelly: Kelly has owned various businesses, including a liquor store, since leaving hockey. The former winger became extremely visible with the Flyers as director of community development—until 2025, he promoted hockey in numerous area schools throughout the years—and as a club ambassador. Nicknamed "Hound," he scored the game-winner in the 1975 Stanley Cup clincher.

Orest Kindrachuk: The relentless center worked in the insurance industry for more than three decades after retiring from the NHL. He then took a job as a consultant for a silicone-coating company. The "Little O" had five goals and nine points in 17 playoff games in 1974.

Reggie Leach: Known as "The Rifle" because of his blazing shot, the electric right winger had 45 goals (plus eight in the playoffs) during the Flyers' 1974–75 season. Leach battled alcoholism, got sober about 40 years ago, and has been teaching hockey skills—and alcohol-related life lessons—to youngsters all over North America.

Ross Lonsberry: The high-scoring and hard-nosed left winger, one of the Flyers' best defensive forwards at that time, died in 2014 at age 67 after a long battle with cancer. After his solid hockey career, he was a commercial insurance broker in Los Angeles.

Rick MacLeish: A three-time All-Star whom Clarke called the most talented player on the Flyers' powerhouses, MacLeish scored the lone goal in the Cup-clinching win over Boston in 1974. He was the NHL's top scorer in the 1974 and 1975 playoffs. MacLeish, 66, who sold insurance after hockey, died in 2016 after battling meningitis and kidney and liver problems.

Simon Nolet: The winger was an important member of the Flyers' first championship team before going to Kansas City in the expansion draft. Nolet later scouted many years for the Flyers—he was responsible for drafting stars Simon Gagné and Claude Giroux—before retiring.

Bernie Parent: Parent had shutouts in the Cup-clinching wins in 1974 and 1975. The Hall of Fame goaltender later was an assistant coach with the Flyers, an author, and a motivational speaker. Parent and his wife, Gini, are involved in lots of charity work, and they reside in South Florida and the Philadelphia area.

Don Saleski: Saleski contributed nine points in the Flyers' 17 playoff games during their first Cup run. After retiring from hockey, the right winger known as "Big Bird" held various high-ranking positions in the corporate world. He now helps run a business that handles physician billing.

Dave Schultz: "The Hammer" has done it all since retiring from the NHL. He has been a standup comedian, author, motivational speaker, singer, minor-league hockey coach and general manager, rink manager, electricity salesman, and limousine-company owner. He is writing a book with Dan Robson, tentatively called *Hammered by Life.*

Wayne Stephenson: The backup goalie during the Flyers' run to the 1975 Cup, Stephenson died of cancer at 65 in 2010. He was the winning goalie in one of the most famous games in Flyers history, a 4–1 victory over the Soviet Red Army in 1976. In five years with the Flyers, "Fort Wayne" had a 93–35–23 record with 10 shutouts.

Bobby Taylor: Affectionately known as "Chief," Taylor was a Flyers broadcaster from 1977 to 1992. The witty former backup goalie later held a similar broadcasting position with the Tampa Bay Lightning.

Ed Van Impe: The second captain (after Lou Angotti) in the Flyers' history, Van Impe was a classic stay-at-home defenseman and an Original Flyer. He remained in the area for many years before selling his insurance company and moving to Vancouver. Van Impe died in the spring of 2025 at age 84.

Jimmy Watson: A five-time All-Star defenseman who was plus-295 in his career, Watson won Stanley Cups in each of his first two full seasons. Watson is one of the owners of the IceWorks in Aston, Pennsylvania, a four-rink complex. Before getting back into hockey, he built houses for about a decade.

Joe Watson: After retiring from hockey in the late 1970s, the dependable and always-colorful defenseman worked for the Flyers until 2021. At different times, Watson was a scout, assistant coach, and advertising salesman for the club. The older brother of Jimmy Watson, Joe collaborated with Bill Meltzer to write *Thundermouth*.

Coach Fred Shero: He was a coach who was way ahead of his time, introducing video, assistant coaches, and morning skates to the hockey world. He also traveled to Russia to study their hockey drills and incorporate some of them into his team's game. "The greatest innovator of his time," Bobby Clarke said. Nicknamed "The Fog," Shero, 65, died in 1990 and went into the Hockey Hall of Fame in 2013.